THE CORRUPTION OF CAPITALISM

THE CORRUPTION OF CAPITALISM

WHY RENTIERS THRIVE AND WORK DOES NOT PAY

GUY STANDING

Biteback Publishing

First published in Great Britain in 2016 by
Biteback Publishing Ltd
Westminster Tower
3 Albert Embankment
London SE1 7SP
Copyright © Guy Standing 2016

ISBN 978-1-78590-044-0

10 9 8 7 6 5 4 3 2 1

A CIP catalogue record for this book is available from the British Library.

Set in Minion

Printed and bound in Great Britain by
CPI Group (UK) Ltd, Croydon CR0 4YY

CONTENTS

GLOSSARY OF ACRONYMS

CETA	Comprehensive Economic and Trade Agreement
ECB	European Central Bank
EU	European Union
GDP	Gross Domestic Product
G20	Group of nineteen major economies and the European Union
ILO	International Labour Organization
IMF	International Monetary Fund
ISDS	Investor–State Dispute Settlement
MGI	McKinsey Global Institute
MPS	Mont Pelerin Society
NHS	National Health Service (UK)
OECD	Organisation for Economic Cooperation and Development (thirty-four mainly industrialised member countries)
ONS	Office for National Statistics (UK)
PAC	Parliamentary Accounts Committee (UK)
PFI	Private Finance Initiative (UK)
QE	Quantitative Easing
TPP	Trans-Pacific Partnership
TTIP	Transatlantic Trade and Investment Partnership
TUC	Trades Union Congress (UK)
UK	United Kingdom
UN	United Nations
USA	United States of America
WIPO	World Intellectual Property Organization
WTO	World Trade Organization

PREFACE

This book is about something worse than corruption by individuals or companies. It is about the uncharted corruption of a claimed ideal – 'free markets' – and how economies are being rigged to favour owners of assets – the rentiers – while depressing incomes from labour.

Some would say that capitalism is inherently corrupt, because those who can cheat successfully for long enough do very nicely and always have. Even many of those who espouse capitalism unreservedly would grudgingly admit to that. Every day there is a report of some economic crime. There are too many rogues whose names are known to us to imagine that corruption does not pay. There is a saying among Russian businessmen: never ask how he got his first million.

Yet that is not what this book is about. It is about how the claims made on behalf of capitalism have been subverted in the construction of a system that is radically different from what its advocates claim. They assert a belief in 'free markets' and want us to believe that economic policies are extending them. That is untrue. Today we have the most unfree market system ever created. It is deeply corrupt because its leaders claim it is the opposite of what it is becoming.

How can politicians look into TV cameras and say we have a free market system when patents guarantee monopoly incomes for twenty years, preventing anyone from competing? How can they claim there are free markets when copyright rules give a guaranteed income for seventy years after a person's death? How can they claim free markets exist when one person or company is given a subsidy and not others, or when they sell off the commons that belong to all of us, at a discount, to a favoured individual or company, or when Uber, TaskRabbit and their ilk act as unregulated labour brokers, profiting from the labour of others?

Far from trying to stop these negations of free markets, governments are creating rules that allow and encourage them. That is what this book is about.

ONE MAN'S NIGHTMARE...

There he was, speaking to the 2015 *Financial Times* Business of Luxury Summit in the principality of Monaco, in the company of glamorous wealth. With a personal fortune of upwards of $5.5 billion – built on a tobacco inheritance and augmented by luxury brands such as Cartier, Chloé and Vacheron Constantin – South African Johann Rupert revealed he had been having nightmares. He could not sleep, he said, because he saw inequality generating envy, hatred and social warfare. He was worried stiff by the prospect of revolt. Addressing his well-heeled audience, he concluded, 'It's unfair. So that's what keeps me awake at night.'

One feels Johann's pain.

On the other side of the Atlantic, in Seattle, venture capitalist and fellow plutocrat Nick Hanauer, another who drew his first fat cheques from a dynastic family business, albeit one making feather bedding rather than cigarettes, was worrying about pitchforks aimed in his direction and his 'fellow 0.01ers'. In his dreams, he feared the *sans-culottes* of the French Revolution, who sent the aristocrats to the guillotine. To avert the threat, he advocated a higher minimum wage, a desirable move but hardly one that would threaten the structures producing the malaise of inequality and insecurity. But at least he recognised that revolt was justified.

Revolt takes many forms. Sometimes it stems from desperation; there is nothing to lose. Sometimes it stems from a dying moment, when the tide of history is drowning the losers, when just standing up is an act of defiance. The miners' strike in Britain in 1984 was like that. It was resistance against loss of a way of labouring that had turned adversity into a community of shared identity. Similarly, the Luddites of the early nineteenth century were resisting disruption to a way of life that weavers had forged over generations as a means of dignifying their community.

Sometimes, though, revolt is more strategic, directed to an end largely understood by those taking part, or by enough of those leading it to give it coherence and sustainable strength. These are the revolts of those wanting to accelerate change and steer it in new directions.

The anger of injustice is combined with a belief that something better can be achieved. In such times throughout history, a collective energy comes from the shared anxieties of people who feel common pressures and a common resentment towards those taking the pickings of society while they are left behind, losing rights they had come to expect. In such circumstances, revolt is against the minority who are gaining from social structures that are anything but natural.

The theme of this book is that conditions have been created in which some sort of revolt is increasingly likely. It will conclude by considering what that might look like and who might be its leaders. Before doing so, the nature of the problem and the scale of the challenge must be understood. Chapter 1 begins by laying out the global context, recalling the decay of institutions and social policies that had served the post-1945 era reasonably well and how they were dismantled. It was no golden age; it was merely better in many respects than what had preceded it.

Chapter 2 considers the institutional architecture that has been carefully constructed to orchestrate the development of a global market system in which rentiers – those living off income gained from property and other assets – are thriving at the expense of most people in most societies. International bureaucracies in Geneva, Washington DC, London and elsewhere have shaped the rules that have made the system so unfree and the gains by the plutocracy and elite so vast.

Chapter 3 deals with one of the dirty secrets of the age: the stealthily built edifice of subsidies that in diverse ways flow to the plutocracy, the elite, their corporate equivalents and other rentiers. Those below them pay the price in higher taxes, lower benefits and worse public services. The rentiers have shunted much of their wealth into tax havens, as the Panama Papers leaked in spring 2016 so comprehensively revealed. No fewer than seventy-two former or current heads of state or government – princes, sheikhs, Presidents and Prime Ministers – were exposed, as well as a wide array of the world's wealthiest. Those tax havens did not come about and persist for many years by accident; they were and remain a means of subsidising the rich, a hand-out they neither earn nor deserve.

Chapter 4 reviews a contrasting side of the global economy, the spread of many forms of debt, which might once have been expected to fade as economies became richer and their residents wealthier. If it is any consolation to those saddled with debts that frighten them into sleeplessness, the reality is that the system has been corrupted to such a degree that it depends on systemic debt enmeshing millions of people. Again, it is not an incidental or accidental feature.

Chapter 5 considers another shocking reality: the way in which the public sphere and the historically created commons nurtured over centuries are being privatised and commercialised. This is accelerating the ecological crisis that threatens all of us and is transferring precious aspects of community life to the rentiers. It must be resisted, before it is too late.

Chapter 6 returns to a theme I have explored in earlier books: the growth of the 'precariat', those living through unstable and insecure labour, in and out of jobs, without an occupational identity, financially on the edge and losing rights. In this book, the focus is on how labour and work are being transformed by the silicon revolution and the growth of new labour relationships. Politicians and trade unions have barely touched on what is happening.

Chapter 7 looks at how the corruption of the free market system has gone in tandem with the corruption and thinning of democracy. The question that hovers in the background is stark: do we have a democracy at all today?

Finally, Chapter 8 poses the biggest question of all: can the corruption that rentier capitalism represents be overcome by normal democratic means? Should we continue to play by its rules?

In sum, this book considers the rise of rentier capitalism and its inherent corruption. While many of the examples are from the UK, the context is the construction of a global architecture facilitating rentiers and the enthronement of property rights over citizenship rights.

Once again, I would like to thank audiences who have listened to talks on this and related subjects in the period in which the book was written. They have helped sharpen the arguments. Thanks are also due to Frances, who helped in so many ways and patiently went through the whole manuscript, to Caroline Wintersgill, who edited and commissioned in her impeccable way, and to Victoria Godden and Olivia Beattie, who shared the final editing. I also want to thank the numerous academics, students and activists who have helped with their questions and suggestions. It would be invidious to single out some without mentioning others. However, they share responsibility for whatever is good or useful in the following. The errors are all my own.

• • •

The UK's referendum on remaining in or exiting the European Union was held as this book was going to press. The shock 52 per cent support for Brexit gives further testimony to the book's primary theme. It was a populist vote against the insecurity, inequalities and austerity induced by a system of rentier capitalism that has channelled more of the income to a minority in a global Gilded Age. That revolt will be followed by others of a similar kind, and politics will grow uglier, unless rent seeking can be curbed and unless the desperate need for basic economic security for all is recognised and met.

Guy Standing
June 2016

Chapter 1

THE ORIGINS OF OUR TIMES

Almost every day a new study reports high and rising inequality. Shock is expressed; newspaper editorials, religious leaders, charities and the usual suspects all assert that something must be done. Then governments continue just as before, blithely making claims about growth, the number of jobs or 'balancing books', blaming their predecessors, disputing the statistics or just ignoring the findings. If protests erupt, a blast of condemnation comes from defenders of the status quo, dismissing the victims or protestors as lazy, irresponsible and inadequate.

As ever more evidence on the deleterious impact of inequality is produced, we are in danger of becoming immune to the shock. When Bernie Sanders started to gain support in the US presidential primaries by focusing on inequality, Hillary Clinton dismissed him as a 'one-issue' candidate. Yet establishment politicians have done nothing about it, instead aligning with financial institutions that are at the heart of the problem. As Sanders reminded his audiences, Clinton had been paid hundreds of thousands of dollars by Goldman Sachs just for speaking.

The twentieth-century income distribution system has irretrievably broken down. In perhaps the most striking reflection of this, Oxfam estimated that in 2015 just sixty-two individuals owned as much wealth as the bottom half of humanity, against 388 individuals in 2010. The top 1 per cent owned more than the rest of the world put together.[1] These may be rough-and-ready estimates, but no one seriously questions the trend or order of magnitude.

In fact, inequality is even worse than conventional figures on incomes and wealth suggest. They are based on money incomes and monetary valuations of wealth. But money income is only part of what can be called 'social income' – income in kind as well as in cash that contributes to the resources people can draw upon. Social income includes non-wage company benefits and perks such as paid holidays and sick leave, maternity and paternity benefits, company pension schemes and subsidised transport. And it includes community benefits – informal support from family, neighbours and friends, and access to public services and the commons. Historically, as argued later, the commons have been an important source of income for those lacking other resources. Their erosion has worsened inequality.

Conventional income statistics also fail to reflect the fact that the same money income is worth more to the recipient if predictable and certain than if unpredictable and uncertain. For example, guaranteed access to state benefits is worth more than access to benefits of equivalent amount that depend on means testing, behaviour testing or the discretion of bureaucratic officials. Income security has a value in itself.

An underlying theme of this book is that social income inequality has grown by even more than income inequality as conventionally measured. A principal reason is the expansion of forms of rent and the consequent 'rise of the rentier'.

THE SPECTRE OF RENT

There is a knock on the door; it has been heard before. The man has come for the rent; he wants it now… On the mantelpiece, the tin is empty.

The landlord and the bailiff have been despised and feared figures for hundreds of years, competing in popular distaste with feudal landowners, who extracted rent from tenants, serfs and peasants. They have always been parasitic, leeching off those in the lower reaches of society. Few have gained their status through 'hard work'.

The power of landlords was meant to wane in modern society, as wealth spread and laws limited their rapaciousness. Yet, today, a tiny minority of people and corporate interests across the world are accumulating vast wealth and power from rental income, not only from housing and land but from a range of other assets, natural and created. 'Rentiers' of all kinds are in unparalleled ascendancy and the neo-liberal state is only too keen to oblige their greed.

Rentiers derive income from ownership, possession or control of assets that are scarce or artificially made scarce. Most familiar is rental income from land, property, mineral exploitation or financial investments, but other sources have grown too. They include the income lenders gain from debt interest; income from ownership of 'intellectual property' (such as patents, copyright, brands and trademarks); capital gains on investments; 'above normal' company profits (when a firm has a dominant market position that allows it to charge high prices or dictate terms); income from government subsidies; and income of financial and other intermediaries derived from third-party transactions.

Classical economists derided rental income as unproductive and undeserved, and poured scorn on rentiers. John Maynard Keynes, the most influential economist of the mid-twentieth century, famously dismissed the rentier as 'the functionless investor' who gained income solely from ownership of capital, exploiting its 'scarcity value'. He concluded in his epochal *General Theory* that, as capitalism spread,

> it would mean the euthanasia of the rentier, and, consequently, the euthanasia of the cumulative oppressive power of the capitalist to exploit the scarcity-value of capital … [W]hilst there may be intrinsic reasons for the scarcity of land, there are no intrinsic reasons for the scarcity of capital … I see, therefore, the rentier aspect of capitalism as a transitional phase which will disappear when it has done its work.[2]

Eighty years on, the rentier is anything but dead; rentiers have become the main beneficiaries of capitalism's emerging income distribution system. Yet the term does not appear in the index of Tony Atkinson's magisterial book *Inequality*, while Thomas Piketty's much-cited tome *Capital in the Twenty-First Century* claims that rentier capitalism has faded.[3]

Keynes was mistaken because he did not foresee how the neoliberal framework built since the 1980s would allow individuals and firms to generate 'contrived scarcity' of assets from which to gain rental income. Nor did he foresee how the modern 'competitiveness' agenda would give asset owners power to extract rental subsidies from the state.

In what follows, a rentier is someone who gains income from

possession of assets, rather than from labour. A rentier corporation is a firm that gains much of its revenue from rental income rather than from production of goods and services, notably from financial assets or intellectual property. A rentier state has institutions and policies that favour the interests of rentiers. A rentier economy is one that receives a large share of income in the form of rent.[4] While textbook examples are resource-rich countries in the Middle East and Africa, rental income in the broader sense, from domestic and foreign sources, accounts for a big chunk of national income in several industrialised countries, including the United States and Britain.

This book argues that the 'euthanasia of the rentier' Keynes described must be part of a strategy to reduce inequality. It will be a struggle. Identifying the target is a first step. And a little social history helps to explain how we reached the current impasse.

SOCIAL DEMOCRACY'S FATAL EMBRACE

The period from the nineteenth century to the 1970s saw what Karl Polanyi, in his famous 1944 book, dubbed 'The Great Transformation' – the construction of *national* market economies.[5] He identified two distinct phases. The first was dominated by financial capital, which sought a free market economy. To aid in this, governments dismantled existing rural systems of regulation, redistribution and social protection that had provided some security and sense of community. Polanyi called this the 'dis-embedded' phase because economic policy required the destruction of existing social structures and institutions.

Widespread land enclosure contributed to falling real wages, as more people were made landless and dependent on wage labour. The resultant impoverishment was met by a novel form of regulatory social security known as the Speenhamland system, first introduced in the eponymous Berkshire village in 1795. The parish topped up low wages with subsidies, related to the price of bread and number of children, on condition that the recipients did not move elsewhere in search of better wages. The system kept rural wages at bare subsistence, just enough to limit discontent at declining living standards. It was to have a 21st-century equivalent, in the form of tax credits.

Over the next three decades, the Speenhamland system was adopted around England. Rural emigration was curbed and farmers gained cheap labour, at the cost of great hardship for the rural population. In 1834, the Poor Law Amendment Act ended the era of wage subsidies and established a free national labour market. Impoverished people flocked to the mills, mines and factories, providing low-cost labour. Concentrated in urban areas, the most destitute ended up in the infamous workhouse. It was a time of workfare, also to have a 21st-century equivalent.

While governments pursued domestic policies of 'laissez-faire' – Polanyi's term for free markets – imperialism provided a flow of rental income from the colonies to financial interests in the colonising countries. This combination intensified inequality and economic insecurity for the emerging proletariat in Britain, continental Europe and the United States.

Although Mark Twain used the term to describe the last three decades of the nineteenth century, the early part of the twentieth century is often called the Gilded Age. It was a time of dizzying wealth, when robber barons and financiers accumulated vast fortunes. However, growing economic and social instability soon paved the way for the Great Depression of the 1930s, which was only ended by the Second World War.

Even before the war ended, it was clear there was no going back to the free market era. Polanyi foresaw a reversal of the trend to free market capitalism in a 're-embedded' phase, with new forms of regulation, social protection and redistribution. The outcome was what is misleadingly called 'the golden age of welfare capitalism'.

Between 1945 and the mid-1970s, rental income subsided. Although there were short-term fluctuations, the shares of income going to capital (profits) and to labour (wages and benefits) were roughly stable.[6] Governments limited the rental income going to financiers and owners of other assets by various means. These included the nationalisation of industries perceived to be natural monopolies, such as the railways and public utilities, and regulation of financial markets to deter speculation and encourage lending for productive activities.

In the USA, a key to understanding the period was the so-called Treaty of Detroit, a five-year contract signed in 1950 between the United Auto Workers and General Motors. In return for renouncing strike action, workers were promised a share of the gains from productivity growth, mainly in the form of rising non-wage benefits and entitlements such as pension plans and medical insurance. This accord was copied across US industry and, to a large extent, in other industrialised countries.

It was the zenith of social democracy. However, the model that underpinned the Great Transformation made 'labour', not all

forms of work, pivotal. Socialists, communists and social democrats all subscribed to 'labourism'. Those in full-time jobs obtained
rising real wages, a growing array of 'contributory' non-wage benefits, and entitlements to social security for themselves and their
family. Those who did not fit this model were left behind. As long
as the latter were a small minority, supported by a means-tested
social safety net, the system worked well enough. The proverbial
worm began to turn when that minority started to grow.

The essence of labourism was that labour rights – more cor-
rectly, entitlements – should be provided to those (mostly men)
who performed labour and to their spouse and children. As workers previously had little security, this was a progressive step. But
it was inherently sexist and hierarchical, privileging those doing
regular paid labour over those doing other forms of work, unpaid
and outside the labour market, such as childcare and work in the
community.

Labourism promoted the view that the more labour people did
the more privileged they should be, and the less they did the less
privileged they should be. The ultimate fetishism was Lenin's dictate, enshrined in the Soviet constitution, that anybody who did
not labour should not eat. Labourism also led to dysfunctional
aspects of the welfare state. To give regular employees labour-
based security, there was a shift from wages to non-wage benefits,
such as company pensions, paid holidays, maternity leave and
sickness benefits.

This cemented a form of structural inequality between those
in stable, full-time employment and those forced to take unstable or casual jobs, or doing more unpaid work than paid labour.
And as non-wage benefits rather than money wages became a

larger proportion of total remuneration, the incentive to labour withered. Doing more labour made little difference to income. In welfare states, this was accentuated by rising social security contributions and income tax rates.

The labourist model frayed in the 1980s, as labour markets became more flexible and increasing numbers of people moved from job to job and in and out of employment. To defend labour-based welfare, social democratic governments turned to means testing, targeting benefits on those deemed the deserving poor. The main aim became 'to eradicate poverty' rather than to defend a solidaristic social protection system in which the fortunate cross-subsidise the unfortunate. The shift to means testing was fatal. As previous generations of social democrats had under-stood, benefits designed only for the poor are invariably poor benefits and stand to lose support among the rest of society.

Labour and social democratic parties everywhere became 'reactionary' – reacting to events rather than forging the future – and regressive, allowing or even fostering inequality. Ironically, it was mainly social democratic parties that shifted policy towards workfare, requiring the unemployed to apply for non-existent or unsuitable jobs, or to do menial, dead-end jobs or phoney train-ing courses in return for increasingly meagre benefits.

Old left parties abandoned notions of solidarity and equality in trying to appeal to the 'aspiring middle class'. This dragged them to the right to compete for votes with libertarian and populist right-wing parties, an unedifying spectacle repeated in country after country.

The Great Transformation had collapsed. The main reason was the end of the closed economy system on which it had depended.

The economic emergence of Japan and newly industrialising countries such as South Korea led to low-cost competition for manufacturing in the developed world that produced repeated balance of payments crises, most notably in the UK.

The tripling of oil prices in 1973 by the Organization of Petroleum Exporting Countries (OPEC) added to the inflationary pressure inherent to Keynesianism, which relied on stimulating aggregate demand to maintain 'full' [*sic*] employment. In an open economy system, Keynesianism in one country could not work, as was demonstrated by President François Mitterrand's ill-fated attempt in 1981 to boost the French economy.

It was the end of the road for that approach. The social democratic model – entailing modest redistribution via high marginal tax rates, labour-based social security, and government as the employer of last resort – had run its course.

Compared with the 1930s, after 1945 capital made concessions to labour. In the 1970s, fear changed sides. The interests of capital grew stronger. They were emboldened by an economic ideology that was to sweep the world.

UNDERSTANDING NEO-LIBERALISM

Around 1980 saw the beginnings of a Global Transformation – the construction of a *global* market system. As with the Great Transformation, the initial phase may be called 'dis-embedded' because the emerging economic system rendered old forms of regulation, social protection and redistribution obsolete or ineffectual.

Politically, every transformation has begun with a repudiation of the certainties of the previous age. This time the attack was on labour-based security, previously the objective of governments of both left and right. Now it was seen as an impediment to growth. Once again, policy changes were dominated by financial capital. Intellectual justification came from the so-called 'Chicago school' of law and economics at the University of Chicago, whose leading lights went on to receive Nobel Prizes. Their agenda, honed in the Mont Pelerin Society set up by Friedrich Hayek and thirty-eight like-minded intellectuals in 1947, evolved into what is now called neo-liberalism.

This meant the liberalisation of markets, the commodification and privatisation of everything that could be commodified and privatised and the systematic dismantling of all institutions of social solidarity that protected people from 'market forces'. Regulations were justifiable only if they promoted economic growth; if not, they had to go.

The agenda involved strict re-regulation of labour markets and only light regulation of financial markets. The argument was that, if left alone, financial markets would reward efficient firms and punish inefficient ones, which would go out of business; meanwhile, financiers could help with mergers and transfers of ownership to the more efficient. This reasoning also bolstered demands for the privatisation of state enterprises, which was soon embraced with almost as much enthusiasm by social democratic parties as by their right-wing opponents – witness the French socialist government of Lionel Jospin and the New Labour government of Tony Blair.

It was soon evident that the effects of financial deregulation were nothing like the predictions of neo-liberal theory. Instead of channelling money from savers to productive investments, financiers indulged in a frenzy of speculative activity to make money from interest, commissions and capital gains. The result was an unstable bubble economy, as investor 'herds' moved *en masse* from place to place. The titans of finance became 'masters of the universe', in Tom Wolfe's famous phrase in *The Bonfire of the Vanities*, his 1987 novel satirising Wall Street, as they mingled with heads of state and spent time in senior government posts before returning to make yet more money from speculation.

The rise of finance was accompanied by more frequent and widespread financial crises, from the Latin American debt crisis in the 1980s to the worldwide banking collapse of 2007–08 and subsequent global recession. Little was done to prevent them, even after the Asian financial crisis of 1997–98 and the related collapse of Long-Term Capital Management, a US hedge fund that boasted two Nobel Prize-winning neo-liberal economists on its board. There was no political will to challenge the might of financial capital.

At the heart of neo-liberalism is a contradiction. While its proponents profess a belief in free 'unregulated' markets, they favour regulations to prevent collective bodies from operating in favour of social solidarity. That is why they want controls over unions, collective bargaining, professional associations and occupational guilds. When the interests of free markets and property clash, they favour the latter. Neo-liberalism is a convenient rationale for rentier capitalism.

THE GREAT CONVERGENCE

It is impossible to make sense of the Global Transformation without appreciating the role of China. With a population of 1.4 billion, it has experienced three decades of rapid economic growth, becoming the world's *de facto* industrial workshop. Chinese wages in the 1980s were about one-fiftieth of those of comparable workers in OECD countries and, although Chinese wages have started to rise amid tales of labour shortages, they have a long way to go to converge with OECD levels.

After the financial crash of 2008, it was China, not the USA as in the past, that supported the world economy. Between 2008 and 2015, US GDP rose by 10 per cent, whereas China's rose by 66 per cent.[7] Wages remain very low, but there are now more dollar billionaires in China (596 in 2015) than in the USA (537).

The emergence of China and other Asian economies has put sustained downward pressure on wages and working conditions in OECD countries. Within emerging economies, the import and adaptation of modern technologies and production chains have led to steeply rising productivity, reducing labour costs despite higher wages. And automation is accelerating. Foxconn, an electronics manufacturing giant that makes Apple's iPhones among much else, employs over a million workers in China (and more elsewhere), but its Taiwanese owner plans to automate 30 per cent of production by 2020. Already one of Foxconn's factories operates on a 24-hour basis without any workers at all.

Some predict that ageing and falling fertility rates will lead to a global labour shortage that will raise wages around the world.[8] This is improbable. Automation will check the demand for labour. But even without it, simple demographic projections neglect rising retirement ages. China has a very low retirement age (fifty or fifty-five for women; sixty for men). The United States, by contrast, has a retirement age of sixty-six, set to rise to sixty-seven. China plans to raise the retirement age in stages from 2017, which will add millions to the world's labour force. Meanwhile, in India, hundreds of millions of people will move from its backward rural economy and informal urban economy into the global wage-labour market. There is little prospect of a global labour shortage pushing up wages in rich countries for many years to come.

China's industrialisation surge has accompanied a sharp decline in manufacturing employment in industrialised countries, particularly since the financial crash. Between 2008 and 2015, the USA lost over 6 million manufacturing jobs. But now over half of China's output is attributable to services, including financial services. It and Southeast Asian countries such as Malaysia and Singapore have become rentier economies, with the means to invest in rich countries and buy up companies and other assets. They have accumulated large cash hoards by keeping labour costs low, which constrains consumption at home. Concentrated in the hands of a few plutocrats and a growing elite, this 'savings glut' has created a stock of funds to invest in assets all over the world, much of it in property.

China has become a special rentier economy. State-owned enterprises spearheaded its export-led industrialisation, helped by subsidies and low wages. The resultant trade surpluses, alongside capital inflows, enabled China to accumulate vast foreign currency reserves. These peaked at nearly $4 trillion in 2014 – almost twenty times what they were in 2001 – and, though they have fallen since, they remain by far the world's largest. A sizeable chunk of the reserves is invested in dollar-denominated US government securities, making China a major holder of US government debt.

Other 'emerging' economies have also built up huge foreign currency reserves. In 2000, the global total was under $2,000 billion, of which emerging markets accounted for just over a third.

By 2015, the global total was over $11,500 billion, with emerging markets accounting for two-thirds of that.[9]

In 2007, China transferred $200 billion from its foreign exchange reserves to create a sovereign wealth fund, China Investment Corp., which has invested in financial assets and 'strategic resources' around the world. And Chinese firms have gone on a buying spree. Foreign direct investment has gone from virtually nothing in 2000 to more than $100 billion a year, making China one of the world's top three foreign direct investors. In buying foreign firms, technology and property, China has gained control of energy and mineral resources on every continent. It has also become a labour export regime, moving hundreds of thousands of workers around the world to work on short-term projects, helping to erode labour standards and decrease wages in host countries.[10]

Between 2000 and 2014, Chinese companies spent €46 billion on over 1,000 direct investments in the European Union, a quarter of which was in the UK.[11] In 2015, EU investments by Chinese firms hit a record €20 billion, 70 per cent coming from state-owned enterprises.[12] Ironically, neo-liberalism, founded on the claimed superiority of free markets and privatisation, created the conditions for Chinese state enterprises to buy European assets, aided by subsidies from the European Union and EU governments. Greece, Poland, Italy and Portugal have ceded control of ports and other parts of their infrastructure. In 2015, after Chinese state enterprises had taken a big stake in North Sea oil, the British government threw subsidies at another Chinese state company in the sensitive nuclear energy sector.

Chinese state enterprises, often heavily indebted, have raised finance on concessionary terms from state-owned banks to buy some of the most iconic corporate names in Europe and America, such as US mobile phone company Motorola, Italian tyre maker Pirelli, Swedish carmaker Volvo and French resort operator Club Med.

Illicit capital outflows have also been enormous. Over $150 billion left China in just one month in 2015, mainly through Macau and underground banks.[13] Capital inflows to China and other emerging markets have also generated considerable private credit. According to Matt King of Citigroup, emerging economies accounted for three-quarters of global 'private money creation' between 2010 and 2015. Flows of $8 trillion into those economies generated $5 trillion of credit annually.[14] Much of that went into fuelling property bubbles at home and abroad.

Ben Bernanke, former chair of the US Federal Reserve, and economists at the International Monetary Fund (IMF) are among those arguing that the combination of loose monetary policy, financial innovation and the savings glut in emerging market economies is responsible for housing price bubbles in Britain, the USA and elsewhere.[15] This has contributed to the growth of wealth inequality and a revival of landlordism. This time, however, many of the landlords are on the other side of the world.

THE SILICON REVOLUTION – APOLOGY TO NED LUDD

'Within the very near future – much less than twenty-five
years – we shall have the technical capacity of substituting
machines for any and all human functions in organisations.'
Herbert Simon, 1960[16]

You do not receive a Nobel Prize for Economics for being right all the time! Simon received his in 1978, when the number of people in jobs was at record levels. It is higher still today. Yet the internet-based technological revolution has reopened age-old visions of machine domination. Some are utopian, such as the post-capitalism of Paul Mason, imagining an era of free information and information sharing.[17] Some are decidedly dystopian, where the robots – or rather their owners – are in control and mass joblessness is coupled with a 'panopticon' state subjecting the proles to intrusive surveillance, medicalised therapy and brain control. The pessimists paint a 'world without work'.[18] With every technological revolution there is a scare that machines will cause 'technological unemployment'. This time, the Jeremiahs seem a majority.

Fortunately, we are still in the early stages, when collective action can assert democratic control. Whether or not they will do so in the future, the technologies have not yet produced mass unemployment. Although measured unemployment is higher than a few decades ago, this must be seen in the context of population growth and globalisation, in which the world's labour supply has more than tripled. There are more jobs than at any time in history.

One difficulty is that many analysts interpret 'disruption' – a favoured word – as the destruction of jobs in general and the simple replacement of labour by robots and automation. This rests on the 'lump of labour fallacy' – the assumption that there is only a certain amount of labour to be done; if machines can do more at less cost, then workers (particularly those with 'low skills') will be displaced. But there is *not* a fixed amount of labour and work to be done.

Sooner or later, commentators cite the Luddite riots that began in 1809, when self-employed weavers smashed machines.

The pejorative term 'Luddite' has come to symbolise opposition to progress. This is unfair towards the fictitious Ned Ludd (also known as Captain, General, or even King Ludd) and towards those who acted in his name. Although worried about machines causing unemployment, their protests were mainly about the disruption to a way of life and mechanisms of solidarity and workmanship nurtured over generations. They were against the herding of workers into factories as employees who had not undergone any apprenticeship and were paid very low wages. They were not against machines per se, or technological progress. They were concerned about losing their independence.

Above all, they were protesting against the destruction of 'work' by 'labour'. Thomas Carlyle recognised this in his 1829 essay *A Mechanical Age*, when he said that the weavers were against becoming 'mechanical in head and in heart, as well as in hand'. They were the 'primitive rebels' of their day, even sending out public letters that began by citing Magna Carta and were signed as from 'Ned Ludd's office, Sherwood Forest', hideout of the equally fictitious Robin Hood. The symbolism was obvious.

Today's technologies are certainly having a disruptive effect. One much-quoted study estimated that nearly half of all jobs in the USA were in occupations threatened by technological change.[19] The Bank of England's chief economist warned that automation could put up to half of all British jobs at risk, implying that mass unemployment was on its way.[20] But such studies imply no such thing. Wages may adjust; occupations may change in character, for better or worse; some jobs may evolve into something else; some may be replaced by others; some technological and organisational changes may induce *more* work and labour.[21]

One of the unsung effects of occupational disruption is, as we shall see, a transfer of rental income from professions and crafts to those who own the technological apparatus.

A once popular theory known as 'Kondratieff long waves' states that every sixty years or so the production structure is transformed by a technological revolution based on some marvellous invention: the water mill in the thirteenth century; the printing press in the late fifteenth century; the power loom and the steam engine in the eighteenth; the steel industry and electricity in the late nineteenth; and the car and Fordist mass production in the early twentieth. While there is little support for Kondratieff's precise theory, clearly there have been periods of breakthroughs interspersed with periods of relative stability. The globalisation era has coincided with a seismic revolution associated with the internet and its offspring in information and communications technology.[22]

For this narrative, two aspects deserve emphasis. First, the new technologies have enabled the outsourcing and offshoring of the production of goods and services and have made it feasible to switch locations at will. Trade in components and tasks has grown relative to trade in completed goods and services. Capital and technology mobility has increased; potential mobility has increased even more. Corporations can de-structure, fracture, offshore or inshore, and outsource or in-source functions as costs and prices dictate, in the interest of profit-making. This fluidity has made the firm itself a variable entity, subject to mergers, acquisitions, takeovers and restructuring at the behest of its ever-changing owners and managers. Firms have become commodities.

Second, the new technologies are contributing to inequality. The ability to move or change the division of labour and job structures gives capital vastly more power over workers than it would have in a closed economy. If workers, or governments on their behalf, push for higher wages or benefits, companies can switch production and employment to somewhere else more accommodating. There is no need for threats; it is just part of the system.

So, while technology is not necessarily destroying jobs, it is helping to destroy the old income distribution system, creating a rental wedge between profits, which are growing and becoming more concentrated, and wages, which are falling and becoming more volatile and uncertain. The threat is technology-induced inequality, not technological unemployment.

THE SECOND GILDED AGE

Today, we are living in a Second Gilded Age – with one significant difference. In the first, which ended in the Great Crash of 1929, inequality grew sharply but wages on average rose as well. The Second Gilded Age has also involved growing inequality, but this time real wages on average have stagnated or fallen. Meanwhile, those relying on state benefits have fallen further behind, many pushed into homelessness, penury and dependency on inadequate private charity.

Since the 1980s, the share of income going to labour has shrunk, globally and in most countries of economic significance, in forty-two of the fifty-nine countries for which there were data, according to one study.[23] The labour share fell in the USA from 53 per cent in 1970 to 43.5 per cent in 2012. Most dramatically, it slid by over twenty percentage points in China and also dropped steeply in the rising industrial giant of South Korea.

Meanwhile, according to the McKinsey Global Institute, corporate profits more than tripled in real (inflation-adjusted) terms between 1980 and 2013 and rose from 7.6 per cent to nearly 10 per cent of global GDP. Multinationals from industrialised countries captured over two-thirds of global profits, helped by big reductions in corporation taxes (which halved in some countries), low borrowing costs and access to cheap labour and materials.[24] After-tax profits of US firms as a share of national income rose to their highest level since 1929.

However, the global corporate landscape is changing fast. So-called 'idea-intensive' firms – in pharmaceuticals, media, finance and information technology – now account for 31 per cent of the profits of Western corporations, up from 17 per cent in 1999. They are global rentiers, deriving income from possession of 'intangible assets' such as patents, brands and copyright under a strengthened intellectual property regime constructed since the 1990s (see Chapter 2).[25] And the industrialised-country share in global profits is set to decline; multinationals from emerging market economies already account for a quarter of the *Fortune* Global 500 biggest companies in the world and McKinsey expects them to account for half by 2025.

In contrast to rising profits, real wages in rich countries have stagnated. Economic growth is no longer a reliable road to wage growth. For instance, between 1973 and 2007, a period of rising national income, average real wages in the USA fell by 4.4 per cent. By contrast, between 1947 and 1973, during the Great Transformation, real wages grew by 75 per cent.

In the economic powerhouse of Germany, the story is equally dire, with real wages falling by more than in any other major economy. The West German economic miracle of the 1960s was made possible by a write-off of debt owed to other European countries in the 1950s. West Germany subsequently benefited from cheap migrant labour, mostly from Turkey. Reunification with East Germany in 1990 gave it yet more cheap labour and, when the Eurozone was established in 1999, the strong Deutschmark permitted an implicit currency devaluation relative to other members, giving German exports a further cost advantage.

To compound the advantage, in 1998 German trade unions made a 'concession bargain' with employers and government that held down wages. Then, in 2004, the Social Democratic government of Gerhard Schröder introduced the Hartz IV welfare reform, which cut unemployment benefits and imposed conditions that forced many to take low-paid 'mini-jobs'. This put more downward pressure on wages, especially at the lower end, so increasing inequality. Real wages were static or fell from the early 1990s onwards. Average wages were lower in 2015 than in 1990, although national income per person had risen by nearly 30 per cent.

In Britain, too, wages have been stagnant for years. Though wages of those in full-time jobs rose a bit in 2015, average weekly pay was still 9 per cent below pre-recession levels. Low-wage earners appeared to benefit most in 2015, helped by a rise in the minimum wage the year before, but this was partly a statistical illusion. The data exclude the growing numbers in so-called self-employment, who now account for about 15 per cent of the 'employed'. Most of the jobs outsourced to 'independent' contractors have been low-paid, so the sample used for calculating average wages has shifted towards higher-income employees. And bonuses paid to higher-income workers boost the average. It follows that if *measured* average wages stagnate, *actual* wages must have fallen. This is a rarely noticed part of the growing inequality in Britain.

Besides falling wages, there has been an increase in wage differentials and a less documented decline in the share of people receiving non-wage benefits, such as occupational pensions, paid holidays, sick leave or medical coverage. Thus worker compensation, in terms of 'social income', has fallen by more than revealed by wages alone.

As a consequence of these developments, 'in-work poverty' has rocketed. In some OECD countries, including Britain, the USA, Spain and Poland, a majority of those in poverty live in households where at least one person has a job. The mantra that 'work is the best route out of poverty' is simply false.

RISE OF THE RENTIER

Meanwhile, rentiers have been the winners of the globalisation era. Using a narrow definition of rental income as income from financial assets, one careful study of patchy data found that across the industrialised world the share of profits in total income rose between the 1960s and the 1990s. But in most of the twenty-nine countries studied the rentier share rose far more, in some cases accounting for all the growth in the profit share. The non-financial profit share also increased in most countries, but by much less.[26]

Excluding capital gains from financial assets, the countries in which the rentier share increased most were, in order: France, the UK, South Korea, the USA, Germany, Australia and Belgium. By 2000, rental income from financial assets accounted for over 20 per cent of income in Belgium, France, the Netherlands and the USA, with the UK and Italy catching up.

If capital gains on financial assets are included, the rise in the rentier share was even greater. Here the USA stands out. The rentier share rose more than sevenfold between 1980 and 2000.[27] By then, rental income, as narrowly defined, accounted for over a third of national income, up from about a fifth before the Global Transformation started. The share of income going to profits in non-financial sectors actually fell.

Meanwhile, deindustrialisation has been relentless. During the early twentieth century, agriculture shrank to less than 3 per cent of US national income, while manufacturing began its steep decline. In 1950, manufacturing accounted for 28 per cent of GDP. By the time of the crash of 2008, its share was down to 11 per cent. The symbolic year was 1985, when financial services (banking, property, insurance, advertising and marketing) first accounted for more of national income than manufacturing. The financial sector's profits – interest, rents and dividends – have continued to rise relative to those from non-financial activity and now account for about 40 per cent of all domestic profits.

It is suggested that the tipping point for being a rentier economy is when 40 per cent of income comes from rent.[28] Even if just interest and dividends are counted as rent, the USA is already at that point. And there has been an even faster rise in the foreign share of financial profits, which has quadrupled since 1950. Non-financial domestic profits have dropped by a third. As the USA now depends on rental income, much of it from abroad, it is scarcely hyperbole to call it an imperialist rentier economy. The rise of finance is reflected in the composition of the American plutocracy. In 1982, according to Forbes, only 8 per cent of the richest 400 Americans made their money from finance; by 2007, that had risen to 27 per cent.

Another study, again looking just at income from financial assets, found that the rise in the rental share coincided with a decline in workers' bargaining power, as measured by unionisation. It was also correlated with interest rate liberalisation, reduced costs of capital mobility and increased returns to foreign financial investment, all desired features of neo-liberalism.[29] The share also rose when there were more right-wing governments.

Banks and other financial firms were at the forefront. But many non-financial corporations also turned to what is known as financialisation, aiming to boost profits through financial investments and trading.[30] Household-name firms, notably General Electric, became rentier corporations, with their own banking arms.

Between 1980 and 2007, just before the crash, the world's financial assets – including equities, private, corporate and government debt, and deposits – quadrupled relative to global GDP.[31] Further, as the 'dis-embedded phase' of the Global Transformation unfolded, financial institutions did all they could to maximise the number of people with debts and the amount they owed, lending recklessly to home buyers, credit card holders, students and others on low incomes. These loans became 'investment products', assets created by bundling loans together and treating debt repayments as an income yield. Financial corporations bought the assets and borrowed against them to make more profit, paving the way for the unravelling that precipitated the crash.

The same mechanism is being used by financial firms today. It is a Ponzi scheme, a sleight of hand that creates a vehicle for generating rental income, until the resultant bubble bursts, as similar bubbles have burst with impressive frequency since the 1980s.[32] If nothing else, the rentier economy creates a rollercoaster ride, causing havoc and misery in its wake.

THE GREAT GATSBY CURVE

Adam Smith, father of mainstream economics, suggested that a man 'must be rich or poor according to the quantity of labour which he can command'. On that basis, today's plutocrats are the richest men (and women) in history, not just because they are wealthier, but because their money gives them unprecedented power. In the First Gilded Age, the world's richest man, John D. Rockefeller, could have hired 116,000 US workers with the income from his wealth. In 2004, Carlos Slim, who rivals Bill Gates as the world's richest man, could have hired 440,000 of his fellow Mexicans with his annual income, not wealth.[33] By 2014, he could have hired 2 million Mexicans.[34]

Growing inequality is commonly attributed to the weakened bargaining position of workers vis-à-vis capital, due to globalisation and technological change. But it also reflects changes in national tax policies. Government after government has cut marginal tax rates on high incomes, which come largely from capital, claiming that lower rates will encourage entrepreneurship, savings and investment, and attract potential investors from abroad. Whatever the rationalisation, reductions in marginal tax rates are inversely correlated with the growth in the share of income going to the richest 1 per cent (and 0.1 per cent). Where marginal tax rates were cut most – in the UK and USA – the growth in the share going to the top 1 per cent increased the most.[35]

It does not stop there. Extreme inequality in one generation reduces social mobility of the next, amplifying inequality. This has been dubbed the 'Great Gatsby Curve', after the novel by F. Scott Fitzgerald.[36] The situation is worse now than at the time of the original Gatsby in the 1920s, meaning that the already low upward mobility of those from poorer families and communities has been cut to a trickle. One reason is that there are fewer occupations in which upward mobility is possible, so people have less opportunity to 'work their way up'. Another is that more of the income going to the plutocracy and elite comes from outside the labour market. In response, mainstream economists have advocated more education. Education is desirable for many reasons, but more of it will not alter the character of the income distribution system.

THE PRECARIAT SMOULDERS

Globalisation, neo-liberal policies, institutional changes and the technological revolution have combined to generate a new global class structure superimposed on preceding class structures.[37] This consists of a tiny plutocracy (perhaps 0.001 per cent) atop a bigger elite, a 'salariat' (in relatively secure salaried jobs), 'proficians' (freelance professionals), a core working class, a precariat and a 'lumpen-precariat' at the bottom. The plutocracy, elite, salariat and proficians enjoy not just higher incomes but gain most (or an increasing part) of their income from capital and rental income, rather than from labour. It is not the level of income that defines their class position, but how they gain it and what form it takes.

The three groups below them gain nothing in rent. Indeed, increasingly they pay rent in some form to the classes above them. First, there is the shrinking proletariat, relying mainly on labour, in stable, mostly full-time jobs, with schooling that matches the skills their jobs require. They gained from twentieth-century social democracy, which provided non-wage benefits linked to workplaces and state benefits mostly linked to labour.

The precariat, which ranks below the proletariat in income, consists of millions of people obliged to accept a life of unstable labour and living, without an occupational identity or corporate narrative to give to their lives. Their employers come and go, or are expected to do so. Many in the precariat are over-qualified for the jobs they must accept; they also have a high ratio of unpaid 'work' to labour – looking and applying for jobs, training and retraining, queuing and form-filling, networking or just waiting around. They also rely mainly on money wages, which are often inadequate, volatile and unpredictable.[38] They lack access to rights-based state benefits and are losing civil, cultural, social, economic and political rights, making them supplicants if they need help to survive.

The precariat is growing all over the world, accelerated by the likes of Uber, TaskRabbit and Amazon Mechanical Turk discussed in Chapter 6. It is in turmoil, reflected in the confusion over perceived class membership. For instance, more Americans today see themselves as in the lower classes. In 2000, according to Gallup polls, 63 per cent saw themselves as middle-class and 33 per cent as lower-class. In 2015, 51 per cent saw themselves as middle-class and 48 per cent as lower-class. Similar trends have been reported elsewhere.

For some years, the precariat has been internally divided and scarcely conscious of its commonality. But this is rapidly changing as more of those in or close to being in the precariat realise that their situation is structural rather than a reflection of personal inadequacy, and that together they have the ability and energy to force transformative changes.

Below the precariat in the social spectrum is what might be called a 'lumpen-precariat', an underclass of social victims relying on charity, often homeless and destitute, suffering from social illnesses including drug addiction and depression. They do not constitute a class, since they lack what sociologists call agency, the ability to act collectively in a strategic way. But they make up a threatening part of the state. Their numbers are rising remorselessly; they are a badge of shame on society.

A TALE OF FIVE SNAKES

The breakdown of the twentieth-century income distribution system arises from the breakdown of basic relationships that characterised market economies in the three decades following the Second World War.

First, rising productivity used to be matched by rising average wages, as enshrined in the Treaty of Detroit mentioned earlier. The two lines on a graph rose in parallel. But, since the 1980s, higher productivity has not led to higher wages. For instance, real wages in the USA have stagnated for over three decades while productivity has risen steadily.[39] Tracing the curves on a graph over time shows the 'jaws of the snake' widening, as the lower jaw (wages) sags while the upper (productivity) gapes upwards. The opening jaw has been a feature of most industrialised countries, including Germany, Australia, the Netherlands and Poland. There has been a break in the link between productivity and real wage growth.

Second, rising employment used to be followed by rising wages. Now, when employment rises, average wages may stagnate or even fall, largely because new jobs pay lower wages than past jobs. Since the 1990s, all US net employment growth has been in non-tradable sectors, such as retailing and personal services, where wages are relatively low and falling.[40] In Germany, too, despite substantial economic growth and declining unemployment between 1995 and 2014, real wages fell over the whole period.[41]

Wages have similarly stagnated in the UK, despite apparent employment growth both before the crash and during the recovery. Ben Broadbent, a deputy Governor of the Bank of England, noted in 2015 that the recovery had been biased towards low-paid jobs, especially compared to the upturn in the 1990s; new jobs were going mainly to people with below-average qualifications and experience, in lower-paid occupations, so depressing average pay growth.[42]

That is linked to a third set of jaws. It used to be that when employment rose, tax revenue from employment rose as well. Now, most notably in Britain, when employment rises, tax revenue may even fall. Since more new jobs are low-paid, and since successive governments have raised the threshold for paying income tax, a higher proportion of those in jobs do not earn enough to pay tax. Thus an increase in UK employment in 2014 accompanied a drop in income tax revenue. This 'jobs-rich, tax-poor' recovery produced what *The Economist* called 'the squeezed state'.[43] Although eventually revenue increased as growth picked up, it is clear that the old relationship no longer holds firm.

Fourth, contrary to the past, rising company profits do not lead to higher average wages. This is partly because profits are more concentrated among firms that do not employ many people. In the USA, employment has grown mainly in low-tech sectors, weakening the links between profits, employment and wages.

Fifth, in much of Europe, while average real wages have stagnated, unit labour costs have been rising. In the UK, for instance, labour costs per unit of output were much higher in 2015 than in 2000, and in Germany they were over 5 per cent higher.

The rise in profits and inequality may be similar to what happened in the early twentieth century when financial capital was last in control, though, as mentioned earlier, the current era differs in one crucial respect. Then, notably in the United States, when profits and inequality rose, real wages also rose.[44] Now, profits and inequality are rising while real wages stagnate or decline. This is not what a free market would predict, and it is not sustainable for long.

The decline in the labour income share and the growth of the capital share is only part of the story. In the USA at least, that has only accounted for a fifth of the increase in inequality.[45] More important has been the growing dispersion of earnings within the labour share itself, first through widening wage differentials *within* firms and later through a greater dispersion of earnings *between* firms. The second reflects the increased domination of large swathes of the US economy by a handful of companies, able to charge high prices (and thus gain rental income) because genuine competition is lacking.[46]

As a result, within the capital share too there has been a widening dispersion of profits, with a few companies able to command
substantial rental income pulling ahead.[47] They pay their key staff
(the elite, salariat and proficians) more generously, which further
increases inequality within the labour share. This is not a matter of
returns to so-called 'skills'. Privileged workers in dominant firms
have gained relative to others with similar skills, sharing the rental
income by way of higher wages, bonuses, shares and perks.[48]

WHY THE PHILLIPS CURVE FLOPS

There is one way in which workers can no longer rely on real
wage growth. Ever since the publication in 1958 of an article
by A. W. Phillips, most economists have accepted that there is
a trade-off between the rate and change of unemployment and
wage and price inflation. As a result, governments have aimed to
influence the 'natural' rate of unemployment or the NAIRU (non-
accelerating inflation rate of unemployment), the rate at which
inflationary pressures are held in check. The so-called Phillips
curve has been used by central banks in operating monetary
policy, and by governments to justify policies increasing labour
market flexibility, on the grounds that more flexibility makes for
a better unemployment–inflation trade-off.

However, in recent years, falling unemployment has not put
much upward pressure on wages. One explanation is that increased wage flexibility means that firms cut wages rather than
jobs in recessions, which some politicians think is preferable.[49] Yet
in addition to causing hardship, lower wages have not bounced

back in subsequent expansions. In the UK, after several years of supposedly robust economic growth, median real earnings in 2015 were still 9 per cent lower than in 2008.

The standard view of the breakdown in the Phillips curve is that unions have been neutered, reducing their capacity to bargain for higher wages. But at least as important is the downward pressure on wages exerted by the global, not merely national, labour surplus. This labour pool has been made more accessible by the unbundling of firms and the technological revolution that has been shaping the rentier economy. As we will see, the new digital platforms have also expanded the effective labour supply by mobilising extra people to carry out tasks on a piecework basis that previously were done by (fewer) full-time employees. The basis of the Phillips curve has been demolished by the globalised flexible labour process.

LIES, DAMNED LIES AND 'AUSTERITY'

> 'The austerity obsession ... is lunatic.'
> Martin Wolf, *Financial Times*[50]

In the early years of the Global Transformation, governments made a Faustian bargain with their citizens.[51] Liberalisation of markets in a globalising economy tripled the labour supply to the world labour market, adding two billion people. This was bound to put downward pressure on the living standards of those relying on labour in industrialised countries. Governments compensated by allowing an orgy of consumption based on rising household debt as well as subsidies such as tax credits that propped up workers' earnings; this increased public debt. When the Faustian bargain came to its predictable end in 2008, governments, financial communities and central, regional and global banks orchestrated a response summarised in a single word: 'austerity'.

The austerity strategy is based on falsehoods intended to create a smokescreen behind which to pursue the political objective of shrinking public social spending. The first falsehood is that the crash was caused by ordinary people 'living beyond their means', requiring them to cut back to 'balance the budget'. In fact, the precipitating cause was a banking failure that started in Wall Street. It arose from the recklessness and criminality of financiers, who had been allowed to gain a rising share of income at the expense of lower-income groups. The austerity strategy deepened that unfairness. The rich rentiers have become richer, while the rest have seen incomes stagnate or decline.

A second falsehood is that cutting public debt will revive growth, along with employment and incomes. In fact, it has a dampening effect, as even the IMF has warned. In Britain, the modest recovery was largely and unsustainably fanned by private credit. In 2014, median household income was still below the level of 2008, according to the government's Office of National Statistics (ONS). And, in another sign of the inequitable thrust of austerity policies, the richest fifth of households were paying 35 per cent of their income in direct and indirect taxes; the poorest fifth were paying 38 per cent.

A third falsehood is that reducing public debt requires cuts in public spending. Margaret Thatcher drew the analogy with family budgets, but that does not apply to governments or firms. Deficits arise from spending exceeding income. But governments can increase income by raising taxes. Instead, they have deliberately cut potential revenue by *reducing* taxes, particularly those on capital and high-income earners. So, to attribute the deficit to overspending on benefits and social services is deceitful. Moreover, it makes sense to borrow to invest for the future, for example, to finance public infrastructure.

Governments do not need to operate with balanced budgets, and even if they wish to do so they can choose whether to cut spending on public services, reduce subsidies or raise taxes. After 2008, successive British governments decided to close the gap largely through cuts in spending. They also reduced taxes and increased subsidies, mainly for the rich, which meant finding more spending cuts. And a commitment to protect pensioners, a political bribe to key voters, meant that a disproportionate share of the costs was borne by younger generations. According to the ONS, pensioner household incomes rose by 7.3 per cent in real terms between 2007 and 2014, while non-retired household incomes fell by 5.5 per cent.

The austerity rhetoric is a confidence trick, aimed at convincing people that they must accept lower incomes in the interest of national recovery, as well as lower taxes on capital to draw financial investment from abroad. The effect has been to further enrich the wealthy at the expense of the less well-off.

THE BRITISH DISEASE

Economists have a theory called the Dutch Disease, named after the Dutch experience following the discovery of gas deposits; this led to a rise in the currency that resulted in lost manufacturing exports and employment. Today, a variant could be called the British Disease, since it is most pronounced in Britain. It arises from the domination of financial capital over the whole economy, stemming from the Big Bang of 1986, when the City of London was deregulated. One outcome has been a persistently strong currency, which has made manufacturing exports uncompetitive and accelerated deindustrialisation. It has also boosted inequality.[52]

Canada suffered similarly after 2008, when money flowed into its financial sector because it had largely escaped the turbulence of the banking crisis. This pushed up the value of the Canadian dollar, causing the manufacturing sector to lose 20 per cent of its capacity. The USA also suffers from the British Disease; finance dominates the economy (and policymaking) to the detriment of its industrial base. It has a huge trade deficit and lost over 6 million industrial jobs in the seven years after the financial crash, while profits and incomes rebounded in financial activities.

The UK is in worse shape. The economic recovery after 2010 was entirely due to the rentier activities of finance, insurance and property, according to the ONS. Manufacturing production and employment have continued to shrink. In 2015, over a million people – about one in twenty-five of all those employed – were in financial services, with another million in associated professions such as accountancy and legal services. The financial sector accounts for nearly 10 per cent of GDP, higher than in any other rich country, and is the world's biggest exporter of financial services.

Increasingly, the City of London has channelled money into speculative or rent-extracting activities rather than productive ones. Net bank lending to non-financial business in 2014 and 2015 was negative, to the tune of over £14 billion. Yet British banks have lent vast amounts to China and other emerging market economies – £800 billion between 2006 and 2015, representing three and a half times their capital, according to the Bank of England.[53] This has provided a flow of rental income, albeit exposing the UK to the growing risk of bad debts in China.

Andrew Haldane, the Bank of England's chief economist, said in October 2015: 'In a nutshell, finance has moved away from serving the economy and towards serving itself.'[54] He and others such as John Kay and Will Hutton[55] have lambasted the 'cult of liquidity' as usurping 'the ethos of long-termism'. This over-romanticises the past. But it is surely the dominant attitude now. When the Bank of England's chief economist concludes that bankers are using ever more sophisticated devices for rent extraction, it is only reasonable to ask why governments have done nothing about it. Perhaps the answer is that they too are short-termist, focused on the next election, and are in thrall to the financial institutions.

In the post-1945 era, a top concern for governments was the trade deficit, which determined the strength of the currency. In the UK in the 1960s and 1970s, failure to reduce the deficit, then about 2 per cent of GDP, caused runs on the pound and the resignation of a Labour Chancellor of the Exchequer. After 2010, the UK ran up a current account deficit that reached nearly 7 per cent of national income by 2015, the highest of any large developed country and the biggest in peacetime since 1830. At over £120 billion, it was also the world's largest deficit in absolute terms, after the USA.[56] Yet there has been little criticism of the government.

Despite the deficit, the exchange rate strengthened, drawing in more foreign investment, mostly to buy property and acquire

British companies, including iconic names of its industrial heritage, such as Cadbury's and Rolls-Royce. The sale of Cadbury's to Kraft of the USA was indicative of the risks that come with foreign control. To secure approval of the takeover, Kraft promised to preserve jobs, only to go ahead with factory closures once the deal was done. Foreign owners will always give precedence to their base shareholders. While British investment in foreign firms abroad has not been successful overall, foreign investment in the UK has done exceedingly well, yielding dividends 30 per cent higher in 2015 than in 2010, according to Capita Asset Services.

In 2010, the Chancellor promised a 'march of the makers' to rebalance the economy towards manufacturing exports. Nevertheless, the volume of goods exported fell by 10 per cent between 2011 and 2015, depressed by an overvalued exchange rate. Britain's last coal mine closed and its last steel mills were under threat.

By 2015, the share of manufacturing in national income was just 9 per cent, well below Germany (nearly 21 per cent), Italy (15 per cent), the USA (12 per cent) and France (over 10 per cent), among others. Two-thirds of remaining manufacturing firms employing more than 500 workers were foreign-owned. Britain had ceased to be an industrial economy.

It is increasingly a rentier economy, living largely off income from financial and other assets at home and abroad. Just as the government can run a budget deficit as long as investors and savers have confidence in the future, so the UK can run a current account deficit as long as foreigners are willing to finance it by putting their savings into British assets. But it is a dependency that will haunt future governments.

CONCLUSION

The labour-based economic and social system constructed in the post-1945 era in the rich industrialised countries imploded in the 1970s and 1980s. It had been progressive by the standards of the past, but it had unattractive features and its contradictions were exposed when the global economy began to take shape.

The neo-liberalism that followed has generated rising inequality of wealth and income, and chronic insecurity for a rapidly growing precariat. Worst of all, it has created a plutocracy and plutocratic corporations linked to concentrated financial capital that are able to gain increasing amounts of rental income by virtue of their wealth. Meanwhile, wages are stagnating. With China, India and other major industrialising economies becoming centres of employment, that stagnation will continue. US economist Robert Gordon has added to the gloomy prognosis about future changes in living standards for those relying on labour, noting that US productivity growth has slowed to a dawdle.[57] It promises to be the same in Europe and Japan and it will stay that way.

The old income distribution system that tied income to jobs has disintegrated. A new system is feasible. But first we need to understand just why and how the rentiers are running away with most of the income and wealth.

Chapter 2

THE SHAPING OF RENTIER CAPITALISM

As neo-liberalism took shape in the 1980s, the concept of 'competitiveness' became almost an obsession. A country could only develop or grow fast if it were more competitive than others, which to a large extent meant having lower costs of production and greater profitability than 'competitors', as well as lower taxes on potential investors.

This was a break with classical political economy. It had focused on trade, driven by a theory of 'comparative advantage'; countries should specialise in those goods and services they were more efficient at producing relative to others. Suddenly, the message seemed to be that all countries had to be better at the same things.

The main economic game became finding ways to attract and retain foreign investment, to boost exports and to limit imports. This led to the political justification for cutting direct taxes, particularly on capital, and providing subsidies to investors. But corporations and financiers have used their new power to induce governments and supranational financial institutions to build an infrastructure that favours their interests.

Aided by the neo-liberal economics community, they have constructed a global framework of institutions and regulations that enable elites to maximise their rental income. It is anything but a 'free market'.

FROM BRETTON WOODS TO CRONY CAPITALISM

In 1944, forty-four allied nations met at Bretton Woods, New Hampshire, in the USA to set up a trio of global institutions. The World Bank was established to rebuild capitalism, the International Monetary Fund (IMF) to maintain economic stability, and the General Agreement on Tariffs and Trade (later to become the World Trade Organization) to liberalise trade.

The World Bank and the IMF, both based in Washington DC, helped Western Europe recover, and then turned to developing countries. By convention, the World Bank is headed by an American nominated by the US government, its largest shareholder. In the 1970s, under Robert McNamara, fresh from masterminding the Vietnam War, the World Bank was made pivotal to the expansion of American interests.

It and the IMF, whose head has traditionally been a European national, became the leading institutions fostering capitalism in developing countries in an increasingly ideological way. 'Structural adjustment programmes' forced on governments in Latin America, Africa and Asia by the IMF obliged them to pursue export-led industrialisation, cut welfare spending, rush privatisation measures, reduce government spending, lower salaries of civil servants and cut their numbers and, above all, enforce private property rights.

Much has been written about the disastrous consequences of

this blueprint strategy. By weakening civil services while directing funds into the privatisation of crucial economic sectors, the scope for corruption and ecological neglect was vastly increased. It created the conditions for 'crony capitalism', enabling well-connected individuals and companies to take control of key sectors and turn themselves into plutocrats through opportunistic networking and clientelism. Carlos Slim became the richest man in the world by acquiring control of Mexico's telecom sector on privatisation. Others elsewhere emerged as billionaires, combining political skills with ruthless commercial acumen.

In industrialised countries in the 1980s and 1990s, the neo-liberal structural adjustment strategy took the form of 'supply-side economics'. The World Bank and IMF were joined by the Organisation for Economic Co-operation and Development (OECD) and fledgling European Community institutions in pushing privatisation, labour market flexibility, lower public spending and so on. This was to lead to more inequality and more unemployment. Those bodies slowly became more intrusive and, by the time of the 2008 financial crisis, in alliance with the European Central Bank, they were able to dictate reforms to struggling European Union members, including Spain, Portugal, Ireland and Greece.

Meanwhile, the Washington institutions gained a new role in the 1990s as the midwives of capitalist development in the numerous 'transition' countries of the former Soviet Union and Eastern Europe, aided by the hastily established European Bank for Reconstruction and Development (EBRD). They adapted the structural adjustment strategy to these countries in what was euphemistically called 'shock therapy'. This had calamitous social and economic consequences, for which the international financial institutions and economists advising them bear a great deal of responsibility.

The worst aspect was the *sequencing* of the reforms. The essence of shock therapy, as devised by arrogant Western economists with little knowledge of the countries' structures and cultures, was simple. First, markets should be established and liberalised. Since there was a shortage of goods and services, this would lead to inflation, which would be controlled by slashing public expenditure and dismantling old state structures. Privatisation was to be rushed, because otherwise there might be more socialistic reform. Private property rights were to be vigorously established. Only after these reforms was the state to be reconstructed with a new system of social protection.

The outcome was predictable and predicted. In the short term, there was hyperinflation, with some countries experiencing price rises that went into thousands of per cent a year – in the case of Ukraine, over 10,000 per cent in 1993. Real wages and living standards plunged, leading to starvation and rising morbidity and mortality. In Russia, male life expectancy fell from sixty-four to fifty-eight between 1991 and 1994, leading to over 2 million premature deaths.

Privatisation was pushed through while senior politicians and civil servants were receiving monthly salaries of $10 or less, leaving them easy prey for bribery or corrupt dealings by those planning to build commercial empires. Outsiders joined in. Economists at Harvard University supposedly helping in Russia's privatisation programme were later found guilty of insider dealing that made them millions of dollars.[1]

Mafioso tactics prevailed in the ex-Soviet Union and in much of Eastern Europe. Out of the morass arose a sinister plutocracy of oligarchs, suddenly multibillionaires with business empires that were to give them unparalleled power and political influence. They were soon to be welcomed and feted in the UK and elsewhere, integrated into the global elite and enabled to fund political parties keen to serve their interests.

As in developing countries under structural adjustment, inequality and oligarchy did not come about as a result of free markets but as the predicted consequence of institutional interventions deploying an ideological agenda. They created a venal form of crony capitalism.

The Economist has constructed an index of crony capitalism based on the wealth of billionaires in sectors such as casinos, oil and construction where, in its view, there is ample scope for rent seeking through cosy relations with government.[2] It claims that rent seeking is worse in emerging-market economies, which account for two-thirds of 'crony wealth', with Russia heading the 2016 rankings of twenty-two countries. Britain, at fourteenth, comes top among industrialised economies, followed by the USA at sixteenth. However, the index does not include technology industries or much of finance as rent-seeking sectors, despite their lobbying power.

In 2014 *The Economist* suggested that crony capitalism had peaked, but in 2016 it acknowledged that there was still reason to worry. Even on its restricted definition of crony sectors, crony wealth accounted for nearly a fifth of billionaire wealth in developed countries and half of billionaire wealth in developing countries. Including hedge-fund billionaires and other financiers would double the crony wealth share of total US billionaire wealth from 14 per cent to 28 per cent. Including the youthful billionaires of Silicon Valley would push it up even more. As *The Economist* admitted, 'If technology were to be classified as a crony industry, rent-seeking wealth would be higher and rising steadily in the Western world.'

Moreover, *The Economist*'s narrow definition substantially understates crony capitalism. Its examples of rent seeking were 'forming cartels' and 'lobbying for rules that benefit a firm at the expense of competitors and customers'. It thus omitted the most insidious way in which crony capitalism is extending its grip: political manipulation by the plutocracy and elite, who are funding politicians and political parties to favour the interest of rentiers (see Chapter 7).

Another aspect of crony capitalism is the spread of corporate rentier devices. Individuals or groups buy firms, saddle them with debt, pay themselves huge bonuses and then declare bankruptcy, thereby privatising profit and socialising losses. Companies buy back their own shares with the intention of forcing up the price, enabling top executives to take windfall gains by selling their shares or realising share options. Or executives take dividends from short-term profits based on borrowing. None of these practices boosts production; they are mechanisms for rent extraction.

Privatisation via structural adjustment programmes has been a way of transferring public assets to private interests, giving selected individuals or firms considerable rental income. One of the most notorious instances was the Treuhand, the trust fund set up by the West German government after the collapse of East Germany, which sold East German state assets at giveaway prices, costing thousands of jobs and enriching a few West German firms.

In 2015, the German government took the lead in imposing

something similar on Greece, forcing its government to sell cherry-picked public assets valued at €50 billion (£35 billion) to help pay off the country's debts. As this was a 'fire sale', made under duress at a time not of the choosing of the Greek government, there was ample scope for corporations or plutocrats to gain assets and thus rental income on the cheap.

Thus financial institutions, and economists working for them, shaped the global economic system in a way that rewarded rent seekers and fostered a pattern of inequality in which an ugly plutocracy emerged. It was not the outcome of autonomous market forces, but of politically driven institutions.

THE GLOBAL ARCHITECTURE OF RENTIER CAPITALISM

The Great Transformation was built by national bureaucracies answerable to national politicians and financiers. But, after the first phase collapsed in the 1930s, bankers were so discredited that when it came to creating the institutions for managing economic issues for the post-1945 era, President Franklin Roosevelt and others excluded all bankers (except one who was regarded as tame) from the Bretton Woods negotiations of 1944. It was only when the Global Transformation took off in the 1970s that bankers and financiers became dominant again. They have played an increasing role in shaping the global economy, largely built by international bureaucracies based mainly in Washington DC and in Geneva.

Geneva has been a centre of the governance of globalisation, and its shifting physical architecture has symbolised the changing character of global capitalism. In 1969, at the peak of the social democratic era, the International Labour Organization (ILO) was housed in an iconic classical-style building by the lake, and in that year received the Nobel Peace Prize.

Shortly afterwards, it moved to new headquarters reminiscent of a massive IBM punch card then used for mainframe computers. Its old building was taken over by the body dealing with trade, GATT (the General Agreement on Tariffs and Trade), which later became the World Trade Organization (WTO). GATT was a midwife of globalisation, orchestrating a series of 'rounds' of trade liberalisation that culminated in the wide-ranging accords of the Uruguay Round and the creation of the WTO in 1995. For a few years, the WTO was the most vibrant part of Geneva's globalising architecture.

However, it soon ran out of steam, unable to finalise the so-called Doha Round, launched in 2001, and ill-equipped to become an institution of governance. It never built itself into a giant bureaucracy. Today, the WTO has ceased to be a centre of reforming zeal, whereas the World Intellectual Property Organization (WIPO), seen as largely ineffectual in the 1970s and 1980s, has become a core organ of global capitalism. In the centre of the UN complex, its new conference centre juts out imposingly.

In 1995, the numbers employed in the WTO and WIPO were about the same, at just over 500. Today, WIPO employs about 1,200 people, nearly twice the number as WTO, and has more staff in Geneva than any international body except the United Nations itself.

At the same time, Geneva has seen a vast expansion of humanitarian organisations, including the UN refugee agency (UNHCR) and the International Organization for Migration (IOM), reflecting the huge growth of distress migration and refugees in the initial phase of the Global Transformation. The number of

UNHCR staff worldwide has almost doubled since 1995 to over 9,300, while IOM now employs 8,400, nearly eight times as many as in 1995. It is symbolic that, on the edge of Geneva airport, a compound for private jets belonging to some of the world's plutocrats abuts cramped temporary accommodation for a growing number of asylum seekers.

On the other side of the Atlantic, in Washington DC, the Bretton Woods agencies have devoted considerable resources to their neo-liberal project. In 2015, the World Bank directly employed over 9,000 staff, a 50 per cent increase since 1995. It and the IMF have channelled huge amounts of money and technical assistance towards liberalising the global economy, through structural adjustment strategies in developing countries, shock therapy in ex-communist countries and supply-side economics in OECD countries. But it is anything but a free market economy they have helped to build.

PATENT POWER

'The granting [of] patents "inflames cupidity", excites fraud, stimulates men to run after schemes that may enable them to levy a tax on the public, begets disputes and quarrels betwixt inventors, provokes endless lawsuits … The principle of the law from which such consequences flow cannot be just.'

The Economist, 1851

In 2011, Google bought the mobile handset maker Motorola Mobility for a hefty $12.5 billion and three years later sold it for

$2.9 billion. On the face of it, this looks like a bad deal. In fact, Google came out on top. It bought Motorola not for its handset business but for the more than 20,000 mobile phone patents that came with it. Royalties and licensing fees from these patents are a nice little earner for Google but, more importantly, ownership of the patents enabled Google to see off a challenge from Samsung to its Android smartphone operating system, increase sales of its own-design Nexus smartphone and further boost its mobile advertising revenues.

Particularly since 1995, intellectual property has become a prime source of rental income, through market power created by the spread of trademarks (crucial for branding), copyright, design rights, geographical indications, trade secrets and, above all, patents. Knowledge and technology-intensive industries, which according to WIPO now account for over 30 per cent of *global* output, are gaining as much or more in rental income from intellectual property rights as from the production of goods or services. This represents a political choice by governments around the world to grant monopolies over knowledge to private interests, allowing them to restrict public access to knowledge and to raise the price of obtaining it or of products and services embodying it.

While governments pay lip service to the need to balance the interests of holders of intellectual property rights with the public interest in access to knowledge, in practice the public interest has been subordinated to the interests of private property, with the USA leading the way. Challenging the grant of intellectual property rights (or upholding rights against infringements) is expensive, especially if, as is often the case, the dispute has to go to court.

Governments have chosen to support investment in innovation

by granting temporary monopolies via patents to private 'owners' of inventions. Other feasible systems of rewarding or encouraging innovation that do not give rental income to inventors, such as prizes or collaborative partnerships, have been relegated to the margins.

As with other aspects of rentier capitalism, the patent system began with the monarchy. From the fourteenth century onwards, European rulers, including the English monarchy, granted temporary monopolies to petitioners through letters of patent, with the professed intention of encouraging new techniques and skills.

However, the system was subject to widespread abuse as a revenue-raising device. Patents were often granted, including on basic commodities, to anyone prepared to pay a fee for the privilege. Modern patent law has its roots in England's 1624 Statute of Monopolies, enacted by Parliament in the reign of King James I to stop him and his successors extracting money in this way; henceforth, the grant of a monopoly was restricted to inventions. Patents to 'promote the progress of science and useful arts' were further legitimised by the American Constitution in 1789. Then, in 1883, the first international agreement on the protection of patents and trademarks was signed: the Paris Convention for the Protection of Industrial Property.

While patents have a long history, there has been an unprecedented surge in the globalisation era. In 2011, over 2 million applications were filed in patent offices around the world, more than double the number in 1995. Over 2.6 million applications were filed in 2013 and 2.7 million in 2014, fuelled by double-digit growth in China. Now the top country for filings, China accounted for more than a third of global applications.

This surge has accompanied new structures that have

strengthened international protection of patents and other forms of intellectual property. When the Uruguay Round of trade talks was launched in 1986, the USA insisted on pushing intellectual property onto the agenda, resulting in the WTO's landmark Agreement on Trade-Related Aspects of Intellectual Property Rights (TRIPS). It came into force in 1995, setting minimum standards for enforcement of intellectual property rights that are binding on all WTO members.

This is in contrast to WIPO treaties, which bind only those countries that sign them (though many more have done so since 1995). Before TRIPS, many countries did not have patent laws or gave patent holders only a few years of rental income. Now, most countries have laws that grant patent holders exclusive rights to a monopoly rental income for twenty years.

Worldwide, an estimated 10.2 million patents were in force in 2014. On one calculation, the global value of patents exceeded $10 trillion in 2009, when there were 6.7 million patents in force.[3] If we assume that the figure has risen in line with the patent 'stock', the value of the global patent stock today would be over $15 trillion, equivalent to nearly 20 per cent of world GDP.

Opposition to the notion that inventions can become the money-making property of an individual, group or corporation also goes back a long way. In 1813, Thomas Jefferson described ideas as natural public goods, since communication of an idea or knowledge to others does not deprive the originator of it: 'Inventions then cannot, in nature, be a subject of property.'[4] He added that patents brought 'more embarrassment than advantage to society', noting that countries that did not grant 'monopolies of invention' were just as innovative as England, which did.

In July 1851, *The Economist* opined: 'Comprehensive patents are taken out by some parties, for the purpose of stopping inventions, or appropriating the fruits of the inventions of others.'[5] It noted that many of the inventions that galvanised the Industrial Revolution, including railways and the spinning mule, emerged without protection by patents. So, there is a long tradition behind the argument that inventions should be part of the 'scientific commons' of society, not converted into a sphere of commercial profits. Why, then, have we been witnessing the biggest and most rapid spread of patents in history?

Unlike traditional societies, which have tended to share ideas, capitalistic societies have institutionalised two claims, that inventors should be rewarded for what is perceived to be their investment and risky endeavour, and that, by providing financial incentives to inventors, patents encourage and support innovation. In addition, the requirement to publish details of patented inventions aims to increase the stock of public knowledge.

Both claims can be contested. Many, if not most, inventions build on the past ingenuity of one or more, perhaps many, people, even over several generations. Faraday's invention of the electric motor followed inventions of the electromagnet (Sturgeon) and the battery (Volta). Moreover, many inventions involve no investment, no cost and no risk, and may even arise by accident.

President John Kennedy's pledge to put a man on the moon led to spin-offs including memory foam, improved radial tyres, freeze-dried food and cochlear implants. Silicon Valley's early start-ups benefited from public spending on research in universities and for defence (including invention of the internet itself, a freely available, publicly funded technology). The research that led to touch-screen displays, GPS and smartphone voice control all had government backing.[6] In effect, government has socialised the risks but not the rewards. Why should all the income from an invention that happens to be commercially successful accrue to just one person or firm, the patent holder?

Furthermore, patent offices, especially the US Patent and Trademark Office (USPTO), have liberally handed out patents for 'inventions' that by no stretch of the imagination satisfy the accepted criteria for patentability. To be eligible, an invention must be novel, involve a not-obvious 'inventive step' and have practical application. Yet the USPTO has granted patents for discoveries of natural phenomena, notably in medicine, such as the breast cancer gene. Though this patent was later invalidated, the American Medical Association estimates that a fifth of the 30,000 human genes are under patent in the USA.

The USPTO has also granted patents for so-called 'business methods', such as Amazon's one-click system for online purchases, and for trivial changes using existing technologies, such as Apple's patent on rectangular tablets with rounded corners. The USPTO even granted a patent for the use of turmeric in healing wounds, later overturned after the Indian government proved in court that this had been known for millennia in traditional Indian medicine.

The claim that patents stimulate innovation can also be challenged. For one thing, patent filings are unreliable indicators of the rate of innovation. A Carnegie Institute survey of why firms chose to patent showed that only 10 per cent of patents had real economic value; the rest were filed to ensure a monopoly or to block potential litigation, that is, for rent-seeking purposes.[7] Other studies have found that 40 to 90 per cent of patents are neither exploited nor licensed out. Meanwhile, data from the European Patent Office analysed by the OECD in 2015 suggest that the average technological and economic value of patented inventions has been falling, probably reflecting growing defensive filings.[8]

Privatising innovation can actually impede scientific advance by making it harder for inventors to build on the inventions of others and by stifling the exchange of ideas. James Watt's patent to protect his invention of the steam engine prevented further development of the technology until after his patent expired.[9] Had César Milstein applied for a patent for his creation of monoclonal antibodies, many advances in cancer treatment would have been delayed.[10] The decision of Tim Berners-Lee and CERN (the European Organization for Nuclear Research), where he worked, not to patent his 1989 invention of the World Wide Web paved the way for an explosion in information and communication technologies. This could not have happened had use of the invention been restricted.

While growth in patent-intensive industries has outstripped growth in sectors with few patents or other intellectual property, there is no consensus on whether patent rights result in more innovation. One study found that patents were good neither at rewarding innovation nor at propagating it.[11] Others could find no correlation between productivity growth and patents. And many patent applications are said to conceal as much information as possible, preventing them from being a vehicle for sharing and disseminating information.[12]

Meanwhile, monopoly pricing by patent holders has blocked access to innovative products and technologies to poor people in all countries, notably in the health and environmental sectors. And the patent system has distorted the direction of research and development, so that resources flow towards areas that promise high rental income, not to areas that would maximise the public good or benefit the less well-off.

PATENT TROLLING AND HOOVERING

In the USA, the monopoly rents gained from patents have spawned a lucrative industry of 'patent trolls': firms that produce nothing themselves but buy up unexploited or undervalued patents with the sole intention of tracking down supposed patent violators and demanding they pay licence fees for use of the patent or face court action. On being threatened by trolls, many corporations pay up simply to avoid lengthy and expensive legal procedures. Nevertheless, there were over 5,000 US lawsuits in 2014, driven by multiple filings by patent trolls, frequently aimed at big tech companies. Apple claimed in 2014 to have been the subject of nearly 100 patent lawsuits in the preceding three years.

Trolling has given additional impetus to the drive by Apple, Google and other powerful multinational corporations to build up huge patent portfolios, strings of patents acquired from individuals or start-up companies, to prevent rivals from entering the market and to entrench their monopoly status. In areas such as pharmaceuticals and information and communications technologies there is also a problem of 'patent thickets', with rival firms holding key patents on some aspect of the overall technology. Witness the 'smartphone patent wars', started between Apple and Samsung, which have involved all the main smartphone manufacturers suing each other in various combinations and in various countries, with damages claims running into billions of dollars.

Patent thickets and patent trolls have become impediments to innovation in the IT sector because companies cannot move without stumbling over someone else's patent and having to pay licensing fees to multiple patent owners. A mobile phone, for instance, may have as many as 3,000 different patents. Similarly, in the pharmaceuticals sector, the development of combined drug formulations for people with Aids has been hampered because the drugs are patented by different companies.

In many cases, as noted earlier, corporations buy up patents less to use them than to defend themselves. A paper for the St Louis Federal Reserve, hardly a hotbed of radicalism, concluded: 'The vast bulk of patents are not only useless, they don't represent innovation at all. They are part of an arms race. Any successful large company needs a large portfolio of patents to fend off potential lawsuits by rivals and by patent trolls.'[13]

Besides hoovering up others' patents, corporations have devised clever tactics to extend patents or the rental income from them. The pharmaceutical industry does this by 'follow-on' patenting or 'ever-greening' (making small changes to drug formulations and claiming a new invention), by clever marketing that maintains demand for a branded product after the patent expires, or by entering 'pay-for-delay' agreements with generic producers, enabling firms to continue to receive rental income beyond the patent term by delaying the entry of cheaper generics on the market.[14]

The USA, European Union members and some other countries have introduced another extension of rental income for drugs by granting pharmaceutical companies 'data exclusivity' and 'market exclusivity' beyond the patent term. During this period, which is twelve years in the USA for biotech drugs known as 'biologics' (five years for chemically derived drugs), ten years in the EU, eight years in Japan and five years in several other countries including Australia, New Zealand, Singapore and Chile, 'data exclusivity' provisions deny generic producers access to research and clinical trial data held by the company that they need to produce and gain regulatory approval for a generic equivalent. 'Market exclusivity' prevents them from putting competitor drugs on the market.

The claimed justification for exclusivity provisions is that costly research would otherwise be replicated by free riders, discouraging innovative research by big corporations.[15] But industry claims that drugs cost up to $2.5 billion to develop are suspect, as is the claim that it needs to charge high prices to fund this research.[16] The US industry spends more on marketing and advertising than on research.[17]

In any case, as much of the research is funded by public institutions and aided by subsidies, the big US corporations could be termed the free riders. On one estimate, taking subsidies and tax breaks into account, private industry pays for only about a third of US biomedical research, yet reaps the lion's share of income from patents.[18]

Another study concluded that the federal government could save up to $140 billion a year on its Medicare and Medicaid prescription drugs bill if there were no patent protection. This would be enough to finance an increase in funding for public biomedical research equal to all the research and development done by the pharmaceutical industry and still leave the government (and the health sector more broadly) with huge savings.[19]

In one well-known example, a Hepatitis C drug, developed after years of high-risk, publicly funded, university-based research, is being sold by Gilead, the patent owner, for $84,000 for a course of treatment, compared with production costs of $70–$140. Although the clinical trials cost about $500 million, this would have been recovered by a few weeks of sales. Gilead earned $10.3 billion from the drug, Sovaldi, in 2014, much of this from payments through Medicare and Medicaid, the subsidised healthcare programmes for the elderly and poor respectively. A US Senate report noted that Medicaid spending on Sovaldi of over a billion dollars in 2014 managed to treat just one person for every forty patients with Hepatitis C.

This is just one example of price gouging by patent monopolists. Of the twelve cancer treatments approved by the US Food and Drug Administration in 2012, eleven cost over $100,000 dollars per patient per year.[20] Such rent extraction has nothing to do with free markets.

THE EMERGING PATENT GIANT: CHINA

China's emergence as the economic giant of globalisation reflected industrial growth based on cheap labour and imported technology. However, in 2011, it overtook the USA as the country with the most patent applications and in 2014 its patent office received nearly a million filings, more than the US and Japanese offices combined. Of the 10.2 million patents in force globally in 2014, the USA still had the most (25 per cent of the total), followed by Japan (19 per cent). But, at 12 per cent, China was catching up.

The majority of applications are filed only with the Chinese patent office and many are for utility models (minor changes) and designs rather than inventions. But there has also been a big increase in Chinese applications filed abroad, signalling their rising commercial value in the global market. In 2015, China came third after the USA and Japan in the number of filings under WIPO's Patent Cooperation Treaty, which enables inventors to file a single patent application for multiple countries. Chinese telecommunications companies Huawei Technologies and ZTE came first and third respectively in the rankings of companies filing the most applications, Qualcomm of the USA being second.

Foxconn, not content with being the world's biggest contract electronics manufacturer, is also a patent heavyweight. As of 2012, the company had filed over 12,000 international patent applications in such areas as electrical machinery and computer and audio-video technology, and was also active in nanotechnology.

The USA, which built its industrial base in the nineteenth century by appropriating technology from abroad, has repeatedly castigated China for doing much the same thing. One study for the US government claimed that Chinese theft of intellectual property was costing US firms $300 billion a year through production of counterfeit goods and 'pirated operational processes'.[21] A much-quoted case involves Pfizer's patent on Viagra. The company was obliged to fight a ten-year legal battle to secure its patent rights in China. During that time Chinese pharmaceutical companies conquered the market with cheaper copycat versions of the drug and, when the patent expired in 2014, were ready to produce generic equivalents.

This is just one example of ongoing tension. The Chinese define indigenous innovation as 'enhancing original innovation through co-innovation and re-innovation based on the assimilation of imported technologies'. Their goal is to transform foreign technology into Chinese with a 'by China for China' tagline. But what they see as adaptation, US multinationals view as a 'blueprint for technology theft on a scale the world has never seen before'.[22]

Yet Chinese firms are increasingly innovative in their own right.[23] While the biggest patenting areas are in alkaloid/plant extracts and pharmaceuticals (much linked to traditional medicines), China ranks with the USA and Japan in digital computing, processing and communication sectors.[24] And since 2005 it has accounted for over a quarter of worldwide patents in the areas of 3D printing and robotics, more than any other country.[25]

In nanotechnology, Chinese applicants make up nearly 15 per cent of filings worldwide, putting China third after the USA and Japan. Many of these come from Chinese universities and public research organisations. As in the United States, the Chinese heavily subsidise the research and development that leads to patentable inventions and innovation, while leaving the income gained from patents in private hands.

• • •

In sum, the spread of patents has been mainly for purposes other than rewarding or supporting innovation. Most patents are acquired to gain or protect a monopoly, acting as a deterrent, not a spur, to innovation. Many of the world's greatest inventions have come without the incentive of patent protection. Yet governments claiming to promote free markets have connived to support the growth of monopoly rental income via patents, which block 'free market' competition. This engine of rental income is out of control.

COPYRIGHT: TAXING KNOWLEDGE

Copyright, the right to a monopoly on literary and artistic works, has also been vastly extended in the globalisation era, through international agreements such as TRIPS and WIPO's 1996 internet treaties and through national laws. Most countries now grant rights to income from literary works for at least fifty years after the death of the author, a rule entrenched in the 1886 Berne Convention for the Protection of Literary and Artistic Works and then TRIPS. The USA, EU members and some other countries have raised this to seventy years, providing rental income to the author's heirs or other copyright owner, even over generations, who have done nothing to earn it.

Copyright rules for music, paintings, sculpture, photographs, videos, films, TV programmes, computer programs and databases have also been strengthened. For sound recordings, the term of protection has risen to seventy years from date of release in the EU and to ninety-five years in the USA, which grants the same term to films made by US movie studios.

In 2014, cross-border payments of royalties and licensing fees for use of all forms of intellectual property (excluding profits from domestic exploitation) were estimated by the WTO at nearly $300 billion, over three times the figure in 2000 and ten times the amount in 1990. These figures do not include trade in audio-visual services – films, music, videos, TV programmes – worth $19 billion in 2013.

The USA accounted for nearly 40 per cent of the payments, followed closely by the European Union (including intra-EU trade). Of the $129 billion in intellectual property exports earned by the

USA in 2013, $45 billion came from patents, $43 billion from software, $17 billion from films, TV programmes, music and books, $17 billion from trademarks and $6 billion from other sources such as live performances and franchising fees.

The leading US firms in three copyright-intensive industries – films, publishing and software – have been much more profitable than their counterparts in construction, transport and mining, and their profit margins have been growing rapidly.[26] A WIPO study of thirty countries in 2011 found that copyright industries accounted for an average of 5.4 per cent of GDP and 6 per cent of national employment.

Historically, copyright – the right to copy – was used by rulers as an instrument of censorship to control what could and could not be printed and disseminated. As with patents, it became a way for a monarch to raise money by charging a fee for permission to print and publish approved works. The forerunner of today's copyright law was the Statute of Anne in 1710 that gave protection to authors for fourteen years.

The US Copyright Act of 1790 also granted copyright to authors for fourteen years, renewable once for another fourteen years. But the present global system, which dates from the late nineteenth century, has not only greatly strengthened protection for literary works, but has extended it to all kinds of creative endeavour. The originator, who automatically owns the copyright at the point of creation (there is no need to apply or register), can keep the rights to rental income, assign them to a publisher or sell them. In 1985, Michael Jackson famously paid $47.5 million for the Beatles song catalogue, bringing him and, later, his estate millions of dollars in rental income annually. As one critic put it, 'Anything and everything is now copyrighted. If you made it, no matter how trivial, you own it, and if someone else copies it you can sue.'[27]

Copyright was opposed by Thomas Jefferson as being a tax on knowledge. But, in the era of rentier capitalism, ever stiffer copyright rules limit access to books and articles, including educational materials and scientific papers. Access is controlled by giant media companies such as Elsevier, Springer, Taylor & Francis and Wiley; they charge enormous subscription fees to libraries of the universities that produced the work (mostly for free) that they are selling back to them, a practice rightly termed 'a notorious rent-seeking boondoggle'.[28]

Elsevier, the biggest academic journal publisher, Taylor & Francis and Springer have profit margins around 35 per cent, more than Facebook (27 per cent).[29] Moves by governments and campaigners to promote open access to scholarly journals, especially for the results of publicly financed research, have paradoxically boosted journal revenues, with publishers such as Elsevier charging authors (or their institutions) up to $2,150 to make their article freely available to the public.

Copyright rules also restrict creators' ability to use images, music or text in new works. In one egregious example, *Selma*, a film about Martin Luther King, was unable to use the actual words of his speeches, including the iconic 'I have a dream' address at the civil rights march in 1963. His famously litigious estate refused permission because it had already licensed the film rights of his speeches to another studio for a planned biopic produced by Steven Spielberg. 'I have a dream' will not be in the public domain until 2039. Similarly, until 2015, when its copyright was overturned, Warner Chappell Music was for many decades able to recoup royalties for public performances of 'Happy Birthday', thought to be the most sung song in the world, and prevent others from using it in films and broadcasts.

Countries vary widely in the extent to which they limit copyright or provide exceptions. In the USA and UK, 'fair use' provisions permit use of copyrighted material for educational purposes or private use. But, there and elsewhere, the interests of big media corporations to earn rental income have prevailed over the public's rights of access to knowledge and culture.

In 2009, the *Financial Times* opposed European extension of the copyright term for recorded music, noting that most revenue accrued to producers and a few superstars. It stated: 'Copyright extension is, in the main, just the well-known strategy of powerful companies: profit-grabbing through lobbying for state protection.'[30] They have usually succeeded. And while internet downloads and streaming have disrupted the traditional music industry model, the end result has been the accumulation of yet more rental income by internet giants Amazon, Apple and Google through their own music delivery services.

THE BRANDING BONANZA

The story is not finished yet. The most widely used form of intellectual property protection is the trademark, a name or logo that identifies a brand, such as Nike, Coca Cola or Apple. Branding has boomed in the globalisation era. Trademark applications have trebled since 1995, reaching nearly 7.5 million in 2014, again aided by a surge in China. Registered trademarks are normally protected for ten years but are renewable indefinitely as long as the trademark is used.

Brands that inspire customer loyalty and trust give firms more market power and enable them to charge more for their products than a simple mark-up over cost, thereby collecting more rental income. As WIPO noted, 'Strong brands can create high barriers to market entry, as new competitors may not be able to bear the high advertising costs of inducing consumers to switch to their products.'[31]

According to WIPO, between 1987 and 2011 US investment in brands accounted for 22 per cent of all investment in intangible assets, exceeding research and development and design. Globally, companies invested $466 billion in brands in 2011 (excluding in-house investment in marketing), with US companies in the lead.

The value of the top 100 global brands was $3.3 trillion in 2015.[32] Brand value can be a high proportion of a firm's market capitalisation – a third, on average, according to a study by Interbrand, but some put it much higher.[33] Coca Cola's brand may contribute one half of its market capitalisation. According to Forbes, Apple, the world's most valuable company, also has the most valuable brand, worth $145 billion in 2015, a fifth of its market value, and its patent portfolio is more valuable still. Microsoft's brand, which came second in Forbes's 2015 list, was worth $69 billion.

According to the Top 150 Global Licensors ranking, retail sales of branded licensed products worldwide were some $260 billion in 2014, having risen rapidly. Disney, the world's largest brand licensor, alone earned $45 billion from licensing use of Disney themes and characters for goods ranging from toys to breakfast cereals. Mickey Mouse, first created in 1928, remains in copyright until 2024. Franchising of branded services – from hotels and fast-food chains to hairdressing – has also grown steadily.

Other forms of intellectual property protection, such as the protection of industrial designs, geographical indications for wines, food and other products, and plant breeders' rights, have also expanded in the globalisation era. They all generate rental income above the market price that would prevail if there were free markets.

TRADE AND INVESTMENT TREATIES

Bolstering these intellectual property protection devices is an expanding set of inter-government deals. The construction of the global market system has been marked by a proliferation of over 3,200 bilateral and multilateral treaties on trade and investment, most of which have never been subject to any democratic mandate or accountability.[34] This is nothing like an open market system, although many of the deals have been depicted as favouring 'free trade'.

The Uruguay Round of trade negotiations that began in 1986 extended the scope of trade talks beyond tariff cutting to non-tariff barriers such as product health and safety rules, liberalisation of services and protection of intellectual property. These accords came into force in 1995 alongside the creation of the WTO. Although there has been no comprehensive multilateral agreement since then – the Doha Round launched in 2001 having run into the sand – there have been more than ten regional deals a year, on average, over that time.[35] But trade deals are far outnumbered by bilateral investment treaties (BITs), part of a murky legalistic system creating a straitjacket favouring commercial interests. Some countries have hundreds of BITs.

By the end of 2015, the USA had concluded twenty bilateral free trade agreements, nearly fifty BITs and sixty-five other investment accords with individual countries or groups of countries, and was hoping to conclude BITs with India and China. It was in negotiation with the EU on a Transatlantic Trade and Investment Partnership (TTIP) and had just finalised lengthy negotiations on the mammoth Trans-Pacific Partnership (TPP), a far-reaching and controversial accord with Canada and ten Asian and Latin American countries accounting for 40 per cent of world output and a third of world trade.

The TPP, though still awaiting ratification, is especially significant as setting a template for future trade deals. It sets a high bar for reductions in tariff and non-tariff barriers to trade in goods, opens up markets for services, including banking and insurance, strengthens intellectual property protection and limits subsidies to state enterprises. While it obliges governments to comply with environmental and labour standards, enforcement provisions are predictably weak.

As one investment banking expert noted: 'It is a mistake to call it a trade agreement. This is really an agreement that's [*sic*] purpose is substantially to weaken nation-based regulation while at the same time strengthening intellectual property protections.'[36]

As is usual in trade agreements involving the USA, American interests prevail and mostly reflect corporate wishes. Under a Congressional mandate, American corporations have an inside track in trade negotiations, being involved as advisors with a direct line to top officials, as well as being powerful lobbyists behind the scenes. This is not just a formal relationship, as was revealed by the release of hundreds of confidential emails between TPP negotiators and industry representatives, obtained under a Freedom of Information Act request. Negotiators privately discussed details of the proposed treaty with corporations when everyone else was denied information on the talks. It is not coincidental that many of the corporate lobbyists were former trade officials.

The USA sees the TPP as a way of increasing its competitiveness vis-à-vis China, which did not join the negotiations, by creating a US-led economic area as a counterweight to China's economic might. And, by binding several of China's key trading partners to regulatory rules and standards that suit American interests, the TPP will put pressure on China to comply with them, whether it joins the TPP or not. While the accord lowers tariffs on agricultural goods, benefiting already heavily subsidised American farmers, the emphasis is on trade in intellectual property-intensive goods and services, such as information and communications technology, Hollywood films and TV programmes, and pharmaceuticals, in which US firms have a comparative advantage.

Already one quarter of US service exports comes from telecommunications, information technology and royalties from licensing intellectual property, according to the US Bureau of Economic Analysis.[37] But this is only part of the rental income gained by owners of patents, copyright, trademarks and design rights. For example, although the latest iPhone is assembled in China from components made in Japan and South Korea, Apple is reckoned to corner 60 per cent of the retail price, wherever it is sold, with gross profit margins pushing 40 per cent. On top of that, it earns rental income from apps sold through its online store. It is no surprise that the USA has relentlessly pressed in trade treaties for strong global protection of its intellectual property.

A particularly controversial aspect of the TPP was the strengthening of patent protection for pharmaceuticals, including a push to oblige all participants to match the US period of data and market exclusivity for 'biologics' of twelve years. While this did not succeed fully, the final accord still obliges countries to provide exclusivity for eight years, or to provide exclusivity for five years and additional regulatory measures to extend protection further. This will boost US pharmaceutical companies' rental income by blocking competition from cheaper generic drugs, to the detriment of patients and health services everywhere, since it will shrink overseas markets for generic producers in India, China and elsewhere.

During the TPP negotiations, the executive director of New Zealand's Association of Salaried Medical Specialists, which represents doctors and dentists, noted that the country's drug-purchasing agency, Pharmac, had previously saved the country billions of dollars by buying medicines at a two-thirds discount, adding: 'But this deal would increase monopoly power of large overseas drug companies. This is not free trade; instead it is introducing the power of big business into our public health service.'[38]

The USA had its own way on copyright too, with participating countries agreeing to extend protection to life plus seventy years, rather than the fifty permitted by TRIPS and the Berne Convention. US negotiators, in thrall to Hollywood, also won stronger copyright enforcement and tougher penalties for piracy. Both will shrink the domain of freely accessible information and increase rental income for the big media corporations.

The TPP will make it easier for foreign financial institutions to enter domestic markets, increasing their income-earning opportunities. Governments will have to open public procurement to foreign bidders and limit subsidies to state enterprises that might otherwise prove more formidable rivals to foreign firms. Some countries agreed to allow foreign companies to provide public services and utilities, while existing privatisation in many areas is locked in. The trade pact is effectively a charter for multinational, particularly US, capital.

Furthermore, the TPP underwrites a contested international dispute settlement process that enables foreign corporations to sue governments for loss of profits and thereby override national environmental, public health, labour and workplace safety regulations (see next section). Investor–state dispute settlement (ISDS) in the TPP will increase rental income by protecting US corporations against policy changes in TPP member countries that might threaten their prospective profits. The fact that the TPP allows tobacco companies to be excluded from ISDS, a carve-out inserted into the accord to win Australia's assent to an ISDS mechanism, is less a point in its favour than an illustration of how multinationals have been using ISDS to undermine decisions of democratic governments. Australia had been defending its controversial cigarette plain packaging law, a public health measure, in an investor–state challenge brought by tobacco giant Philip Morris, maker of Marlboro and other cigarette brands. Philip Morris is pursuing a similar case against Uruguay.

The TTIP is equally ambitious. The American ambassador to the EU said it would 'provide the economic equivalent to NATO', hardly a minor institutional force. As in the TPP, US pharmaceutical companies are pushing for tough data and market exclusivity provisions; the USA and Europe account for 80 per cent of global pharmaceutical sales. And US negotiators want ISDS mechanisms written into the TTIP, expanding ISDS to 50–60 per cent of US foreign direct investment, against 15–20 per cent covered by existing treaties. This would rise to over 80 per cent of US investment with the TPP and mooted EU/China and US/China investment pacts.

Faced with fierce opposition to ISDS from campaigners and pressure from the European Parliament and others, in 2015 the European Commission proposed setting up a specialised court of appointed judges with a right of appeal. The so-called Investment Court System would also circumscribe cases that could be brought to the court and make clear governments' right to regulate. But this would still allow multinationals to sue governments if those regulations affected their profits. And it remains to be seen whether this ISDS-lite will be acceptable to US negotiators. A particular worry is the potential use of ISDS to block new environmental protection regulations in Europe. Environmental cases account for 60 per cent of the 127 ISDS cases already brought against EU countries under bilateral trade agreements in the last two decades, according to Friends of the Earth Europe.

The TTIP could also prevent any future British government from reversing privatisation of parts of the National Health Service or renationalising the rail network, both of which have strong public support. Poland and Slovakia were sued by private health and insurance providers when they attempted to reverse some privatisation of their healthcare systems. And in the TPP and other agreements, the USA has pushed hard for severe restrictions on state-owned firms. This obviously impinges on national sovereignty.

The economic impact of the TPP and the TTIP is disputed: the negotiators claim they will have growth benefits, while independent studies predict job losses, a decline in worker incomes and greater inequality.[39] In reality, these agreements are a smokescreen for strengthening rentier capitalism. As *The Economist* acknowledged, 'Trade deals have relatively little to do with tariffs; they focus instead on deeper regulatory issues such as rules governing capital flows and competition policy.'[40]

Negotiations on a Trade in Services Agreement (TISA) represent another controversial prospective deal aimed at liberalising trade in services such as finance, telecoms, healthcare and transport. Driven by the USA and the EU, the secret talks involve fifty mainly developed countries that together account for 70 per cent of global services output. Although the European Commission has said it will not open publicly funded services such as health, education and social services to foreign companies, US negotiators are pursuing a corporate agenda to make it easier for foreign companies to enter service markets of all kinds and limit the ability of governments to regulate them in the public interest.

Free trade and investment treaties have limited national sovereignty and extended the sovereignty of corporations. As Evgeny Morozov has noted, trade agreements 'describe a world devoid of any other political actors; it's just companies out there.'[41] When a defender of the TTIP asserts that 'it is not about labour standards', he ignores the wider implications of free trade.[42] Trade deals such as the North American Free Trade Agreement (NAFTA) with Mexico and Canada have allowed US corporations to shift jobs to lower-wage countries within a free-trade area and export back to the USA duty-free. If such agreements result in lower wages or weaker bargaining power of workers, because they facilitate relocation of production and employment, they must affect labour standards. The benefits of trade and investment agreements do not accrue to workers through jobs or higher wages. It is the owners of rent-providing assets who have done very nicely.

WHY GLOBAL CAPITAL LOVES DISPUTES

Any economic activity involves risk, which represents a cost against income. The main argument for patents is that they are a reward for risk. But, quietly, the global rules have been changed to minimise risk for multinationals. The investor–state dispute settlement (ISDS) process, incorporated into over 3,000 trade and investment accords, enables them to sue governments for compensation for any policy changes or action deemed to threaten their profits. Risk reduction raises net income for this select group, amounting to a form of rental income.

The policy originated in the late 1950s in Germany, where a business group came up with the idea of an arbitration system to protect their investments in developing countries. The group was led by the chairman of Deutsche Bank, who called the idea an 'international Magna Carta' for private investors. It was taken up by the World Bank, which launched the International Centre for the Settlement of Investment Disputes (ICSID) in 1964, in spite of opposition from twenty-one developing country members, at whom the plan was directed.

Later the US administration included ISDS in trade agreements with developing countries, taking advantage of their need for investment and claiming they did not have adequate legal systems to protect foreign corporations. It was incorporated into the 1994 NAFTA and copied around the world. Recent trade and investment agreements incorporating ISDS include the Trans-Pacific Partnership (TPP) and the Comprehensive Economic and Trade Agreement (CETA) between the EU and Canada, negotiated in 2014. While fewer than 100 claims were made between 1959 and 2002, the number has accelerated, with nearly 700 claims reported by the end of 2015, involving over 100 governments.[43] This litigation has been a rich source of income for multinationals and their lawyers.

Whereas early cases were mainly concerned with egregious violations of agreements such as the expropriation of corporate property or flagrant breach of contract, many cases now intrude directly on public policy, including policies to protect health or the environment. ISDS arbitrators have steadily extended the system's reach to cover any regulatory action with an adverse impact on foreign investors. Notions of 'fair and equitable treatment' and 'indirect expropriation' have been expanded to encompass anything that could affect a company's cash flow. And the definition of investor has been enlarged to include anyone with a financial interest.

As of 2015, twenty ISDS cases had been filed against the Spanish government, by investors ranging from the Abu Dhabi sovereign wealth fund to German municipalities to US brokerage firm Schwab Holdings, for suspending renewable energy subsidies worth €6.5 billion in 2014.[44] Arbitrators have also allowed 'forum shopping', the practice of setting up in a particular jurisdiction solely to exploit a relevant treaty, as Philip Morris did when it transferred its regional headquarters to Hong Kong in order to sue Australia for its plain packaging law.

The ISDS system does not conform to the most basic principles of justice. Cases are heard in secret by arbitration tribunals, the main one being the ICSID based in the World Bank in Washington DC, though there are also tribunals in London, Paris, Hong Kong and The Hague, among others. Three tribunal members, almost always highly paid corporate lawyers, are appointed to adjudicate. One is selected by the multinational, one by the state concerned, and the two then must agree the tribunal president. In ICSID cases, if they cannot agree, a president is appointed by the World Bank president, an American citizen, who also appoints all three members of the Annulment Committee, a last recourse after an award has been made. The system is rigged. As a minister in the Ecuadorian government, hit hard by ISDS rulings, noted, 'The US has not lost one case as a defendant.'[45]

Tribunal members are not required to follow precedent and rulings are made by majority vote. As one vote is automatically in favour of the corporation, the multinational need only convince one of the two other corporate lawyers. This is made easier by the fact that the lawyers who act as arbitrators in one case can act as counsel for a corporation in another, setting up conflicts of interest. Yet decisions are final and binding; there is no right of appeal. If governments do not pay the fines awarded, their assets can be seized in most parts of the world.

Alfred-Maurice de Zayas, a UN independent human rights expert, summed up the reasons for multinationals' success in ISDS cases:

Why? Because the arbitrators are corporate lawyers, today working for the corporation, tomorrow as advocates, day after tomorrow as lobbyist, the day after that as arbitrators. These are situations of conflict of interest and lack of independence.[46]

In his September 2015 report on trade and investment pacts to the UN Human Rights Council, he argued that

the dispute settlement mechanism has mutated into a privatised system of 'justice' ... whereby three arbitrators are allowed to override national legislation and the judgments of the highest national tribunals, in secret and with no possibility to appeal. This constitutes a grave challenge to the very essence of the rule of law.

The ISDS has spawned an industry of legal connivance weighted in favour of capital and against governments. Over half of the cases concluded by 2015 resulted in an award to the investor or a confidential settlement. The state was the winner in just 37 per cent of cases. Yet, even if it wins, it must pay its costs as there is no 'loser pays' rule. Legal fees to fight ISDS tribunal cases have averaged over $8 million; some have cost $30 million. Moreover, the threat of being sued for huge sums is bound to have a chilling effect on contemplated regulatory changes, even if these are in the public interest.

Many ISDS claims exceed $1 billion. Although the compensation awarded is generally much lower, Occidental Petroleum was awarded $1.8 billion against Ecuador, equivalent to 2 per cent of its GDP, for what was a lawful termination of an oil concession contract, and in 2014 arbitrators awarded compensation of a staggering $50 billion against Russia for forcibly nationalising oil company Yukos. (In 2016, a Dutch court approved Russia's application to set this award aside, but Yukos's former owners plan to appeal.) That sort of payment will put off governments from taking on corporate might. Guatemala allowed a controversial gold mine to remain open after warnings that the Canadian company could invoke ISDS. New Zealand deferred anti-tobacco measures after the Philip Morris case against Australia. There will be many other examples.

US supporters of ISDS state that, if incorporated in all trade treaties, 'this mechanism would protect US firms against predatory regulatory interventions by member governments'.[47] US-based companies are already by far the biggest users of the ISDS system, bringing about 130 cases by 2015. This was nearly twice as many as Netherlands-based companies, which ranked second. In contrast, only fifteen cases had been brought by foreign companies against the USA.

At the G20 Summit in Brisbane in November 2014, speaking about concerns over ISDS in the TTIP, David Cameron said: 'We've signed trade deal after trade deal and it's never been a problem in the past.' The special advisor to the House of Lords' inquiry into the TTIP said, 'In reality, ISDS does not affect the UK much.'[48] These comments are highly misleading.

While only two cases have been brought against the UK, UK-based investors have been the third biggest users of the ISDS system, filing over fifty cases so far. It has been a way for British corporations to extract substantial sums from developing countries that have changed policies. For example, UK power investor Ruralec successfully sued Bolivia, receiving over $30 million in compensation, after the government nationalised the country's largest energy provider in which Ruralec had an indirect stake. Although ISDS is supposed to be a neutral forum for investment disputes, the British government covertly lobbied on behalf of Ruralec with the Bolivian authorities.

Argentina has been most subject to pressure from the ISDS. When the country suffered a financial crisis in 2001–02, the worst in its history, it introduced measures to stabilise the economy. The crisis resulted from the government's adoption in 1991 of a liberalisation programme recommended by the IMF and World Bank; this involved substantial privatisations, which included guarantees and benefits for licensee foreign companies. When the economy crashed, the governments that followed (there were five presidents in ten days) introduced emergency measures, again under advice from the international financial agencies.

These measures led to a spate of demands by foreign companies for compensation, based on the numerous bilateral investment treaties Argentina had been induced to sign in the 1990s. Between 2001 and 2012, fifty cases were brought for claims totalling $80 billion, 13 per cent of Argentina's GDP.[49] Of the twenty-seven cases stemming from the emergency measures, 30 per cent were settled out of court, 44 per cent resulted in a condemnatory award in favour of the corporation, and just 15 per cent ended up in complete favour of Argentina. Final rulings resulted in Argentina having to pay $900 million, not counting legal costs.

One of the government's lines of defence was that the measures were taken out of necessity. All the tribunals rejected this, even though none had any economic expertise. Most ruled that Argentina had contributed to the crisis, due to 'excessive public spending', 'inefficient tax collection', 'delays in responding', 'insufficient efforts at developing an export market' and 'political dissension'. Others ruled, based on superficial analysis, that the measures taken were not the 'only available' means to avoid the crisis, positing hypothetical alternatives that would not affect foreign investors, such as 'dollarisation of the economy' and debt restructuring.

The intention of the ISDS is unambiguous, to protect corporations from government actions they do not like. ISDS clauses in trade agreements have strengthened the power of corporations to oppose democratic actions. They are putting a straitjacket on democratic societies, restricting and directing national sovereignty.

Thus the Swedish nuclear energy group Vattenfall is reportedly claiming €4.7 billion from the German government for lost prospective profits due to the decision to phase out nuclear energy following the Fukushima disaster.[50] The company reached a settlement in a previous dispute with the government over environmental protection rules imposed by local authorities on a coal-fired power station near Hamburg, which Vattenfall claimed were too strict. The settlement allowed it to use more water from the river and weaken measures to protect fish. Other cases have trumped national social policies. For instance, the French waste and energy group Veolia sued the Egyptian government after it raised the minimum wage, claiming that this hit production costs and thus profits.

'The ultimate question … is whether a foreign investor can force a government to change its laws to please the investor as opposed to the investor complying with the laws they find in the country', said a lawyer defending El Salvador in a case lodged by an Australian mining company against the government's refusal to allow it to dig for gold.[51] The government said this was because the firm failed to obtain rights to much of the land (many farmers refused to sell) and did not have the requisite environmental permits.

One ironical aspect of the ISDS process is that corporations are using arbitration claims as collateral for loans, based on their expectation of winning. And investment fund companies have emerged to provide financial backing for companies filing claims, in exchange for a cut of any eventual award, in effect treating claims as a new 'asset class'. Thus the claim itself is a source of rental income. It has nothing to do with production.

In sum, ISDS is a crude system for extracting rent. It gives foreign corporations exclusive access to a system that overrides national laws and courts, access denied to domestic companies and citizens who must seek remedy in the national justice system. There is no reciprocity: governments cannot bring ISDS cases. The process does not conform to juridical principles and compromises national sovereignty and democratic decision-making.

THE FIRST THREE LIES OF RENTIER CAPITALISM

So, what can be concluded from this review of the institutional architecture of globalisation? It is claimed that global capitalism is based on free markets. This is the first lie of rentier capitalism. Given the spread of intellectual property rules, development of the global capital-risk insurance system and the rent-seeking abilities of the plutocracy in crony capitalism, the existing situation is probably the most unfree market system in history.

There has been a commodification of ideas, knowledge and information. While Paul Mason has interpreted the abundance of information as indicative of 'postcapitalism',[52] the reality is actually a deepening penetration of capitalist logic and rules, in which rent seeking has been legitimised and strengthened by new global institutions and structures. Use of the word post-capitalism is revealing, as any word beginning with that prefix suggests a lack of direction. Rather, capitalism has mined the sphere of ideas as a lucrative source of income for rentiers. That is not post-capitalism, or a stepping stone in that direction.

This leads to the second lie of rentier capitalism. In defence of intellectual property rights, the claim is made that these encourage and reward risk takers. But many patented inventions are based on publicly subsidised research, in public institutions. It is the global public that pays, through taxes that finance the research, higher prices for patented products and, in the process, loss of the intellectual commons.

Moreover, most innovations that yield large returns in rental income through patents and so on are actually the result of a series of ideas and experiments attributable to many individuals or groups. As Gar Alperovitz has said, Bill Gates made a pebble of a contribution to a Gibraltar of technological advances.[53] There is no moral reason for him to receive the whole Gibraltar of reward for the endeavours of those who went before him. One could repeat this metaphor for many breakthroughs that have yielded a few individuals billions of dollars.

The third lie of rentier capitalism is that the institutional structure of global capitalism built in the globalisation era is 'good for growth'. It has actually hindered growth and made the growth that has occurred less sustainable, with rising ecological costs that are partly the outcome of rentier mechanisms put in place. The ISDS should be singled out for particularly sarcastic assessment in this respect, but it is only the most egregious aspect.

There is no evidence that investment accords promote foreign investment, their ostensible purpose. Most studies have found weak or non-existent correlations between investment treaties and investment flows, which have unsurprisingly gravitated towards the most promising markets such as China and Brazil. Neither country has signed up to ISDS. Nor is there much correlation between opening up to foreign investment and economic growth. Instead, the correlation is with financial instability.[54]

Many of the rent extraction practices that have flourished in recent years are opportunistic rather than derived from rules. An aim of the neo-liberals since the 1980s has been the privatisation of all possible spheres. The World Bank and IMF were charged with accelerating privatisation and have put enormous pressure on countries to do so. The rentiers of the world have cause to be grateful to them. The WTO has also played a role, through its construction of regulations favouring private capital, and organisations like the OECD have tried to give privatisation an intellectual legitimacy.

In sum, the institutional architecture of rentier capitalism has created a fearsome edifice for siphoning income into the hands of the plutocracy, an elite receiving income from capital, and some other favoured groups. None of this should occur if there were 'free markets' or strong democratic systems that could change the rules.

Chapter 3

THE PLAGUE OF SUBSIDIES

'Whosoever hath, to him shall be given, and he shall have
more abundance: but whosoever hath not, from him
shall be taken away even that he hath.'
Matthew 8:12

Subsidies for rentiers are the dirty secret of the unfree market system. An extraordinary feature of globalisation is that governments everywhere have splurged on an increasing array of subsidies to asset holders of all kinds, giving out public money to selected private interests. Subsidies that go to owners of land, property, mineral rights, intellectual property and financial assets are rental income; they are not gained from 'hard work' or production. And they are worsening inequality while giving rental income to some very undeserving individuals and corporations.

Subsidies of all kinds account for over 6 per cent of GDP in most rich countries and even more in many developing countries. Whether in the form of direct payments, price or cost reductions, or tax concessions, they are given ostensibly to encourage or reward certain types of behaviour. This means they distort 'free markets' by tilting economic activity towards sectors or types of firm receiving them, to the detriment of others. Some subsidies might be acceptable from an economic viewpoint if they were designed to compensate for 'externalities' (public benefits not reflected in the market price) and thus promote desired behaviour, such as investment in renewable energy or land conservation. However, most are not designed for this purpose and have nothing to do with creating or sustaining free markets.

Subsidies involve moral hazards, inducing people or firms to behave in unethical ways just to qualify to receive them. Employment subsidy schemes exemplify one type of moral hazard known as the 'deadweight effect'. Widely practised in industrialised countries, these costly schemes pay firms that increase employment. Evaluations have found that as many as nine out of every ten jobs for which the subsidy was paid would have been created anyway, without the subsidy.[1] Politicians deceive in claiming that all those subsidised jobs result from the subsidy scheme, yet journalists report such claims as gospel.

Another moral hazard is associated with subsidies that pay firms to take on particular types of worker, such as youth or the long-term unemployed. This is 'substitution' – firing existing workers in order to take on others for whom the firm can claim a subsidy.[2] In reality, moral hazards arise with most subsidies.

Politically, one advantage of subsidies is their relative invisibility. Most who do not receive them are unaware of how much they are worth for those who do, or even that they exist. Governments can dispense largesse to favoured interests, who can repay them with votes or donations. By contrast, taxes are felt by most people.

SEEKING 'COMPETITIVENESS' VIA SUBSIDIES

Subsidies to corporations are transfers of unearned rental income to capital. They have become part of the rhetoric of competitiveness. Quietly, countries are waging economic war using subsidies to attract capital, patent holders, property tycoons and other plutocrats, and to help exporters, with export incentives and credit guarantees. One study concluded that 90 per cent of exports from the world's poorest countries had to compete with subsidised commodities from richer countries.[3]

Some developing countries have tried to respond to the growth of subsidies in industrialised nations, with mixed success. China has used subsidies extensively to help dominate global manufacturing. But Vietnam is now questioning its generous incentives to foreign investors such as electronics giant Samsung. And in Brazil, an austerity drive to combat rising government deficits threatens cuts in subsidies, tax incentives and state bank-subsidised lending, on which Brazilian firms have depended to compete.

Subsidies to promote trade and investment are protectionist devices that run contrary to free trade. Yet the same politicians who spout their love of free markets have been leading the charge for more subsidies. The subsidy state is an expensive defence mounted by rich countries to arrest the logic of globalisation. But it has become an impediment to global growth while worsening inequality and market distortions. And many subsidies, such as those for fossil fuels, have been ecologically destructive.

• • •

Subsidies to rentiers can take the form of selective tax rates, tax breaks of various kinds and opportunities for tax avoidance (and evasion), as well as direct subsidies. Tax credits to top up low wages are also subsidies to capital, because they reduce firms' labour costs.

SELECTIVE TAX RATES

> 'The hardest thing in the world to
> understand is the income tax.'
> Albert Einstein

Most countries operate a regressive tax system in which the mix of taxes and subsidies favours the rich. Governments tax different sources of income differently, for the benefit of certain groups or interests. Often, income from assets and wealth is taxed less than income from employment. This is a subsidy for rentiers. Everyone else pays, in higher taxes and lower public spending.

In the USA, the UK and some other European countries, income from dividends or capital gains is taxed at a much lower rate than income from wages.[4] Warren Buffett, one of the world's richest men, whose income comes mainly from owning chunks of corporations, famously noted that he paid a lower tax rate than his secretary. Mitt Romney, who ran for US President as the Republican candidate in 2012, paid a tax rate of only 14 per cent on his $22 million income in 2010, because most of it came from investments. The US advocacy group Citizens for Tax Justice has calculated that removing this subsidy to capital would raise $533 billion over a decade. Wealthy US hedge fund managers, four of whom paid themselves over

$1 billion in 2015, also benefit from having their earnings treated as 'carried interest' and taxed at capital gains rates.

Another selective tax rate that privileges the rich is the low or zero inheritance tax in many countries. US inheritance tax only kicks in on estates over $5 million. In the UK, the government has raised the threshold for such tax to £1 million for wealthy, home-owning couples (and there are ways of minimising the tax through trusts and the like). In Australia and New Zealand, there is no in-heritance tax at all, while in many European countries the tax is minimal for family members. Inherited wealth is rental income, unearned, from having assets in the form of wealthy parents.

In most of the industrialised world, corporation tax levied on profits has been cut to well below the standard rate of income tax. This enables firms to pay out more to their owners and share-holders. According to the IMF, corporation tax rates internation-ally have halved since 1980. In the UK, the rate was slashed from 52 per cent in 1980 to 30 per cent between 2000 and 2007 and 28 per cent in the last two years of the New Labour government. The coalition government cut the rate further, to 20 per cent in 2015, foregoing revenues of £7–8 billion since taking office in 2010, according to the Institute for Fiscal Studies. Yet the Conservative government plans a further reduction to 17 per cent by 2020.

In Spain, corporation tax was cut from 30 per cent to 25 per cent in 2016. Portugal is reducing it from 25 per cent in 2013 to 17 per cent by 2018. Norway plans a further cut to 22 per cent to match reductions in Sweden and Denmark. Canada, Australia and Japan have all lowered rates in recent years. Ireland, whose 12.5 per cent rate is the lowest in Western Europe, has lured multinationals such as Apple and Facebook to set up European headquarters there. This may have some effect on the geographical distribution of employment – Ireland has 160,000 workers employed in foreign companies – but the net effect of 'beggar-my-neighbour' cuts in corporation tax has been to increase the rental income of corporations and their owners and shareholders.

The orthodox claim is that lowering corporation taxes encourages investment, which in turn boosts employment, incomes and tax revenue. But investment does not seem responsive to cuts in corporate tax. Instead, profits are stashed offshore or paid out in dividends, share options and bonuses, while tax receipts fall. Official UK figures show that small companies pay nearly 60 per cent as much in tax as large companies, compared with about 17 per cent in 2001, an indication of how big corporations have gained. Facebook paid just £4,327 in corporation tax in 2014, contriving an accounting loss after paying over £35 million to UK-based staff in a share bonus scheme.

It was later revealed that in the same year, 2014, six of the ten biggest British companies paid not a penny in corporation tax, in spite of making combined profits of more than £30 billion.[5] Speaking at a tax conference in Oxford in June 2015, Philip Baker QC remarked: 'I don't think in the last twenty years or so one can say that governments have driven corporation tax policy. It's the large companies that have driven the direction of corporate tax policy.'[6]

Coordinated international action is required to curb tax competition. Yet Britain, Ireland and others have repeatedly stymied any such proposals. The British government, like the Irish, has made tax competition part of its economic strategy. Tax advantages have motivated multinationals such as Aon, Fiat Industrial and Starbucks to set up 'headquarters' in the UK, often with few staff. This contributes nothing to production, while tax competition lowers revenue all round.

In 2015, the OECD published proposals aimed at reducing 'base erosion and profit shifting' (BEPS) by closing some of the most blatant loopholes in the international tax system. But it backed off recommending needed structural reforms, due to opposition by rich-country governments. As one critic noted, the project 'could have gone much further if they had not made so many concessions to tax advisers, who have much invested in the current system, and to governments, who want to retain powers to give concessions to business'.[7]

Earlier, in June 2015, the European Commission floated a plan to introduce common rules on where company profits arise, known as the 'common consolidated corporate tax base', to stop firms exploiting differences in national tax regimes. The same week, the UK minister in charge of tax policy told members of the European Parliament that Britain would not accept the proposals. 'He was very clear that the UK is insisting on tax competition. It was really a shock from the minister,' a German MEP said after the meeting.

'NON-DOM' STATUS AND TAX

A feature of the tax system in Britain has been the favourable treatment extended to wealthy residents deemed to be domiciled abroad. So-called 'non-doms', who include UK-born citizens as well as foreign plutocrats, enjoy special privileges, notably a limit on the tax they pay on foreign income. One prominent beneficiary is Viscount Rothermere, a British-born billionaire and hereditary peer who owns the *Daily Mail*, a right-wing tabloid that special-ises in scurrilous attacks on impoverished benefit recipients.

Following a public outcry, the government announced timid plans to end inherited non-dom status. But, as the Treasury ad-mitted, most non-doms will be little touched by ending tax privi-leges for those resident for fifteen of the previous twenty years. The Chancellor said that non-dom tax status 'plays an important role in allowing those from abroad to contribute to our economy'. In other words, the government wants to give some privileged people something for nothing.

The non-dom system is part of a class-based migration policy op-erated by half of the EU's twenty-eight members, which includes the selling of residency rights and/or passports.[8] While governments are raising barriers for poorer migrants, they are offering inducements to a rich minority, no matter from where their money might have come. To say they are all 'contributing to our economy' is bogus.

TAX BREAKS

A second type of subsidy reduces the tax bills of individuals or companies for certain types of spending, such as investment, debt repayments, pension contributions and health insurance. Tax breaks are subsidies just as much as direct payments. But they are less visible because they take the form of tax foregone rather than more public spending. Most tax breaks are regressive and distort markets by favouring certain firms or sectors. They are for special interests, electoral or otherwise, and are unrelated to production.

Tax breaks for individuals are regressive since they are worth most to those paying higher tax rates. For those too poor to pay tax, they are of no use at all. Of a UK labour force of 30 million, a sixth have incomes below the income tax threshold of £11,000 and gain nothing from tax breaks or further increases in the threshold. The Institute for Fiscal Studies estimated that raising the threshold between 2010 and 2015 cost the Exchequer £12 billion (the same amount as the extra planned cuts to the welfare budget). Most of the benefit went to higher-rate taxpayers.

The affluent can usually take more advantage of tax concessions. In many countries, pension contributions, childcare and health insurance premiums are tax-deductible. All of these are more valuable to higher income-earners, who spend more on them. In the UK, higher-rate taxpayers obtained half the gain from pension tax breaks costing £35 billion a year. In the USA and many European nations, taxpayers can deduct mortgage interest payments, a subsidy that goes to the wealthy who own houses or apartments.

The scale of tax subsidies is awesome. According to IMF calculations, the USA spends over 7 per cent of GDP on tax breaks, Australia and Italy 8 per cent or more and the UK 6 per cent.[9] Just seven of the personal tax breaks in the USA – for health insurance, mortgage interest, pension plans, earned income tax credit for low-paid workers, deductions for state and local taxes, charitable donations and untaxed social security benefits – will cost $3 trillion in lost revenue between 2014 and 2018.

Over half of US tax breaks go to the richest fifth of households, according to the Congressional Budget Office. The poorest fifth obtain less than 10 per cent. The mortgage deduction alone costs

$70 billion a year, with three-quarters going to homeowners with annual incomes of over $100,000.[10] Four times as much goes to the wealthiest fifth in mortgage interest deductions as on social housing for the poorest fifth.

Some tax breaks that do not amount to much in total are worth a great deal to the few who gain from them. The USA gives tax breaks to wealthy owners of racehorses and professional sports teams – halving the $2 billion price that Steve Ballmer, billionaire co-founder of Microsoft, paid for the LA Clippers basketball team. UK tax breaks include £3 billion a year in reduced capital gains tax for individuals selling their businesses. According to Richard Murphy of Tax Research UK, in the tax year 2013/14, £1.8 billion of this benefited just 3,000 people, who each sold their company stakes for more than £1 million.

Landed estate owners in Britain have enjoyed a special tax break introduced in 1994 by John Major's government, which exempted 'sporting estates' from business rates (local property taxes). In 2015, Scotland's SNP government announced plans to scrap the concession as a measure to widen land ownership in a country where half of all privately owned land is held by just 432 people. This prompted David Cameron's stepfather-in-law, Lord Astor, who inherited a vast deer-stalking estate in Scotland (now owned through a Bahamas-based family trust), to write a newspaper article preposterously comparing the plan to the forcible eviction of white landowners by Zimbabwe's Robert Mugabe.

Then there are tax breaks on savings. The UK's 'individual savings allowance' (ISA), launched in 1999, enabled people to gain tax-free interest from annual savings in designated accounts up to a certain amount. In 2016, the cash ISA was replaced by exempting from tax the first £1,000 of interest earned on savings and current accounts. This is a nice subsidy to those who can afford to save. The precariat has debts, not savings.

Less publicised have been the stocks and shares ISA and its forerunner, the Personal Equity Plan (PEP), introduced in 1987. The stocks and shares ISA allows savers to invest their tax-free allowance in equity and bond funds, free of tax on dividend income and capital gains. Again advantageous to higher-rate taxpayers, it has allowed some to make tax-free fortunes. John Lee, a minister in the Thatcher government, who invested £150,000 in both schemes from 1987, had a portfolio worth £4.5 million in 2015, on which he will pay no income or capital gains tax at all.

Tax subsidies for corporations are even more generous. They include tax breaks for investment, research, business expenses (a convenient catch-all) and many other concessions. The USA has thousands of such subsidies, including one for corporate jets that costs taxpayers $3 billion a year and another worth millions for tuna companies operating in American Samoa. Of course, the definitions of 'investment', 'research' and 'business expenses' are stretched by tax advisors to the limit.

One US subsidy allows corporations to deduct from taxable profits 'performance-related' bonuses for executives. This has predictably encouraged them to pay their CEOs ever more munificently in share options, dressed up as performance-related, even when performance has been poor. As a subsidy to the elite it is thoroughly regressive. Scrapping it would save $50 billion over ten years. The US Government Accountability Office has calculated that tax breaks reduce the official 35 per cent corporation tax to an actual rate of 13 per cent, saving corporations $200 billion annually.

Tax breaks for corporations are also another form of protectionism, a bribe to induce multinationals to locate, stay or expand in the country. This is rental income, bypassing market mechanisms. As Mario Monti, a former EU Competition Commissioner (and Prime Minister of Italy from 2011 to 2013), once noted, such tax breaks constitute disguised trade- and investment-distorting state aid that is hidden from public scrutiny because it does not appear on company balance sheets.

One study estimated that US state and local governments spend $80 billion a year on incentives and subsidies to companies, accounting for 7 per cent of their budget. Much of this goes on 'beggar-my-neighbour' subsidies to win jobs and investment at the expense of other states – a zero-sum game. General Motors has extracted $1.7 billion over the years from sixteen US states, which has not stopped it closing factories in places that have given it cash. Shell, Ford and Chrysler have received over $1 billion each, Amazon, Microsoft, Prudential and Boeing over $200 million each.[11]

Then there is the widespread practice of allowing firms to deduct debt repayments from taxable earnings. Dating from 1853, when the UK first made interest paid by firms on loans or debts tax-deductible, today it is a feature of tax systems everywhere.

In 2007, before the crash, the annual value of lost revenue due to tax breaks on debt payments was 2.4 per cent of GDP in the Eurozone (1.9 per cent for company debt; 0.5 for mortgage debt) and 3.5 per cent in the UK (all attributable to company debt, as mortgage interest payments are not tax-deductible). To put it into context, this was more than those countries spent on defence. In the USA, the lost revenue was a staggering 4.9 per cent of GDP, with company debt accounting for most of it. Tax relief on debt servicing by financial firms accounted for three-quarters of all the tax fore-gone in Britain and the USA; in the Eurozone it was over half.

These subsidies amount to giving the affluent a lot of 'something for nothing'. Even in 2013, when interest rates were close to zero, US debt subsidies cost the federal government over 2 per cent of GDP, more than it spent on all nationwide policies to assist the poor.

In the austerity era, governments have claimed that public debt must be reduced, making it necessary to slash social spending and welfare benefits. Yet, in giving subsidies to private debtors in the form of tax breaks they are deliberately foregoing revenue that would make many spending cuts unnecessary.

Tax breaks for debt have other adverse effects besides loss of public revenue. Tax relief on mortgage payments lowers the cost of borrowing to buy property, inducing those able to do so to borrow more to buy more expensive property. This raises house prices, providing rental income from capital gains, as well as more from letting. Of course, the tax benefits and the rental income they stimulate go mainly to the better-off.

Similarly, tax breaks for debt skew corporate decision-making, making it cheaper to borrow rather than issue shares. With tax advantages in mind, firms borrow not for productive investment but to buy assets via mergers and acquisitions, or to refinance their own assets. This enriches the financial industry but does little for anyone else. Moreover, economies that encourage the use of debt are more fragile because in downturns the obligation to repay is more likely to lead to bankruptcies. By contrast, equity financing through stock markets means shareholders bear the losses of downturns and the gains of upturns. Companies are at less risk of going bust.

Another corporate tax break is the so-called 'patent box'. In the UK, this was proposed in 2009 by New Labour and introduced in 2013 by the coalition government, which cut the tax rate on profits deemed to derive from patented inventions to 10 per cent. After complaints from other EU countries, notably Germany, the rules were tightened to tie the concession more closely to patents linked to research and development in Britain. But companies can still claim a reduced rate on patents they have bought in or that arise from outsourced research.

France, Luxembourg, Spain, Portugal, Italy and the Netherlands (which has a concessionary rate of just 5 per cent) are among countries that operate a patent box. Ireland, which under pressure closed a related tax-dodging loophole known as the 'Double Irish', is introducing a patent box with a concessionary rate of 6.25 per cent.

The ostensible purposes of patent boxes are to encourage firms to do more research and to attract 'knowledge-intensive' multinationals. But they are in reality another beggar-my-neighbour subsidy that leaves no one better off except the corporations. The money to make up the loss must come from higher taxes on labour and consumption or from cuts in public spending. But, as detailed in Chapter 2, here is little evidence that patents stimulate innovation or raise productivity and growth. The tax break is a gift to multinationals.

TAX AVOIDANCE AND EVASION

The borderline between tax avoidance (legal) and evasion (illegal) is wafer-thin. They have similar effects – loss of government revenue that must be paid for by others in taxes or spending cuts; similar opportunities – the arrangement of an individual or company's financial affairs to minimise tax; and similar causes – they do not come about by accident, but by action or lack of it by governments.

A review of the UK tax system by James Mirrlees in 2010 concluded that marginal tax rates above 40 per cent dampen government revenue, not because they discourage people from doing more labour but because they encourage tax-avoidance measures. For example, a large gap between corporation tax rates and tax rates on earnings encourages high earners to be paid through companies set up for the purpose. In 2012, it was revealed that 2,400 high-paid British government officials were being paid through companies or other intermediaries, even though they were regular employees.

Similar situations arise in other countries that have large gaps between income and company taxes. In Australia, where the top income tax rate is 49 per cent and the corporation tax rate 30 per cent (28.5 per cent for small firms), Prime Minister Malcolm Turnbull noted, 'People with substantial assets ... are able to structure their affairs so that the bulk of their income is earned through corporations.'

Tax breaks encourage the rich to devise ingenious schemes to avoid tax. As tax authorities clamp down on one abuse, an industry of accountants, lawyers and financial advisors puts its collective mind to coming up with others. UK tax-avoidance devices listed by the *Financial Times* in November 2015 included putting money into companies leasing refuse collection vehicles to local councils, funding crematoria and investing in unproven start-ups. These companies, whose business model is based on taking advantage of tax breaks, charge hefty fees for their services.

They and their wealthy clients are taking rental income, for which others pay.

Charitable donations are another tax-avoidance device much used by the wealthy, some of whom set up charities for the purpose. Tax breaks on donations cost the UK Treasury £3.5 billion a year. Total tax relief to the charitable sector has been put at £4.5 billion, including exemptions from taxes on income from trading, rents, investment, capital gains and business rates.

In 2013, one UK charity, Cup Trust, was exposed as a front for a tax-avoidance scheme, having donated just £55,000 of its £176 million income to charitable causes. While its attempt to claim tax relief was foiled, other schemes are surely still operating. In the USA, where charities benefit from numerous tax breaks, Lady Gaga's Born This Way foundation raised $2.6 million in 2012 but gave away only $5,000. Cancer Fund of America spent less than 1 per cent of donations on charitable activities. Over ten years it paid $5 million to the founder's family and $80 million to fundraisers, but gave just $890,000 to cancer patients.

Other tax-dodging devices include setting up trusts and parking assets in offshore (and in some countries, onshore) tax havens, of which there are over fifty, serving as domicile for 2 million companies and thousands of banks, funds and insurers. While no one knows exactly how much is stashed away, some estimates put it at over $20 trillion. We are not talking just about Caribbean islands or Panama. In 2013, the US state of Delaware, a tax haven, was home to 945,000 mostly shell companies, more than its 917,100 population.

Corporate tax avoidance skirts illegality. The European

Commission is investigating a 'sweetheart deal' between Apple and the Irish authorities, which allegedly allowed it to shelter profits from tax in return for maintaining jobs in Ireland. The commission, which claims the deal is illegal state aid, has already ruled against tax arrangements granted by the Netherlands to Starbucks, by Luxembourg to Fiat Chrysler and by Belgium to twenty-five companies. Luxembourg's arrangements with Amazon and McDonald's are also under investigation, following revelations that it had made secret deals with hundreds of companies.

Whatever their legality, these schemes are a means by which firms obtain substantial rental income. Even more egregiously, some multinationals have exploited anomalies in the tax rules of different jurisdictions, using devices such as Google's famous 'Double Irish with a Dutch sandwich' to move profits to tax havens such as Bermuda where the corporate tax rate is zero. In 2011, nineteen subsidiaries registered in Ireland used the 'Double Irish' to avoid tax on €33 billion of profits, equivalent to a fifth of the country's economic output that year.

Perhaps the biggest source of corporate tax avoidance is the parking of profits offshore by US companies, induced by the US tax system. While most countries operate a territorial tax system, taxing only profits deemed to arise in their jurisdictions, the US taxes companies and individuals on their worldwide income. But profits are only taxed once repatriated. So, by keeping profits elsewhere (preferably in low-tax jurisdictions), companies avoid federal corporation tax of up to 35 per cent, one of the highest headline rates in the world.

According to Bloomberg, in 2014, US corporations were holding over $2 trillion in profits offshore.[12] The top ten accounted for a third, led by General Electric. Although Apple does not count all its overseas holdings as parked profits, including them would take its offshore hoard to $180 billion, easily topping the list.

With interest rates close to zero, US companies have funded domestic spending through cheap loans at home (on which they get tax relief) rather than repatriate profits. This has enabled corporations to invest those parked profits in financial markets, and in acquiring physical and intellectual property, fuelling asset prices everywhere and boosting the wealth of those who receive their income by non-working means.

In 2014 alone, the value of the total cash hoard rose by 8 per cent, while corporations were tapping domestic financial markets to pay out record amounts in dividends, buybacks (purchase of their own shares) and acquisitions of other firms. Two-thirds of large company profits in Europe and the USA have been spent on buybacks and dividends in recent years.[13]

Another device for avoiding corporation tax, much used by pharmaceutical companies, has been the 'inversion deal', buying or merging with a foreign firm for the purpose of switching domicile to shield overseas profits from US tax. In 2014, inversion deals accounted for 9 per cent of all mergers and acquisitions, saving corporations billions in avoided tax. A trick used by inverted companies, known as 'earnings stripping', piles debt onto the US 'subsidiary' or has it borrow from the foreign 'parent' in order to deduct the debt from its US tax liability.

London, with its financial centre and low tax rate, has been the domicile of choice for many, including Coca Cola. Ireland is favoured by pharmaceuticals. In 2015, US-based Pfizer caused outrage when it agreed a $160 billion merger with Allergan, itself the product of an inversion deal, and announced its intention to shift its 'principal executive office' to Ireland while keeping its global headquarters in New York. The proposed merger, which would have saved Pfizer billions in taxes, was subsequently called off after the Obama administration introduced new rules aimed at putting an end to inversion deals.

Other drug-makers have used a different avoidance strategy, channelling patent royalties to low-tax countries, notably Ireland. Gilead has transferred the patent rights to its Hepatitis C drug, which sells for $1,000 a pill, to an Irish subsidiary, saving hundreds of millions of dollars in tax. Regeneron Pharmaceuticals has made Ireland the tax base for sales outside the US of its big-selling eye drug Eylea.

The IMF has put the revenue loss from profit shifting by multinationals at $600 billion a year; the OECD puts it at $240 billion – lower but still equivalent to 10 per cent of global corporation tax revenue. An analysis by the Tax Justice Network suggested that profit shifting by US companies now accounts for 25–30 per cent of their total profits, compared with 5–10 per cent in the 1990s. In 2012, according to the network, shifted profit amounted to 27 per cent of gross profit, nearly 1 per cent of world GDP. Over half was parked in jurisdictions with near-zero effective tax rates, mainly the Netherlands, Ireland, Bermuda and Luxembourg.

Nearly three-quarters of firms on the Fortune 500 list of biggest US companies have tax haven subsidiaries, according to a report by Citizens for Tax Justice. These 358 firms maintained 'at least' 7,622 tax haven subsidiaries.

DIRECT SUBSIDIES

The number of direct selective subsidy payments, and the amount spent on them, is mind-boggling. Ostensibly aimed at reducing costs, encouraging innovation or raising employment, they are a deeply regressive form of rental income that mocks the idea of free market capitalism.

It is ironic that one of the biggest UK beneficiaries is Iain Duncan Smith, Secretary of State for Work and Pensions from 2010 until his abrupt resignation in 2016, who made it his mission to cut welfare spending. Over the past decade, his family has received well over £1 million from the EU's Common Agricultural Policy (CAP), £160,000 in 2014 alone, because his wife inherited 1,500 acres of farmland. He did not do a single day of farm work to acquire that land, let alone the subsidy.

When the European Commission proposed to cap the subsidy for large-scale landowners, the British government refused to apply the cap in England (though Scotland, Wales and Northern Ireland decided to do so). Meanwhile, Duncan Smith was capping payments to the unemployed and housing benefit claimants, averring that nobody should receive more in welfare than in a job.

About 90 per cent of CAP subsidy payments to the UK, £3.6 billion annually, go to the richest 10 per cent of farmers. Among the biggest beneficiaries are the Queen (perhaps the world's wealthiest woman) and the Duke of Westminster (with a fortune of £8.5 billion), who claimed nearly £1 million in 2014.

This is not just a European boondoggle. In the USA, most of the $20 billion paid annually in farm subsidies goes to rich farmers; fifty billionaires have received taxpayer-funded farm subsidies since 1995.[14] Large corporations and rich individuals with farmland receive subsidies even when it is not used for farming.

The European subsidy habit stems from a deal between Germany and France at the outset of what became the EU, which ensured subsidies for German steel workers and coal miners in return for aid for French farmers. Despite subsequent attempts to curb the most egregious subsidies, others with equally distorting effects have proliferated. A case in point concerns the German discount retailer Lidl, which has received loans of $900 million from the World Bank and the EBRD to help it expand in Eastern Europe. Dieter Schwarz, Lidl's owner, is estimated to be worth some $16 billion. Why is taxpayers' money being used to help a plutocrat expand his business?

Some subsidies are ideologically inspired. Poland received over €100 billion from the EU between 2007 and 2013 and is due to receive €106 billion more from 2014 to 2020. This is equivalent in today's money to twice all Marshall Plan spending on European reconstruction after 1945. Poland was singled out in the 1990s as the country in which the neo-liberal agenda had to succeed. Money was poured into infrastructure and farm subsidies as the old state was dismantled and new institutions erected. Poland's current relatively good economic situation can be attributed largely to that subsidy.

In the USA, federal subsidies for corporations cost $100 billion a year, according to the right-wing Cato Institute.[15] They include farm subsidies, housing subsidies, research subsidies (including billions for defence contractors), innovation subsidies, fishery promotion subsidies, energy subsidies, subsidies to carmakers such as Ford and Nissan to develop 'greener' cars, rail and shipyard

subsidies, subsidies to airlines for 'essential services', loan guarantees, and subsidies to small businesses. As the Cato Institute said,
corporate welfare 'undermines the broader economy and transfers wealth from average taxpaying households to favored firms'
and fosters 'crony capitalism' by creating ties between politicians
and business that fuel corruption.

Some subsidies miss the intended recipients. The US Research
and Development Tax Credit was meant to encourage mid-sized
companies to increase R&D. Instead, 80 per cent has gone to
mega-corporations like Google, Intel, Boeing and Apple.[16]
Moreover, the Bayh–Dole Act of 1980 enabled institutions gaining from public research funding to commercialise the outcomes
by taking out patents and licensing the exploitation rights to private firms. Margaret Thatcher introduced a similar system and
other countries followed. Taxpayers pay twice over for this, first
by funding the research (which reduces the firm's risk as well as
its costs) and then through higher prices, due to the ability of
firms with a patent monopoly to charge more.

In the UK, while cutting spending on public-sector research,
the coalition government increased subsidies for private industry
research and development, allowing firms to patent or otherwise
appropriate the outcome. These subsidies came to £1.6 billion
in 2011 and were supplemented by £1.1 billion in tax relief.
According to the National Audit Office, 70 per cent of the latter
went to large companies, including foreign firms. Between 2013
and 2015 Nestlé received £487,000 to invent an energy-efficient
machine for making chocolate; PepsiCo was given £356,000 to
develop ways of drying potatoes to make crisps.

Among the worst direct subsidies are those that help the fossil fuel industry, including subsidies to keep down prices for consumers. According to the International Energy Agency, these came to $550 billion worldwide in 2014, four times the subsidy for renewable energy. It estimated that scrapping them would cut carbon emissions by a fifth. The Overseas Development Institute (ODI) estimates that G20 countries, the world's twenty leading economies, spend $88 billion a year supporting fossil fuel exploration.

There is also an enormous indirect subsidy, because prices do not reflect the true costs of burning fossil fuels arising from air pollution, climate change and congestion. The IMF reckons direct and indirect subsidies together cost $5.3 trillion a year, equivalent to over $1,000 for every person in the G20 countries. Those with above-average subsidies include Saudi Arabia, Russia, the USA, China, South Korea, Canada, Australia and Japan.

Perversely, the UK government in 2015 announced that it would slash subsidies on renewable energy such as solar and onshore wind projects, the cheapest forms of clean power, while increasing subsidies for fossil fuel companies, mainly through tax breaks to boost declining North Sea oil production. It is also subsidising polluting 'diesel farms' to provide stand-by power to the National Grid, directly and via tax breaks, at a time when the renewable subsidy cuts have driven several solar energy companies out of business and threaten community projects attempting to reduce energy costs for low-income households.

The ODI estimated that UK fossil fuel subsidies already amounted to £6 billion a year in 2013 and 2014, nearly twice as much as subsidies for renewable energy before the cuts, which followed intense lobbying from the fossil fuel industry and opposition to onshore wind farms in rural Tory heartlands. It may be no coincidence that in 2013 David Cameron appointed as his personal advisor on energy and climate change a former lobbyist for British Gas, while several fossil fuel company employees were seconded to the Department of Energy and Climate Change to help draft energy policy.[17]

In the USA, the balance has been similar. In 2014, Oil Change International, a campaigning research group, calculated that taxpayers subsidised oil, gas and coal exploration and production to the tune of $21 billion a year, while the fossil fuel industry spent $1.8 billion between 2010 and 2014 on lobbying, notably for subsidies.

In the UK, corporate welfare is estimated to exceed £93 billion every year, of which direct subsidies and capital grants account for £14.5 billion; tax benefits £44 billion; transport subsidies (especially for rail companies) £15 billion; energy subsidies £3.8 billion; and benefits from public procurement £15 billion.[18] Disney was given millions in tax credits to make films in Britain. Amazon, another firm paying virtually no UK corporation tax, was wooed with millions to build distribution centres in Scotland and Wales.

While giving so generously to British and foreign firms, the UK government has argued that spending on social services and benefits must be cut by £20 billion more by 2020 to 'balance the books'. This is a policy driven by ideology, not economics. The popular media are equally hypocritical, focusing endlessly on alleged false claims for paltry benefits by deprived families, while keeping quiet about the vast amounts received by corporations that they have done nothing to justify and that have no known benefits for the economy or society.

Overall, direct subsidies given to rich corporations and rich individuals are distortionary, inefficient and regressive. Removing them would improve growth and ecological sustainability and, above all, reduce inequality.

THE FOLLY OF TAX CREDITS

Tax credits used to top up low wages in the USA, UK and elsewhere bear an uncanny resemblance to the Speenhamland system of the early nineteenth century, described in Chapter 1. They were the last throw of social democracy in the globalisation era. 'Third-Way' thinking was that the market should determine wages, unions should be constrained and government should correct for distributional outcomes through tax credits. It was paternalistic, allowing workers' bargaining strength to weaken while assuring them that government would look after the losers.

Tax credits started modestly in the 1970s with the US Earned Income Tax Credit (EITC). The Clinton administration expanded it in the 1990s. Nowadays, costing $78 billion a year, it matches food stamps as the world's most expensive welfare scheme. In the UK, after similar modest beginnings in 1999, working tax credits (and child tax credits for low-income parents) were introduced in 2003 and became central to New Labour's approach to labour market and social policy reform. Other countries have moved in the same direction.

Tax credits look like welfare payments, but they are in reality a subsidy, providing capital with unearned rental income. They make it easier for employers to pay low wages (and employ part-time rather than full-time staff), since low wages can be topped up by taxpayer-financed tax credits. An investigation by Citizens UK found that retailers such as Tesco were benefiting more from wage top-ups for their low-paid employees than they were paying in tax.

In the UK, between 1999 and 2015, the cost of working and child tax credits ballooned to £30 billion a year. Including housing and council tax benefits for those in jobs, spending to compensate for low wages rose to £76 billion annually, representing a third of all expenditure on welfare and the biggest welfare item apart from pensions.[19] The number of people in jobs dependent on tax credits rose from more than 2 million in 2003 to over 3.3 million ten years later. This is not a free labour market.

In the USA, according to University of California (Berkeley) researchers, taxpayers spend $153 billion a year on tax credits, food stamps and other benefits to support people on poverty wages working for the likes of McDonald's and Walmart. A quarter of all Americans are now eligible for tax credits, reflecting the failure of the labour market and the seductiveness of subsidies. And research has shown that, because of their complexity, about a quarter of all tax credit payments have been issued in error; they have also increased inequity in the tax system.[20]

Tax credits weaken workers' incentive to press for higher wages (or to join a union to bargain for them), since the tax credit will shrink if wages rise. Unless the wage is pushed up beyond the qualifying level for tax credits, workers will be little better off. So tax credits deepen poverty traps faced by the precariat, acting as a disincentive to labour. In an example from New Zealand, another country using tax credits, one mother pointed out: 'The more I earn, the less Working-for-Families [the New Zealand tax credit] we get and childcare subsidy is also decreased. Therefore I'd be going back to work for diddly squat and also giving up precious time with my children.'[21]

Another mother calculated that if she returned to full-time nursing earning NZ$50,000 a year the family would be no better off due to the loss of means-tested benefits and tax credits, and extra transport and childcare costs. Poverty traps are endemic wherever benefits and subsidies are means-tested.

After the 2015 general election, the UK government changed tack. The Chancellor announced swingeing cuts in tax credits alongside a fanfare announcement that employers would be required to pay a national living wage – higher than the minimum wage – for anyone aged over twenty-five. Breaking with tradition, the Treasury did not issue a report on the distributional impact, which the Institute of Fiscal Studies calculated would cost 3 million people an average of £1,000 a year. The Chancellor meanwhile raised the income threshold for the higher rate of income tax, benefiting the better-paid.

The tax credit cuts were eventually abandoned following an outcry that they would hit the very 'hard-working families' the government was pledged to support. But there was no back-track on plans to reduce benefits under the 'universal credit' scheme scheduled to replace tax credits. This will cut spending by just as much as the abandoned cuts in tax credits, according to the Office for Budget Responsibility, and hurt low-income families just as much.

The government may hope that a living wage will reduce the tax credit bill. At the time, nearly a quarter of all employees –

6 million people – were being paid less than the living wage, half of them in social care, retail or hospitality. But as the wage is an hourly rate there is ample scope for firms to reduce working hours or jobs to keep payroll costs down. Alistair Darling, former Labour Chancellor, admitted as much when he wrote that tax credits 'support many who will not benefit from the minimum wage'.[22]

Tax credits are a subsidy to capital, distort labour markets and hold down wages. Research suggests that employers gain a quarter to a third of their value through paying lower wages.[23] The unions have erred in supporting them, since they are a poor substitute for collective bargaining and reduce the incentive for low-paid workers to join unions. They are also bad for productivity, since they result in an under-valuation of labour, reducing the pressure on employers to be efficient. They also encourage firms to use low-paid workers rather than higher-wage employees.

By definition, tax credits raise the income of those receiving them, thereby helping them out of poverty. However, this comes at the cost of lower wage rates, not only for recipients, who thus benefit by less than the amount of the tax credit, but for others competing with them for jobs at the low end of the labour market.

Tax credits are also trade-distorting because they are a subsidy that reduces labour costs, thus affecting competitiveness. Logically, free traders (and international financial institutions) should condemn them.

One toxic aspect of the UK 'Brexit' debate was the government's decision to make in-work benefits (tax credits) the main issue in 're-negotiating' certain membership terms ahead of the June 2016 referendum on whether or not to leave the European Union. As a result, EU migrants could be blocked from receiving in-work benefits for four years. If the measure goes through, in or out of the EU, nobody should be surprised if other European countries hit back at British migrants there.

THE SUBSIDISED CHARITY STATE

One great achievement of the social democratic state was to marginalise charity. Society's response to deprivation and trauma was turned over to the public sector, with government expected to provide benefits and services to deal with the vicissitudes of life. Fewer had to rely on discretionary charity. They ceased to be supplicants.

The neo-liberal agenda has focused on cutting public spending so as to facilitate tax cuts and privatisation. But this has left a widening gap in the provision of services for those in need. To fill it, governments have provided subsidies to encourage the growth of charities and philanthropy.

This shift is driven by an ideological recklessness that has yet to receive the criticism it deserves. If the state provides a statutory service, there is a democratic guarantee that it will continue. If provided by charity, it can be withdrawn arbitrarily or without notice.

When the UK austerity regime began, public spending cuts were partially offset by subsidising charities expected to fill the vacuum. This lessened the impact of the cuts on children, the elderly and disabled. But the subsidies needed by charities rose with successive reductions in benefits and care services. Following the austerity logic, the government then argued that charities too must share the burden.

According to the National Council for Voluntary Organisations, between 2010 and 2013 government grants and contracts to charities fell by 11 per cent, and those for charities for children and youth by 18 per cent. The main reason was the financial squeeze on local councils, forcing them to cut assistance to charities, because they had to slash all non-obligatory (non-statutory) spending.

Charities had to curtail activities or collapse. In August 2015, Kids Company, a government favourite, which had cared for disturbed children and teenagers for nineteen years, went bankrupt. It will not be the last charity to fail and leave people in dire straits. Poor financial administration had gone unchecked for years, during which it had received £46 million in public funds, according to the National Audit Office. But the main point is that vital social functions should not be left to charity and unaccountable organisations, however 'noble' those involved might be.

BANK 'BAILOUTS': RENT FOR FAILURE

Banking is one of the few occupations never to have been professionalised, that is, made subject to professional qualifications, codes of ethics, and procedures for entry and exit through a professional guild. Anyone can be a banker. So it should be no surprise that, throughout history, banks have been vehicles for amoral behaviour, fraud and corruption.

However, three new features have emerged in the globalisation era. First, governments have ended democratic control of central banks and monetary policy. Since 1980, dozens of countries have given their central bank independence. Indeed, among the

triumphs of neo-liberalism was persuading even social democratic governments to privatise their central banks in all but
name. One of Gordon Brown's first acts on becoming Chancellor
in 1997 was to give the Bank of England independence to set
monetary policy. The surprise decision was greeted with delight
by the Conservative opposition and the City of London. It was an
act of financial appeasement.

Henceforth, the bank's Monetary Policy Committee (MPC),
although nominated by the Chancellor, was free to set interest
rates based on loose guidelines. This soon led to penetration by
special interests. For instance, in 2015, the Chancellor appointed
to the MPC a Belgian economist and partner of a hedge fund
that makes money from predicting interest rates. With the bank's
agreement, Gertjan Vlieghe initially planned to retain his stake
in the firm while stepping down from 'active' involvement during
his three-year MPC term. Following public protest, including
from the cross-party Treasury Select Committee, he suspended
his ties with the hedge fund. But it is scarcely conspiratorial to
surmise he will favour hedge fund interests.

The abdication of government control was based on the flimsy
proposition that this would de-politicise monetary policy and
stop governments inflating their way out of trouble or engineering booms to win elections. In reality, it was one of the final
failings of twentieth-century social democracy, reflecting accept-
ance of neo-liberal economics.

It was hardly surprising that the coalition government went to
the next stage, which was to appoint a foreigner to run the Bank
of England. Mark Carney was prised from being head of Canada's
central bank at vast public expense. Whatever his qualities, this

was unprecedented. Could one imagine a foreigner being appointed to run the US Federal Reserve or France's national bank?

A second feature has been the resort by governments and central banks since the crash to inject cash into the banking system, to bail out failing banks and to pump up the money supply to stimulate growth via 'quantitative easing'. QE is discussed later in this chapter. Here it is enough to recall the self-serving statement used to justify the bailouts, that the banks were 'too big to fail'. The cringing justification for giving them vast amounts of public money was that if they went bankrupt due to their recklessness the contagion effects would have sunk the whole economy. So their owners and managers were helped to restore their lavish earnings.

A third feature has been growth of non-bank financial intermediaries, including some inside non-financial corporations. The new types include payday lenders, such as the notorious Wonga, equity crowdfunding such as UK-based Crowdcube, and peer-to-peer online lending platforms, whereby investors put up money for lending and receive returns based on debt repayments. The platforms do the credit scoring and earn income from arrangement fees, not from the spread between lending and deposit rates as traditional lenders do.

Peer-to-peer lending is still modest compared with retail banking, but by 2015 the biggest – Lending Club, Prosper and SoFi in the USA; Zopa and RateSetter in London – were lending at a rate of over $10 billion a year.[24] In Britain, peer-to-peer investors can put over £15,000 a year into tax-free savings accounts, representing another nice subsidy for the affluent and profit for the platforms.

The crash of 2007–08 was an international banking failure. Yet every OECD government had backed the regulatory and institutional regime that allowed the financial bubble to grow over the previous two decades. In response to the crash, governments rushed to bail out the financial sector, in contradiction to the neo-liberal preaching about free markets. When it came to the crunch, they just gave more to financial asset holders.

In effect, they gave fortunes to financial institutions and their bosses *because they had failed.* The bailouts were pure subsidies that bankers had done nothing to deserve. Many of those responsible for the debacle were paid huge salaries and bonuses by their bailed-out institution. Others who had waxed lyrically about the wonders of free markets, and who had been at the heart of the crash, were put in charge of clearing up and paid handsomely to do so.

The USA set the lead, doling out billions to Wall Street. From 2008 to 2012, $4.6 trillion was spent in bailing out nearly 1,000 banks, insurance companies and other financial institutions, while guarantees from the Treasury, Federal Reserve and other agencies totalled $16.9 trillion. Europe followed. In 2012–13, the ECB lent €1 trillion to Eurozone banks to avert a funding crisis. At its peak, UK government support to prop up ailing banks totalled £133 billion in cash and £1 trillion in guarantees and indemnities.

Bernie Sanders, the Vermont senator who campaigned for the presidential nomination in 2016, listed twenty profitable corporations that had received taxpayer bailouts while operating subsidiaries in tax havens to avoid taxes and even receiving tax rebates. Bank of America received $1.9 billion as a tax refund in 2010, even though it made $4.4 billion in profits. During the crisis, it received a $45 billion bailout and $1.3 trillion in near-zero-interest loans. At the same time, it was operating 371 subsidiaries incorporated in tax havens, 204 of them in the Cayman Islands (zero corporate tax rate). That enabled it to save $2.6 billion in federal income taxes. Goldman Sachs received a bailout of $824 billion in cash and low-interest loans. In 2008, it paid no federal income tax and instead received a $278 million tax refund, even though its profits were $2.3 billion. It would have owed $2.7 billion in federal taxes had it not been using offshore tax havens. In the UK, New Labour rescued the Royal Bank of Scotland, using £45 billion of taxpayers' money to buy 79 per cent of its shares. In 2015, the Conservative government, advised by Rothschild & Co., started to sell the shares, initially 5 per cent of them, to selected City investors and hedge funds, at a loss to the public of £1.1 billion. It announced there would be a series of sell-offs of the remainder before the next election in 2020, even though the share price was expected to remain well below the bailout price. This is another example of a government supplying rental income to its financial friends rather than operating in the public interest.

The government also began selling the 43 per cent of shares it acquired in Lloyds Banking Group, after it returned to profit. With the exception of a planned £2 billion sale in 2016 to retail (small) investors at a 5 per cent discount to the market price, the sales have been to carefully selected private investors, enabled to reap the gains from a publicly funded bailout.

In 2015, the UK government also sold a £13 billion package of mortgages and loans formerly issued by Northern Rock, which collapsed in 2007, to the US private equity group Cerberus; Cerberus promptly sold a quarter of the loans to another bank. The once-toxic mortgages, with an interest rate of nearly 5 per cent, had come good mainly because of a rise in property prices.

So public assets were sold on favourable terms to the financial elite based on an ideological commitment to privatisation and a desire to finance tax cuts.

Other countries, such as Greece, Ireland, Italy, the Netherlands, Portugal and Spain, have done much the same, recapitalising failing banks or taking them into state ownership, only to sell them once profitable into the private sector. Irish banks required a bailout of an astonishing €64 billion, close to two-fifths of GDP. Portugal's banks received over €7 billion of state aid as part of a bailout programme agreed with the EU and IMF in 2011. Weeks after emerging from that programme in 2014, the Portuguese government forked out another €4.9 billion from bailout funds to capitalise a 'good bank' from the collapsed Banco Espírito Santo, one of the country's largest banks. It planned to sell the 'good bank' while taking assets of the 'bad bank' into public ownership.

Bailing out banks has given billions in rental income to financial capital. Although the banks claim that most of the bailout loans have been repaid, those cheap loans kept them in business when they were facing ruin and enabled financial rentiers to rebuild their personal incomes.

Ironically, many institutions given public money were subsequently fined billions for acknowledged wrongdoing. By mid-2015, the five biggest US banks and twenty biggest European ones had paid fines and litigation costs of over $260 billion, with another $65 billion to come, for transgressions such as rigging foreign exchange markets, manipulating interest rates, money laundering and mis-selling mortgages and payment protection insurance.

These transgressions should have led to criminal prosecutions and prison sentences. Yet only a few people in Europe, and several dozen in the USA, were jailed and others were given non-custodial sentences. No top executive was charged. Fred Goodwin, former head of Royal Bank of Scotland, was stripped of a knighthood. A senior executive of HBOS, owned by Lloyds Bank, was fined and banned from financial services. Top executives of Lloyds lost part of their bonus packages but were not charged with any crime. By contrast, Iceland jailed twenty-six financiers for their role in the economic meltdown in 2008.

The financial institutions have protected their own by agreeing to costly settlements. And US banks have even been able to claim most of the fines as tax-deductible expenses, so saving themselves $15 billion.[25] Bank of America was allowed to deduct $12 billion of a $16.6 billion settlement with the Justice Department. JPMorgan Chase was allowed to deduct $7 billion of a $13 billion settlement.

QE AND CHEAP MONEY

> 'Bankers have been the biggest beneficiaries, with their twenty- or thirty-times leveraged balance sheets. Asset managers and hedge funds have benefited, too. Owners of property have made out like bandits. In fact, anyone with assets has grown much richer. All of us who work in financial markets owe a debt to QE.'
> Paul Marshall, chairman of Marshall Wace,
> a London-based hedge fund

The clunky term quantitative easing, QE, entered the popular lexicon in the wake of the 2008 financial crash. It involves creating money for banks and other financial intermediaries to lend to companies and consumers. The central bank does this by buying government bonds and other debt from the banking sector, giving it low-cost funds to finance investment.

All the major central banks – the US Federal Reserve, the Bank of England, the European Central Bank and the Bank of Japan – have operated QE and related 'cheap money' policies. Their aim has been to avoid deflation (falling prices) and to stimulate economic activity, mainly by lowering interest rates; in theory, this not only reduces borrowing costs but has knock-on effects, devaluing the currency, boosting exports and shoring up the value of financial and other assets, raising wealth and spending.

To this end, the USA spent $4.5 trillion on QE, the UK £375 billion. Both countries are holding on the asset stock they accumulated. Japan continued its QE of $650–700 billion into 2016. The ECB initially planned to spend €1.4 trillion – €60 billion a month – over the two years to March 2017 and in March 2016 raised that to €80 billion a month. Yet economic activity has remained sluggish and deflation remains a threat.

'Ultra-loose monetary policy' has instead provided a subsidy to the finance industry to acquire and drive up asset prices, on its own account or as loans for others to do so.[26] The IMF estimated that in 2012 the subsidy to banks from cheap money was worth up to $70 billion in the USA, $110 billion in the UK and Japan and $300 billion in the Eurozone. The total was bigger than Sweden's GDP and more than the net profit of the 1,000 biggest banks.

In an open economy system with capital flows in all directions and ample opportunities for rent seeking, any increase in the money supply will be directed to where it can earn the highest return. So money has poured into property and other assets that offer the prospect of higher returns or capital gains. This has pushed up prices and created destabilising asset bubbles. The printing of money has been a wonderful source of unearned rental income for bankers, shadow bankers and other financiers.

When central banks buy bonds, their price rises. As bonds pay a fixed amount of interest, a price rise decreases the interest rate or yield. Investors then look for riskier assets that promise a better yield, driving up their prices as well. QE thus raises asset values all round, producing a wealth effect. By making people feel wealthier, higher asset values are supposed to make them more inclined to spend or invest in productive activities. Instead, they have fuelled yet greater speculative investment in financial assets and property, setting the scene for another crash.

Since 2000, throughout the industrialised world, banks have been lending more to buy residential property than to businesses, encouraged by international banking rules that classify mortgages as half as risky as corporate loans. QE has further contributed to house price 'bubbles' by lowering mortgage interest rates, raising house prices by encouraging prospective homeowners to take on bigger mortgages. Between 2010 and 2015, average house prices rose in the UK by 15 per cent, in Norway by over 30 per cent and in Germany by nearly 25 per cent.

Lower interest rates benefit debtors and hurt savers. However, in practice it is middle- and upper-income groups that gain from lower borrowing costs and higher asset prices, not the precariat, who have few assets and short-term, high-interest debt. Lower investment yields have also hit pension funds and other retirement savings. For many people, this has offset any inducement to spend from the wealth effect. Instead, they have tried to save more and have invested in riskier assets with higher yields to preserve future income.

Meanwhile, QE has lowered corporate borrowing costs. This accounted for 20 per cent of the increase in profits of US non-financial corporations between 2007 and 2012. Yet little of the profits were invested in productive activities; they went on dividends, share buybacks and company acquisitions.

By inflating asset prices, ultra-loose monetary policy worsens inequality, between rich and poor, between young and old, and between regions.[27] By maintaining high bond and stock prices, central banks are further enriching the elite. The Bank of England calculated that the top 5 per cent of households held 40 per cent of the assets boosted by QE, while the prices of things the rich buy – prime property, paintings, fine wine and classic cars – have soared.

As UBS and PwC put it in their *2015 Billionaires Report*, 'Billionaire wealth creation over the last two decades has been largely correlated to the financial markets.' The plutocracy gained from rent extraction, not by producing anything of value.

By lowering interest rates, QE also aims to lower the value of the currency so as to boost exports. The US, Japan, the UK and the Eurozone did succeed temporarily in engineering devaluations, but it could not last as others followed. In any case, devaluation now appears to have little effect on trade, because large companies rarely cut prices in response.[28] It does, however, pad profits, since foreign earnings are worth more in terms of the domestic currency. Devaluations thus provide more rental income for capital.

Besides QE, central banks have subsidised investors speculating in bonds and equities through assurances that they will act to buoy stock markets and keep interest rates low. This raises capital values and asset prices by reducing the risks of speculation. The most well-known instance is what has become known as the 'Greenspan put'; Alan Greenspan, when Chairman of the US Federal Reserve, let it be understood that the Fed would cut interest rates to stop a stock market rout. Successive rate cuts duly propped up US stock markets during the 1990s and early 2000s. Some economists have even argued that central banks should buy shares in the open market to underpin 'reasonable' price-to-earnings ratios, as China's did in 2015 by providing cash for a stock-buying fund.

The assurance of intervention amounts to a regressive subsidy to the affluent, who own shares. There is no macroeconomic justification for propping up stock markets. Research shows that declines in equities have little long-term adverse effect on the economy, since they affect only the wealthy. Central bank intervention also creates a moral hazard, since the message is passed that investors can take risks with impunity. It thus encourages rent-seeking speculation, making money from money, not from producing anything. This is one way by which independent central banks have pursued regressive policies, storing up problems for the future.

Monetary policy has been recalibrated as central banks have become more secure from democratic accountability. As mentioned earlier, the initial justification for making them independent was that governments were prone to use monetary policy to boost employment and wages, making it inherently inflationary. A mantra of monetarism associated with Milton Friedman is that monetary policy – control of the money supply and interest rates

– should be used to control inflation, leaving microeconomic policies to influence employment and wages.

Independent central banks were accordingly given terms of reference that gave priority to restraining inflation. In recessionary times, with inflation low or even negative, they have moved further into economic policymaking by giving more emphasis to job creation and growth. But their prime focus has been to maintain the price of bonds and stocks, guaranteeing the incomes of financiers. This is not 'letting the market work'; it is manipulating the market in favour of the privileged. Economically, it is hard to justify. Morally, it is impossible to do so. The only answer is to re-assert democratic control of central banking.

Working in tandem with central banks are the big investment banks, headed by Goldman Sachs. One of its money-making 'services', from which it makes hundreds of millions of dollars, has been advising governments on sovereign debt. In 2001, it arranged a secret loan of €2.8 billion for the Greek government, disguised as an off-the-books 'cross-currency swap', in order to make the country's debt look smaller.[29] Subsequent market movements nearly doubled that debt, because of the way Goldman Sachs had structured the loan. For the privilege of being deeper in debt, Greece had to pay Goldman Sachs €600 million for services rendered. That is just one way by which Wall Street firms profit as intermediaries.

Their leaders also make fortunes flipping between the private sector, senior government posts and strategic positions in international financial agencies. Mario Draghi was director of Goldman Sachs's international division when the secretive Greek loan was developed. Then, as President of the European Central Bank, he played a part in the 'troika' (the ECB, European Commission and IMF) that forced Greece to cut pensions and public-sector employment and privatise public assets as conditions for successive bailouts, including funding to keep its banking system afloat. Having interfered with the domestic policies of a democratic country, the ECB then added to the pain by excluding purchase of Greek bonds from its QE programme.

The resort to QE since 2008 reflects the hegemony of financiers. While they claim to perform a service, they are in reality receiving 'something for nothing'. No productive activity earns these transfers. It is rent pure and simple.

SUBSIDISED LANDLORDISM

'There is no place for dirty money in Britain'
David Cameron, 28 July 2015, referring to foreign owners
of London properties

According to the National Crime Agency, buying London properties has become a way for foreign criminals to launder billions of pounds, using anonymous offshore companies to conceal ownership from their own tax authorities.[30] In their desire to attract affluent migrants, successive UK governments have allowed foreigners to buy up properties in London and elsewhere, with few questions asked about the source of the money. Cameron himself cited the case of a former Kazakh secret police chief (since murdered) who had built a London property portfolio worth £147 million.

In some posh streets, most houses and flats are foreign-owned, many empty most of the time. According to WealthInsight, London is the most popular city for second homes, ahead of New York, Los Angeles and Monaco. In central London, a third of residential sales are to foreigners, as homes or for letting.

As other buyers are pushed down the housing chain, inflation at the top of the market ripples down. This has contributed to the escalation of house prices and rents, making housing unaffordable for most wage-earners. Between 2010 and 2015, London house prices leapt by about 50 per cent. And while the housing crisis in London is most acute, prices have also risen steeply in the rest of the country.

The previous trend towards more people owning their homes has gone into steep reverse. More are living in overcrowded or inadequate accommodation; more young adults are living with parents, unable to set up a household of their own; and homelessness is increasing, including among families with children.

In Britain and elsewhere, low interest rates and tax breaks have propelled property prices to levels that have put home ownership out of reach for many and, coupled with the abolition or erosion of rent controls, generated an increasingly expensive private rental market. Landlordism has become a feature of global rentier capitalism. It has not been resurrected by chance or by free markets.

The UK's present housing crisis has its origins in Thatcher's decision in the 1980s to give council tenants the 'right to buy' their homes at a substantial discount, a subsidy scheme that decimated the stock of social housing. Nearly 2 million tenants have since taken advantage of the scheme. Financial liberalisation also meant mortgages became easier to obtain. Home ownership peaked in 2003, when 71 per cent of homes in England were owned outright or with a mortgage. Subsequently, while outright ownership went on growing, the share of mortgaged housing plummeted.

Something similar happened in the rental sector. The share of social housing continued to decline, spurred by the coalition government's decision to increase the 'right-to-buy' discount. The number of households renting from private landlords more than doubled between 2001 and 2015 to 5.4 million, a fifth of all households. By 2025, a quarter will be renting privately, according to predictions by PwC, the accountancy firm.[31] For those aged twenty to thirty-nine, 'Generation Rent', a majority will be doing so.

The number of landlords has also increased, from 1.5 million just before the financial crash to over 2 million. They own 5 million properties, including more than a third of all former council houses sold under the 'right-to-buy' programme. While 80 per cent of landlords own just one property, according to the Bank of England, the remaining 420,000 own on average eight properties. Some own hundreds.

In a market of contrived scarcity, the shrinking supply of affordable properties for home-buyers and tenants has pushed up rental incomes and prospective capital gains. According to mortgage lender Kent Reliance, in 2014–15 landlords made £112 billion in rent and capital gains, an annual return of 12.5 per cent per property. The average property made a gross return of £24,221; in London, it made £59,455. Landlords collected £4 billion each month in rent.

The value of private rented housing has passed the £1 trillion mark. The Wriglesworth Consultancy estimated that landlords had enjoyed returns of 1,400 per cent since 1996, far in excess of rewards offered by shares, bonds or cash. Unsurprisingly, institutional investors, including foreign companies, have flocked into rental housing, to the tune of £2 billion a year.

This bonanza has been fuelled by subsidies. Lenders used to treat landlords like small businesses, typically requiring a 50 per cent deposit and charging a higher interest rate than for owner-occupiers. But, in 1996, lenders introduced 'buy-to-let' mortgages on more favourable terms. Like owner-occupiers at the time, landlords received a tax break for mortgage interest.

In 2000, Gordon Brown abolished mortgage interest tax relief for owner-occupiers, which he rightly described as 'a middle-class perk', but not for landlords. This tilted the balance in favour of buy-to-let, as a way of capitalising on rising property prices. Between 2005 and 2015, buy-to-let mortgages doubled as a share of all mortgages, to 15 per cent, with a rise in 'amateur landlords' supplementing other income.

Like other businesses, landlords can also claim tax deductions for a wide range of expenses, including insurance, maintenance and repairs, utility bills, cleaning and gardening, and legal fees, all costs that homeowners must meet in full. In the financial year 2012/13, tax breaks for landlords reached a record £14 billion; mortgage interest tax relief alone came to £6.3 billion.[32] There is also a little-publicised tax break for those renting spare rooms to lodgers, introduced in 1997. From 2016, they can receive up to £7,500 a year in rent tax-free.

Landlords also make money from housing benefits paid to low-income tenants. This has increased inequality, as rents have risen faster than pay or benefits. In 2013/14, the government paid £24 billion in rent subsidies, twice as much as a decade earlier, with over a third going to private landlords. Yet private tenants live in the worst accommodation and have the highest housing costs, paying on average 40 per cent of their gross income in rent.

As Gillian Guy, chief executive of Citizens Advice, pointed out, 'Dodgy landlords make as much as £5.6 billion a year from renting out homes that don't meet legal standards and £1.3 billion of this bill is picked up by the state in the form of housing benefit. Tenants must pay soaring rents despite severe damp, rat infestations and even the risk of explosions.'

There have been some modest improvements. In 2015, the government announced a cut in tax breaks for landlords, who will also have to pay more stamp duty on purchases of buy-to-let properties. From 2017, landlords will no longer be able to deduct mortgage interest from their rental income to reduce their declared profits. And higher-rate taxpayers will no longer receive tax relief at 45 or 40 per cent, but only at the basic rate of 20 per cent.

Landlords whose mortgage interest is a high share of their income may struggle. Some will raise rents; some may form companies to bypass the rules; some may offload properties, which might lower prices, but not by much, as demand will still exceed supply. The wealthiest, who can buy without a mortgage, will be unaffected.

All this is like closing the stable door after the horse has bolted. Fergus and Judith Wilson, Britain's biggest buy-to-let landlords, announced in December 2015 that they were selling their entire property empire – about 900 houses – for £250 million, to a consortium of Arab investors. These houses will remain in the private rented sector. A fifth of all MPs, and a quarter of Conservative MPs, are landlords, some with many properties. They will continue to receive subsidies that owner-occupiers do not. Richard

Benyon, reportedly Britain's richest MP, lives in an inherited stately home and owns a land and property empire. Apart from receiving subsidies from the EU's Common Agricultural Policy, his company made £625,000 in one year from housing benefit in just one local council area.

The growth of landlordism, and the associated rental income, should be seen in the context of the shrinking ability of all but the affluent to own a home. House prices have risen far faster than wages. By 2015, the average house cost over five times average annual earnings, up from three times in the 1980s.

Yet the government's response has been to pile on more subsidies that make the situation worse. It has stoked demand for homes to buy, raising prices further, while the supply of affordable properties is dwindling, worsened by extending the 'right to buy' to housing associations and forcing local councils to sell their most valuable properties. The subsidies help the better-off with the wherewithal to start on the housing ladder, magnifying inequality.

The 'help-to-buy' scheme, introduced by the coalition and expanded in 2015, has been billed as the biggest home ownership programme since Thatcher introduced the 'right to buy' for council houses. The £22 billion scheme, which runs to 2020, comprises interest-free loans and a subsidised savings account (Help-to-Buy ISA) for a deposit to buy new-build homes up to £250,000 (£450,000 in London) and mortgage guarantees to buy homes up to £600,000. These are available to anyone, with no upper income limit, making the impact regressive, as they will benefit those able to save, or with cash from parents or grandparents, who could buy without the subsidies.

The UK's main housing problem is a shortage of affordable homes. In the 1970s, four-fifths of public spending on housing went on new homes, mostly for rent. The Thatcher council house sell-off depleted the social housing stock, but the New Labour government compounded the shortage, building even fewer houses than its predecessor. By 2000, most subsidies were going to support demand rather than supply. Today, subsidies for rent and ownership are twenty times those for housebuilding.

Moreover, the limited subsidies for housebuilding are going mainly to developers, not for social or affordable housing. Expanding a New Labour scheme to subsidise construction of private housing for letting at 'market rents', the government has set up a fund providing state-backed loans for 'build-to-rent' projects, mostly purpose-built flats. The requirement to include a proportion of affordable homes has been weakened.

In 2015, the government announced it would pay £2.3 billion in subsidies to developers to build 200,000 'starter homes' for sale at a 20 per cent discount; these can be resold at market prices by lucky recipients, who will be among the better-off, with money for a deposit and an income to support a mortgage. Another plan is to encourage 'shared ownership', where people buy a share of a house and pay rent on the rest, with an option to buy in full later. None of this helps low-income groups.

Housing wealth has been key to rising inequality in Britain and elsewhere. One study argues that the rising share of income going to capital identified by Piketty in *Capitalism in the Twenty-First Century* is largely attributable to increased payments to house owners.[33] In seven rich countries, capital income from housing accounted for 3 per cent of the total in 1950 but 10 per cent today.

These results may be exaggerated, since rental income has been growing from other sources too. But, without doubt, housing-based inequality has been fuelled by government subsidies that have neither moral nor economic justification.

THE FOURTH LIE OF RENTIER CAPITALISM

A fourth lie of rentier capitalism is the claim that profits reflect managerial efficiency and returns to risk-taking. Rather, the increase in the share of income going in profits reflects the development of regulatory structures discussed in Chapter 2, the rise in regressive subsidies, and the effects of inequality on the structure of aggregate demand. The increased profit share has gone mainly to those receiving rental income, much of it linked to financial assets. There has been no increase in managerial efficiency and no increased risks to investment.

The carefully woven web of subsidies is regressive and distorts all sorts of markets. In spite of the claims of special interests, there is little evidence that subsidies boost growth or development. Few are subject to objective evaluation and most merely represent rental income to their recipients.

Chapter 4

THE SCOURGE OF DEBT

'Neither a lender nor a borrower be.'
Polonius, *Hamlet*

The debtor has long been associated with condemnation and moral disdain. In some languages, including German, Dutch and Hebrew, the word for debt is etymologically linked with guilt. But, in reality, the notions of debt and credit, and debtor and creditor, are socially constructed. And it is primarily creditors who construct debtors.

If debt and debtors are 'bad', then creditors should not escape moral opprobrium. Never has this been truer than now, when rent-seeking lenders have proliferated and when debt has come almost to define the age.

Global rentier capitalism loves debt. Financiers and other holders of assets thrive on creating debt, because they are enriched by interest payments and fees. And they are constructing new forms of debt as well as maximising old ones. The result is that global debt, both public and private, has climbed relentlessly to record, destabilising levels. Another financial crisis is looming, possibly triggered by stumbling and highly indebted emerging market economies.[1]

It is conventional to distinguish public (central and local government) and private (corporate and household) debt. After the 2008 financial crash, an enormously influential study purported to show that public debt exceeding 90 per cent of GDP slowed economic growth.[2] Governments, notably in Britain, used that argument to justify savage cuts in social spending intended to reduce government borrowing. Sadly, only three years later another study showed that the first had been flawed.[3] And the direction of causation could be the reverse. As European countries subject to austerity have found, slower growth tends to raise public debt by lowering tax revenue and increasing the cost of unemployment and other benefits.

The IMF subsequently questioned the wisdom of concentrating on reducing public debt. It found no evidence of a public debt threshold,[4] whereas high private debt appeared to be much more detrimental to economic growth, deepening recessions and slowing recoveries. That is because a build-up of private indebtedness eventually becomes unsustainable, forcing defaults, foreclosures, bankruptcies and big cutbacks in spending and debt levels. To the extent that reductions in public debt intensify private debt, governments may achieve short-term gains at the cost of longer-term fragility. Several studies have concluded that it was a sharp rise in household debt that turned the financial crash of 2008 into a slump.[5] It was fundamentally a debt crisis, precipitated by the recklessness of financial institutions.

Household debt can be divided into three types. 'Entrepreneurial' debt arises from borrowing to boost income. 'Strategic' debt consists of borrowing for personal investment, to buy a home or pay for schooling or university. 'Distress' debt arises mainly from borrowing more than a person can afford, to pay for essentials or because of an increase in previously supportable debt due to higher interest rates or changes in circumstance.

The main narrative in the age of rentier capitalism concerns the growth of distress debt. This has contributed to inequality and intensified economic insecurity for a growing proportion of the population. Those on low incomes have the highest debt relative to income and face the highest interest rates, another reason why inequality measured by money incomes understates social income inequality.

In particular, the precariat is living on the edge of unsustainable debt, knowing that one accident, illness or financial mistake could unleash a spiral leading to homelessness, dependence on charity, alcoholism, drug addiction and other social illnesses. Maurizio Lazzarato, an Italian sociologist, has depicted 'an indebted subjectivity' – a sense of facing infinite debt that feeds into a psyche of nervousness and social passivity.[6]

Among the causes of mass indebtedness is a historically unique situation: people are trying to maintain a past living standard in the context of declining and more volatile real wages. Since the establishment of capitalism, society has been conditioned to expect that each generation will have a higher average standard of living than its predecessors. This is no longer the case.

Our perceived needs are formed by our life experience, by the living standard attained by our parents and our peers, who set the income and consumption aspirations of each generation. People borrow to keep up, but keeping up has become harder. One reason is the conversion of the 'social commons' – public services and amenities – into commodities. Instead of being free

or subsidised as part of social income, more of these involve payments. As discussed later (Chapter 5), privatising the commons
increases the fragility – lack of resilience – of those on the edge of
unsustainable debt in meeting daily or life cycle needs.

High and rising debt testifies to rentier capitalism's relentless
expansion. In 2014, global debt reached a record $199 trillion,
equivalent to nearly three times global income, according to the
McKinsey Global Institute. This was 40 per cent more than in
2007, far outstripping economic growth in the period. Although
the biggest factor was government debt, in most countries private
debt also rose. Public and private debt quadrupled in China to
nearly three times GDP, contributing over a third of the worldwide increase in 2007–14. If and when the global debt bubble
bursts, the world economy will be unable to rely on China to
come to the rescue as it did after 2008.

Japan was the most indebted, with total debt four times GDP. But
the UK is moving that way. Despite spending cuts, government debt
rose by fifty percentage points and total debt by thirty percentage
points, leaving it among the most highly indebted rich countries,
with total debt two and a half times GDP. And although households
and companies ran down debt after 2007, by 2014 the trend was upwards again. The Office for Budget Responsibility forecast in 2015
that by 2020 the average British household would have debts equivalent to more than 180 per cent of annual income, even higher than
the pre-recession level, and far above levels prevailing in earlier decades. In the 1980s, household debt was under 100 per cent of income.

In 1981, US household debt was less than half of GDP; by 2007,
it was equal to 100 per cent and net household saving had fallen
to zero. By 2014, household debt had fallen to 77 per cent of GDP

but, as in Britain, was expected to start rising again. Household debt was even higher elsewhere. In Denmark it was 129 per cent of GDP (an astonishing 275 per cent of household income), in the Netherlands it was 115 per cent and in Australia 113 per cent.

Creditors and financiers have done well from this mountain of debt. Andrew Ross has described the USA as a 'creditocracy', in which Wall Street calls the political shots and three-quarters of households are in serious debt.[7] In 2015, nearly 7 million US homeowners had 'under water' mortgages, owing more on their homes than they were worth. Still, most lenders want debtors to keep on paying. If distress debt continues to increase, the resultant financial crash could be more threatening to the global economy than in 2008: the debt is greater, more global and out of control. Some countries may be able to shift part of the debt abroad, and others may shuffle the shares held by government, corporations and households. But, as the lead author of the McKinsey report told the press, 'It is like a balloon. If you squeeze debt in one place, it pops up somewhere else in the system.'[8]

Today's situation stems from developments in the 1980s, when financial intermediaries multiplied channels of credit, taking advantage of globalisation's downward pressure on real wages in rich countries. Governments eagerly facilitated the spread of cheap credit as part of the Faustian bargain essential to their survival. Easily accessible, low-cost credit, coupled with the modern Speenhamland system of tax credits, allowed consumption to gallop ahead.

When the spending binge came to an abrupt end in 2007–08, household, corporate and government debt had reached unprecedented shares of national income. The austerity era made matters worse.

AUSTERITY: TURNING PUBLIC DEFICITS INTO PRIVATE DEBT

The austerity strategy is shifting debt onto private households, by cutting state benefits and privatising services. Cutting benefits for low-income families has forced many to borrow just to keep from going under. Downward pressure on already low wages, due to competition for jobs by more desperate jobseekers, is forcing more into deeper debt. At the same time, many costs of living are unavoidable and are fixed or rising, due to cuts in public services. People have to pay more for such essentials as housing, bus fares and childcare.

In early 2008, the Money Advice Trust, a British debt charity, estimated that the average person had only enough money to survive for fifty-two days if they lost their job; a third would run out of cash in just two weeks. So, there was little scope for resilience even before the financial crash. The subsequent shift of the debt burden onto households has made another financial crisis more likely.

Adair Turner, former head of the UK's Financial Services Authority, who took over days after the collapse of Lehman Brothers in 2008, has also argued that the 2008 crash was due to the stoking of household debt by the financial sector, especially to buy property.[9] Traditionally, banks took deposits from households and lent to businesses to invest to expand production. These days, most lending is for property, mainly to buy existing assets rather than create new ones. In 1928, across seventeen industrialised countries, only 30 per cent of bank lending was for property; by 2007, the proportion was nearly 60 per cent.[10]

When central banks cut interest rates to practically zero or indulge in quantitative easing, more money flows into the property market, raising house prices, enriching landlords and encouraging speculative property buying. Eventually, this precipitates an asset crash and a 'debt-deflation' recession in which firms and households, faced with dwindling asset values, slash spending to try to meet increasingly onerous debt repayments.

There is a historical parallel. Early in the twentieth century, financiers in industrialised countries sowed the seeds for debt deflation by channelling funds into imperialistic ventures, drawn by promises of spectacular riches in exotic places. This led to what the British economist John Hobson depicted as systemic underconsumption at home. In the USA, critics such as Thorstein Veblen saw finance distorting production and, in Germany as early as 1910, Rudolf Hilferding warned against financial capitalism for similar reasons.

Finance fuelled the imperialistic rivalries that contributed to the First World War. Once an exhausted peace had been restored, Europe was afflicted by debt deflation, partly due to US demands for payment for armaments it had supplied to the UK and France. They in turn pushed impoverished Germany to pay heavy war reparations, plunging it into economic depression and paving the way for Nazism.

Meanwhile, the elite in the USA and Europe continued their lavish lifestyles, mostly funded from rentier income, until the bubble burst in the Great Crash of 1929. The slump became global. The final scene in the tragedy was the failure of the 1933 London Economic Conference, called to decide on debt relief and other measures to induce international recovery. The refusal to write off the debt that had dragged all economies down deepened the Great Depression that was only ended by the Second World War.

Domination by financial capital created the conditions and

governments failed to prevent the tragedy from unfolding. Their modern equivalents are more culpable, since they have history books to remind them what happened the last time rent-seeking finance was allowed to stoke debt to its advantage.

Flash forward to today and consider the refusal of those representing international finance to write off Greek sovereign debt, despite the hardship imposed on the Greek people. Ironically, Greece was among the countries that agreed to write off German sovereign debt under the London Debt Agreement of 1953, the aim of which was to avoid a repeat of the 1930s. Total debt forgiveness amounted to 280 per cent of German GDP between 1947 and 1953, setting the scene for the 'German miracle'. It would have cost much less to do the same for Greece.

The refusal to write off Greek debt followed similar refusals for Ireland, Portugal and Spain. All of these countries saw their economies nosedive, with rocketing unemployment, poverty rates and homelessness. Debt became more deeply ingrained.

Rising debt is associated with subsequent falls in output and a permanent reduction in potential growth.[11] This is because 'debt overhang' – excessive debt – comes to dominate the decisions of governments, corporations and households in ways that make it harder to reduce debt without economic and social pain. Ominously, the world faces a *global* debt overhang, with the USA, China and Eurozone countries all struggling with excessive debt.

Orthodox responses to excess credit expansion hold out little prospect of lasting success. Requiring banks to hold more reserves or tighten lending criteria is likely to accelerate the shift to less regulated non-bank intermediaries such as the peer-to-peer platform lenders discussed later in this chapter. The only solutions are to reduce the 'demand' for debt, channel credit into productive investment and oblige lenders to bear more of the risk.[12]

Before turning to how debt has been promoted for the benefit of rentiers, two further points are worth noting. While banks and corporations have been enabled to borrow or carry debt at unprecedentedly low cost – with interest rates at or close to zero – those forced into distressed debt face extraordinarily high costs. The inequity has always existed, but never to this degree.

Then there is the collective action dilemma. If just a few countries pursue the austerity path by cutting spending, with relatively little burden placed on taxes – the British route – then they may succeed to some extent, by attracting rent-seeking investment from abroad. But if many countries do that, there is a high probability of generalised deflation. By 2015, the rush to austerity had put the global economy on edge, leaving economic growth both anaemic and fragile. Repeated doses of QE may have avoided a relapse into recession, but at a cost of more debt. Meanwhile, rentiers living off the proceeds were flourishing. The Second Gilded Age continued, as the plutocracy, elite and some in the salariat wallowed in luxury.

DEBT AS EXPLOITATION

Debt has again become a systemic mechanism of worker exploitation. In the early days of industrial capitalism, employers commonly put workers in debt, often via a company store, to oblige them to stay in their job. Leaving without having paid off the debt risked the wrath of the law. That practice went out of fashion, partly due to union pressure. For a while, workers received wages with few deductions and plenty of additions. But deductions have crept up, while those additions have been disappearing. And costs of working have been shifted onto workers.

Banks and other lenders like clients to be permanently in debt, since that means a continuing flow of income from fees and interest. As the chief counsel of the US Comptroller of the Currency said in March 2005, 'Today the focus for lenders is not so much on consumer loans being repaid, but on the loan as a perpetual earning asset.'[13] For many years, the financial industry has tried to induce people to borrow more, with great success.

In the UK, stagnant wages have pushed more people into chronic debt. By 2014, over 3.2 million households – one in eight – were spending over a quarter of their income on servicing unsecured debts such as bank overdrafts, credit card and store debt, up from 2.5 million the year before, according to research commissioned by the Trades Union Congress and Unison, drawing on official data.[14]

Some 1.6 million households, two-thirds on low incomes, were spending 40 per cent or more of their income on repayments of non-housing debt. The debt advice charity StepChange reported that between 2012 and 2014 it saw a 56 per cent rise in the number of people seeking help, with unsecured debt averaging £15,000. The introduction of a living wage (which is based on an hourly rate) and modest rises in wages of full-time employees will not overcome these unsustainable strains.

Falling behind with repayments has broader repercussions. In 2012, a study for Demos revealed that 47 per cent of US employers ran credit checks on job applicants before hiring.[15] Many UK employers do the same. It is unlikely to be much different elsewhere.

HOUSING DEBT

Almost everywhere in the industrialised world, the main reason for rising household debt before the 2008 crash was a rapid increase in housing debt. Much of the increase was due to government policies that made subsidised credit available for house purchase to potential voters who could not afford housing without subsidies and the assurance of rising incomes. In particular, the US administration created the conditions for the sub-prime mortgage bubble by encouraging imprudent lending deliberately targeted at low-income groups.

These policies exacerbated debt due to rising property prices. In the 1970s, US house prices represented about twice annual family income; by 2005, they were about five times annual income. Middle-income homeowners were running down retirement funds to maintain mortgage payments, as homeowner stress fed into old-age insecurity. In Spain, between 2003 and 2007 around a million sub-prime mortgages were peddled to vulnerable households, increasing household indebtedness nationwide.

Similar pressures built up in Britain, inducing more to take on debt commitments well beyond their means. House prices have trebled in real (inflation-adjusted) terms since the early 1990s. The Nationwide Building Society calculated that the ratio of house prices to average earnings rose from under three times in the early 1990s to over five times in 2015 (and from five to more than nine times in London). Area statistics show an even more dramatic picture. According to the Office for National Statistics, house prices averaged nearly nine times *local* incomes in England and Wales (and far more in sought-after areas), compared with 6.4 times in

2002, when data were first collected. House prices are beyond the means of a growing proportion of the adult population.

In 2015, a first-time buyer would have needed to earn at least £41,000 a year in order to obtain and service a mortgage, at a time when the median wage was £22,000. In fact, the average buyer had an income of nearly £50,000, in the top 30 per cent. In London, where the average home costs half a million pounds, buyers would need an income of at least £77,000, against the average London wage of £28,000.[16]

Unsurprisingly, there has also been a sharp rise in high-risk mortgages. Between 2010 and 2015, there was a 64 per cent increase in new mortgage loans for upwards of 4.5 times household income, which the Bank of England regards as unsustainable in the event of a rise in interest rates, a recession or a personal mishap. This is a bubble waiting to burst and Britain is not alone. Canada, Australia and New Zealand are among countries the OECD regards as vulnerable to a price correction.

Every British government promises to increase home ownership. Yet, since 2003, ownership has been in decline, while renting from private landlords has risen. This has particularly affected those aged twenty-five to thirty-four; in 2004, 60 per cent of that age group owned their own home; by 2015, it was just over a third. The shift to private renting would have been even greater were it not for the fact that many in their twenties and thirties stayed in or returned to the parental home, while others were crowded into group lets.

The availability of social (council and housing association) housing has shrunk too. This has reduced the stock of affordable housing and pushed more low-income families into expensive private rental accommodation, making indebtedness more likely. Extension of the 'right-to-buy' subsidy scheme to housing association tenants will make the situation worse by further reducing the social housing stock. Everything is subordinated to the desire to privatise and commodify housing, for the benefit of landlords and property speculators.

The right-to-buy scheme, which allows tenants to buy their home at a big discount to the market price, has enriched a few, none of whom has worked for that windfall. A council flat in London's Covent Garden area, sold for £130,000 in 1990, went for £1.2 million in 2015. This example, though not typical, is indicative of what the right-to-buy policy implies. What was built as a public asset provided somebody with private riches.

While the government was boasting of economic growth, with national income supposedly at a record high, nearly 450,000 families were in overcrowded accommodation and homelessness was on the rise, including the 'hidden homeless' camping in the homes of friends or in squats.

Yet there were 25 million unoccupied bedrooms, reflecting a 50 per cent increase in under-occupation in the previous decade.[17] This unprecedented market failure is mainly due to elderly people continuing to live in the family home after their children have left. It will be further encouraged by inheritance tax reform that allows homes valued at up to £1 million to be left tax-free to descendants, a change for which there is no moral or economic justification.

Britain is not alone in having a dysfunctional housing market. Homelessness has been growing across the rich part of the world, including most European countries, the USA and Australia. A survey in the USA in 2015 counted over half a million homeless people, a quarter of them children, sleeping on the streets, in cars, in hostels for the homeless or in temporary accommodation. The number of hidden homeless, or homeless for at least a period during the year, is thought to be much higher.

Trailer parks have become a growth industry. Surely only in America could there be a Mobile Home University. Based in Orlando, it teaches people how to make profits from buying trailer parks and renting out spaces to those made homeless by the financial crisis. According to the US Census, an astonishing 20 million people – 6 per cent of the population – now live in trailer parks, in the richest capitalist economy in the world. Some plutocrats have been making a lot from the growing business. Sam Zell, who is worth about $5 billion, is America's largest mobile homes park owner through his Equity Lifestyle Properties. He owns 140,000 trailer parks, earning $777 million from them in 2014. Warren Buffett, with $67 billion to his name, owns the biggest mobile home manufacturer and the two biggest mobile home lenders.

In Spain, at the peak of the crisis in 2012 over 500 families were evicted from their homes every day. In 2014, evictions were still taking place at the rate of more than 100 a day. The number of unoccupied houses and apartments rose sharply, many repossessed by the banks after homeowners were unable to pay their mortgages. By 2015, 3.4 million homes lay vacant.

In Spain, as in Ireland, people remain liable for mortgage debt, complete with penalties and interest, even after repossession. But while the British authorities continue to welcome plutocratic property speculators and create yet more incentives for under-occupation, in parts of Spain a new breed of politicians has taken action. The mayor of Barcelona, a housing activist elected in 2015, has fined banks for keeping properties empty and negotiated the temporary transfer of apartments for use as social housing. More than 100 other Spanish municipalities have taken similar powers.

Although local authorities in England can levy extra council tax on long-term empty properties, many do not use these powers, and the levy is capped at 50 per cent of the normal rate – too low to make much difference.

LANDLORD DEBT

The private rental sector in the UK has been growing by over 4 per cent a year since 1999. In 2012, private renting overtook social housing as the second most common form of tenure after owner-occupation, and by 2015 it accounted for about a fifth of all households. Rising property prices, easily obtained cheap credit, tax relief on buy-to-let mortgages and other subsidies encouraged many people to become landlords; others have become landlords in the need for extra income. As a result, most landlords are now individuals. The Private Landlords Survey of 2010 found that over 90 per cent were part-time, with other income-earning activities in addition. In 2011, just 1 per cent of private rentals were owned by institutions, compared with 13 per cent in the USA and 17 per cent in Germany.[18]

In 2014, four-fifths of all new mortgages were landlord loans. Beneficiaries have included Tony and Cherie Blair, who have accumulated more than two dozen apartments to let since Tony Blair stepped down as Prime Minister, as well as highly valuable properties used by his family. In 2015, worried by the extent of debt and the growing housing bubble, the government raised taxes and reduced subsidies on buy-to-let properties. While this may deter some from starting or expanding buy-to-let activities, it does nothing to shrink the pool of existing buy-to-let debt. Landlords with large mortgages will be in trouble if interest rates rise. This new form of debt seems as risky as any other.

PREDATORY CREDITORS: CREDIT CARDS, CATALOGUES AND PAYDAY LOANS

'I use Mastercard to pay Visa.'
Bumper sticker

Rent-seeking capitalism relies on inducing people to spend more than they can safely afford. This contrasts with the old Fordist model, in which corporations were encouraged to pay decent wages – a practice started by Henry Ford for his employees – on the grounds that workers had to be able to buy the goods and services being produced. Today, wages are kept down on grounds of 'competitiveness' with wages in some other part of the world, while desired domestic consumption is fanned by easy credit.

Since the UK emerged from the Great Recession, consumer debt has grown rapidly. By late 2015, Britons owed £180 billion on consumer credit, while over 3 million people were struggling with their debts.[19] The mechanisms to induce overspending have been refined. In the midst of austerity, retailers devised a 'buy-now-pay-later' Christmas in the form of 'Black Friday', a day of discounted deals at the end of November designed to generate a frenzy of Christmas-oriented sales. Not surprisingly, the Bank of England expressed concern at the growth of personal loans, but was reluctant to raise interest rates, which would have plunged many debtors into crisis.

This revival of the Faustian bargain has stimulated growth, but it is unsustainable. It is scarcely the model of the prudent house-wife, on which Thatcherite economics was based. It has increased the fragility of the economy and the probability of another finan-cial crash.

Payday loans, credit card and catalogue debt are the bane of the precariat. Finance imposes extra costs on the economically disadvantaged. Those in and out of casual jobs, with fluctuating low incomes, dependent on state benefits, or with a record of debt, however petty or short-lived, are often denied cheaper forms of credit and must borrow or obtain credit from lenders who charge much higher rates. This further increases social income inequality.

Payday loans, perhaps the most parasitic rent-extraction practice, came to prominence after the financial crash of 2008. These very short-term loans at eye-watering rates of interest aim to tide people over for a few days before payday when their low wages run out. In the USA, payday loan storefronts outnumber McDonald's restaurants and are the prime source of credit for 90 million unbanked Americans. The average unbanked house-hold pays more than $2,400 each year for storefront financial services, even though they are banned in fourteen US states. And some of these lenders are operated or backed by the very Wall Street banks that refuse cheap loans to poor people.[20]

In Britain, the coalition government eventually introduced rules to limit the predatory behaviour of payday loan companies, which were charging financially illiterate people as much as 5,000 per cent annual interest and deducting money from borrowers' bank accounts without their say-so. Even after the new rules came in, Wonga (the lender that came to symbolise the sector) was still able to charge an annualised rate of 1,509 per cent, and QuickQuid one of 1,212 per cent.

A new breed of online lender, expanding rapidly in the USA with names like ZestFinance and LendUp, provides short-term small loans with annual interest rates of up to 390 per cent per annum. Some do not charge interest but levy a flat fee. A feature of all these companies is that they require full access to their clients' bank accounts and other personal data, which they use to determine whether to provide loans, what interest rate to charge and for how long to lend.

THE PLATFORM DEBT MACHINE

The misnamed 'sharing economy' is also fostering indebtedness. App-based taxi services, such as Uber and Lyft, have tie-ups with lenders that enable drivers to buy vehicles on credit. Big car companies are becoming involved. In January 2016, General Motors announced a deal with Lyft, under which it would supply rental vehicles to Lyft drivers. In 2015, Ford introduced a pilot scheme in London and six US cities allowing customers buying cars on credit to rent them out through peer-to-peer car rental platform companies.

The idea is that customers will be more likely to buy a car through Ford Credit, and keep up regular instalments, if they can earn extra income by renting it out. The scheme represents a novel way of generating debt and rental income, both for Ford and for the platform companies, easyCar Club in London and Getaround in the USA. Like other platforms (see Chapter 6), they act as brokers, charging fees for each rental transaction. In easyCar Club's case, the basic fee is 10 per cent of the transaction. Getaround charges a whopping 40 per cent commission on rentals as well as booking fees and charges for data network access.

More generally, lightly regulated peer-to-peer (P2P) lending platforms have been seizing business from banks by enabling investors to earn a higher return through lending directly to individuals and enterprises. The leading names are Lending Club and Prosper in the USA, and Funding Circle, which operates in the USA as well as the UK, its home country. Politically well-connected individuals, such as former US Treasury Secretary Larry Summers, are on the board of Lending Club, the biggest P2P platform. While the platforms may be vulnerable to financial crises and defaults, in the meantime they are generating a lot of rental income. Renaud Laplanche, co-founder and chief executive of Lending Club, told the *Financial Times*: 'The sky is the limit – there is no practical limit to how big we can get.'[21]

There does indeed seem to be no limit to platform-driven debt creation. The system's solvency will only be tested when the bubble bursts. Meanwhile, rental income is being amassed in ever more innovative ways. The latest manifestation is the emergence of loan brokers, websites that for a fee (£50 or more in the UK) offer to put desperate people needing a loan in touch with potential lenders. Brokers may share bank details and other personal information with up to 200 companies, which then also attempt to levy charges on the individual. Rent extraction is a polite term to describe their activities.

STUDENT DEBT

Probably the most spectacular new form of debt in the twenty-first century has been mass indebtedness associated with tertiary education. More and more young people are accumulating more and more debt, due to rising fees and costs and the conversion of educational grants into student loans.

Yet teenagers and their parents are under pressure to extend tertiary schooling, a consequence of the 'credentialism' used in recruitment by most firms and the changing structure of jobs. Lack of a degree diminishes a person's economic prospects. But the surge into universities and colleges means a majority of youth now emerge with significant debt. It is a new mechanism of inequality: students with affluent parents can avoid or minimise debt, the rest struggle. And it is not just the debt itself that boosts inequality but the effect it has on economic risk-taking. It is hard to take entrepreneurial risks if bailiffs or debt collection agencies are lurking.

In many countries, including the UK and USA, going to university or college has gone from being a right to education, funded by grants and subsidies, to being a phase of preparation for adulthood and the labour market, funded by public and/or private loans. Leaving education with major debt can blight life for years. It is a form of exploitation, a substantial deduction from income stretching into the future. Debt becomes normal, a weight on the conscious and sub-conscious psyche. And it creates yet another 'poverty trap', since in most cases the debt need not be repaid until earnings exceed a certain threshold.

In the USA, private college loans grew from $2 billion in 1996 to $17 billion in 2007. In May 2012, student debt reached the $1 trillion milestone. It has become a hallmark of rentier capitalism, a huge source of rental income shaping the lives of millions of young Americans. By 2013, over 7 million ex-students were in deep arrears. They were not alone. In Japan, students owe the equivalent of billions of dollars. In Sweden, where universities are still nominally free, over 85 per cent of students graduate with large debts, a higher proportion than in the United States. Similar figures can be cited for other countries.

In the UK, student loans are rising remorselessly. Student debt held by the government reached a record £73.5 billion in March 2015, more than double the amount in 2010, boosted by a tripling of undergraduate tuition fees in 2012/13. And the situation was about to worsen, following a 2015 decision to end grants for poor students and oblige them to take loans instead. This will deter some potential students from low-income families from going to university. The Institute for Fiscal Studies estimated that the poorest 40 per cent of students would graduate with debts of up to £53,000 at the end of a three-year course, up from £40,500 before the change.

More face the prospect of being unable to pay off their loans and other debt accumulated during their university years. Former students at English universities must start paying off the debt once their income passes a certain level (currently £21,000), which turns it into a tax. This creates a poverty trap. Someone passing the threshold would pay income tax at 20 per cent, national insurance contributions of 12 per cent and 9 per cent on loan repayments, giving a marginal tax rate of 41 per cent. Marginal tax rates above 40 per cent are commonly claimed to act as a disincentive to labour.

All the time the debt incurs interest, so that if repayment is deferred the amount a student must repay rises even after studies have finished. Only 47 per cent of those who graduated in 2013 were earning enough in 2015 to have started repaying their loans.[22] The government itself has estimated that 45 per cent of lending will not be recovered.[23] One credible report concluded that a majority of undergraduates would still be paying off their debt in their forties and fifties, with nearly three-quarters unable to clear it before it was written off after thirty years.[24] The Sutton Trust's Director of Research, Conor Ryan, summed up the implications: 'For many professionals, such as teachers, this will mean having to find up to £2,500 extra a year to service loans at a time when their children are still at school and family and mortgage costs are at their most pressing.'[25]

In 2014, 59 per cent of recent graduates were in jobs that did not require a university degree, and thus were likely to be relatively low paid. In effect, the costs of their education are way out of step with its 'market value'. Forty per cent of UK students surveyed in 2016 said their expected debt levels were not an 'acceptable' investment in their future career, up from 18 per cent in 2012, and 40 per cent said long-term debt was a 'major' source of stress.[26]

For many if not most graduates, student debt will be a proverbial albatross around the neck, with severe psychological and financial implications. Though student debt in the UK does not count against credit scores, mortgage lenders must take repayment capacity into account when deciding whether to lend for house purchase, and heavy debt obligations are also likely to constrain saving for a deposit.

The UK government is copying the Americans in privatising student debt. A law introduced in 2008 permits the sale of the 'student loan book' through 'securitisation', bundling the debt into income-generating assets to be sold to private investors. They will gain rental income from debt repayments, which would otherwise contribute to government revenues. Privatising student debt will also make it harder for any future government to ease repayment conditions, since investors will lobby against any reduction in their income flow.

While early attempts at selling securitised student debt flopped, the government still hopes to sell a large chunk of the loan book by 2020. Raising the interest rate on past loans was proposed in a government-commissioned report on student debt privatisation, but rejected after an outcry. An alternative proposed was a 'synthetic hedge' that would guarantee investors compensation for any loss due to favourable loan terms, yet another taxpayer-funded subsidy to rentiers. However, a sale on the basis of a guarantee would not get student loans off the government's books.

Most likely then will be the 'tranching' of loans – splitting the loans into risk categories for sale at differential prices reflecting the degree of risk. This would be an implicit guarantee of positive returns to investors, at the cost of a loss for taxpayers, especially since private buyers of discounted debt are not shy of using aggressive tactics to elicit repayment. Turning debt into a new type of income-generating asset to be privatised is a phenomenon unique to the age.

In the USA, the average cost of a college degree has doubled in the past fifteen years, largely due to withdrawal of public funding.

Nearly 70 per cent of 2014 graduates had student debt, averaging $29,000 per borrower. Rising default rates and slowing repayments have prompted US federal programmes to ease repayment schedules and make them more affordable. But most students have private loans in addition or instead. It is these that are being bundled into investment assets, known as SLABS (student loan asset-backed securities), and sold off to financial institutions, which earn rental income from the debt repayments.

Even so, slower rates of repayment and higher rates of prospective default have hit the price of bonds backed by student debt as the assets are seen as riskier and less attractive to financial investors. Symptomatic of an emerging crisis, in September 2015 US Bancorp dropped an effort to sell a $3 billion portfolio of student loans because the bids were too low.[27] As many portfolios are sold to raise money for making further loans to students or consumers, this incipient crisis may drive up the price of loans to students, or even result in a shortage of loans to fill the contrived secondary market. This is not a 'natural' market. It arises from converting a public good into a commodity.

The scale of outstanding student debt in the USA is astonishing. According to MeasureOne, a San Francisco firm that tracks the market, as of mid-2015 outstanding loans amounted to $1.27 trillion, more than all credit card debt. Repayment obligations are operating as a drag on the US economy, limiting spending on other things. As in Britain, millions of young Americans are delaying setting up as independent households and starting a family, while house purchase is increasingly out of reach. Even more corrosively, debt is likely to prompt graduates to shun lower-paid but essential jobs such as teaching or social work and opt for higher-paid jobs that will make loan repayments easier.[28] High student debt has also been shown to inhibit risk-taking and entrepreneurship.[29]

Student debt has become an asset for financial capital, a means of extracting rent, by converting the 'educational commons' into a private necessity and then forcing students to rely on loans that produce debts greater than their additional prospective earnings. Those likely to join the precariat are losing an acquired social right because the cost of education is becoming prohibitive. And they are losing a political right, since tertiary education is being converted into a commodity, without its historical enlightenment features.

STUDENT ACCOMMODATION DEBT

Student housing in Britain is another growing niche of the rentier economy, attracting private investment of a record £6 billion in 2015, more than double the amount in 2014. This worrying trend is pushing up student indebtedness, as high-cost accommodation replaces often scruffier but more affordable housing.

One reason is the building by private developers of purpose-built, luxury student dwellings, often boasting a private gym and gaming room, spurred partly by rising numbers of affluent overseas students attending British universities. The gentrification of accommodation is helping to sell universities in the global marketplace, where they are increasingly competing on the basis of a 'total experience': for the lifestyle on offer rather than just the perceived value of their degrees and diplomas.

Meanwhile, keen to maximise profits or to overcome cost pressures, universities have been selling their previously low-rent student dwellings to private investors, creating space for global finance to expand in a semi-captive market. By 2013, over 80 per cent of student accommodation was being provided by profit-making firms. Rents have soared. The average cost of accommodation of £124 a week in 2013 consumed 95 per cent of the maximum student loan, leaving next to nothing for other living costs, and the situation is certainly worse today. As well as forcing students to take term-time jobs (three-quarters had paid employment in 2015 against 57 per cent in 2013),[30] this has resulted in yet more debt. In 2014–15, some 40 per cent of students said they needed to borrow more to pay the rent, according to Shelter's Private Tenant Survey.

The student accommodation 'industry' has become a favourite for global finance, attracted by the high returns that look set to continue as demand for student accommodation far outstrips supply. US investment bank Goldman Sachs has set up a student housing venture called Vero Group, which aims to become the UK's leading student accommodation provider. The biggest current operator, Unite, has 46,000 beds across the UK. Much of the investment comes from overseas, notably from North America, Russia and Middle Eastern countries, all looking to extract rental income. As one property consultant told *The Observer* in 2015, it was the latest 'must-have asset class'.[31]

SOCIAL POLICY AS DEBT CREATOR

Personal and household debt is also being propelled by the restructuring of welfare benefits and services. Instead of benefits paid promptly as entitlements to cover, in Beveridge's famous words, 'interruption and loss of earning power', governments have engineered a complex system of delayed social assistance requiring myriad checks and assessments. More people are pushed to rely on short-term loans to pay for living costs during the long delays.

The UK government has also forced the unemployed to wait at least seven days, rather than three as before, before they can even apply for jobseeker's allowance. Once enmeshed in debt – or, in the case of the newly unemployed, in deeper debt than before they lost their job – they will find it extremely hard to escape.

Conservative MP Kwasi Kwarteng has proposed that unemployed youth who have not had a job, and thus have not paid national insurance contributions, should receive their jobseeker's allowance as a repayable loan. This would impose a rental charge on a state benefit, turning a benefit into a debt. It would be yet another way by which a person would lose social rights. It would be yet another way by which financiers could make rental income.

SECURITISATION: THE RENTIER'S JOKER CARD

'Securitisation', the commercial practice of turning debt into an income-earning asset, has become big business, house mortgages and student loans being the two most prominent examples. What is involved is remarkably simple – making rentier income, lots of it, from bundling up people's debts and selling them for handsome income flows for years ahead. Securitisation was at the heart of the sub-prime mortgage scandal in the USA, which precipitated the financial crash that ruined lives and intensified inequality and economic insecurity. It is still going on.

An egregious case in Britain was Northern Rock, a lender that borrowed heavily on UK and international capital markets during the pre-2007 housing boom to give mortgage loans of up to 125 per cent of the property value. Like its counterparts in the USA, the firm bundled up these risky mortgages and sold them as income-generating assets to investors, using the proceeds to help pay its debts.

When the credit crunch came in 2007, the demand for securitised mortgage assets dried up and Northern Rock was unable to meet debt commitments. There was a run on the bank, the first UK bank run in 150 years, and in 2008 it was taken into state ownership. Billions of pounds of outstanding mortgages remained, many in arrears. The government held on to them until the market picked up. Then, in 2015, it sold a 'book of loans', the collective mortgage debt of 125,000 households, to an American private equity group, Cerberus, for £13 billion. This made it the biggest-ever sale of a loan portfolio, described effusively by the Chancellor of the Exchequer as the largest sale of financial assets by a European government.[32]

The deal immediately attracted controversy. Cerberus, which specialises in 'distressed investing', was still mired in a scandal over its earlier purchase of £1.3 billion in Northern Ireland property loans, following allegations that it had promised payments to individuals involved in the sale.[33] Moreover, the British government had not sold the debt portfolio to the New York-based Cerberus, but to a Dutch subsidiary, enabling it to pay much less in corporation tax. It was already known that Cerberus was assiduous in channelling its European deals through low-tax jurisdictions. Critics noted that Britain would lose tax from the deal, but still it went ahead.

Cerberus is well connected to the US Republican Party. Its founder, Stephen Feinberg, is a major donor, and former US Vice-President

Dan Quayle and former Treasury Secretary John Snow are co-chairs. The firm has become the biggest owner of financial loan assets, having bought more than €27 billion of European loan portfolio assets in 2013–15 alone. Most were bought at knock-down prices, giving it ample scope to make huge profits. To this was added the Northern Rock portfolio, which by 2015 was a low-risk asset, since 96 per cent of the mortgages were up to date and not in arrears.

As far as the British economy is concerned, the income flow over many years was sold in return for a lump sum that could help pay down the government's short-term budget deficit. But, as with other similar sales under way or being contemplated, it recalled a famous saying by Harold Macmillan that sooner or later you will have sold off the family silver. You impoverish your tomorrows.

In the USA, mortgage loans in default are being sold at a discount by both private and public lenders to hedge funds or hedge-fund-backed operations, which have had little compunction in insisting on full payment or selling the properties and evicting families from their homes. Other multi-billion-dollar corporations specialise in buying up bad debts that they then try to collect for themselves, acquiring vast portfolios of delinquent credit card and other debt for just a few cents in the dollar. Encore Capital and Portfolio Recovery Associates, the industry leaders, each collect $1 billion from US consumers every year. Roughly half of that comes from filing hundreds of thousands of court cases against often poor unrepresented debtors, without the means to challenge payment demands that may leave them short of money for food, utility bills and other essentials.[34]

SLABS (student loan asset-backed securities), mentioned earlier, are an even more speculative form of debt asset. Starting in the USA in a modest way in 1992, SLABS have exploded in size, enabling several venture capital-backed companies to become financial giants. As of 2015, the largest such company was SoFi (Social Finance), which in that year re-financed over $1 billion in student debt held by 13,500 graduates in 2,200 colleges. With similar securitisation of mortgages and personal loans, SoFi's deals passed the $3 billion mark. Another major company in the student debt sector is CommonBand. Both have targeted top students from brand-name universities, who have the lowest default risk. This raises a familiar aspect of privatisation – cherry-picking. It paves the way for stratification of the student finance market, leaving those deemed to be relatively high-risk paying higher interest rates. SoFi boasts that it has not had one borrower default in the first three years of their loan repayments. But this reflects the stated practice of choosing students doing subjects promising to yield high incomes and excluding those doing subjects that do not. The market rules, but education was never meant to be like that.

CONCLUSION

'If anyone owe a debt for a loan, and a storm prostrates the grain, or the harvest fail, or the grain does not grow for lack of water, in that year he need not give his creditor any grain, he washes his debt-tablet in water and pays no rent for this year.'
The Code of Hammurabi, 1792 BC

Historically, every economic crisis, sooner or later, has required the restructuring and write-off of debts.[35] Debt cancellations started long before King Hammurabi showed his wisdom. They were done badly and patchily after the First World War and more systematically and relatively well for Germany after the Second World War. They were done partially and patchily after the financial crash of 2007–08. The world is paying a heavy price for that lack of wisdom.

A term that has cropped up occasionally since it was formulated in 1927 is 'odious debt'. This refers to debt foisted on the public by devious means that make it illegitimate and thus suitable for a moratorium. A contemporary example is the borrowing by successive Greek governments to finance spending on armaments, through deals between corrupt politicians, armaments companies, and foreign governments keen for their arms exporters to bring in foreign exchange. Glib commentary that Greeks were living above their means financed by borrowing is wrong, as the gains went mostly to foreign arms dealers and financial intermediaries. Should ordinary Greeks be forced to repay such debt? The fault lay with the German and French governments and financial and military interests, which had induced the Greek authorities to borrow excessively.

In recent years, citizens' audits of public debt have been conducted in various countries, many in Latin America. An audit for France, coordinated by economist Michel Husson, concluded that 60 per cent of French public debt was illegitimate because the main cause of the increase was not higher public spending, which had fallen, but tax reductions for the wealthy. The report also noted that the identities of holders of French public debt are confidential. The bonds issued by government to finance the debt are sold to authorised banks, which in turn sell the bonds on the global financial market. The state pays interest to the bondholders, but their identities are unknown to the public.

The French audit, and many other audits, raise questions about the legitimacy of public debt and point to the fact that they are politically constructed. The growth of public debt in most industrialised countries is largely due to tax cuts for the wealthy and subsidies for selected interests. Cutting public debt, if desired, could be done by raising taxes and eliminating regressive and inefficient subsidies.

One final point should be made about societies relying on debt, as all rentier economies do. Psychologists have shown that debt adversely affects mental health and mental alertness and leads to a more passive and conservative mindset.[36] Insecurity associated with debt makes people less resilient and less resourceful. Having large numbers of people deeply in debt and exposed to circumstances that make indebtedness more likely is also chipping away at freedom, which requires non-domination by external pressures.

Chapter 5

PLUNDER OF THE COMMONS

'Inclosure came and trampled on the grave
Of labour's rights and left the poor a slave'
John Clare, *The Mores*, c.1815

'**P**roperty is theft,' thundered Proudhon. We may dispute that endlessly. But what cannot be denied is that, through the ages, much of what was once the commons, in 'public' owner-ship, has been taken, often by coercion or devious means, and converted to private land and other forms of private property.

The commons symbolise the humanity and history of our society, with deep emotional connections. The young Karl Marx was initially radicalised in 1842 not by some action by a local mill-owner, but by observing the enclosure of the commons in his native Moselle Valley, where the descendants of generations of peasants who had collected vital firewood from the forests were suddenly confronted by land privatisation that denied them the means to reproduce their way of life.

The commons have always stood for a collaborative way of living, suggesting shared access by rough equals. The notion of the commoner is a heart-warming figure of British history, lauded in early photographic accounts of village life.[1] The archaic verb 'to common' meant to participate and share in activities in the commons. Edward Coke, the jurist who rescued Magna Carta in the early seventeenth century, stressed 'to common' to mean doing a customary *activity*, not as a thing or a resource to be used for commercial profit.[2]

The commons are not just public in terms of ownership and use; they are a zone of freedom from private restriction and domesticity. Handed down through the generations, the commons represent what has been gained for society. Often, they have been created for posterity, bequeathed as acquired rights. They cannot legitimately be taken away by private interests or exploited for private profit.

Although the 'spatial' commons – such as common land – are what most people think of as the commons, they are by no means the only form. We can conceive of social, civil, cultural and intellectual (or educational) commons as well. All are threatened by erosion, enclosure and conversion into sources of rental income. And all are more important for the precariat than for those above them in the class spectrum. For that reason, as suggested later, the precariat has the most interest in recovering the commons from rent seekers.

Ironically, the neo-liberal era has brought about the realisation of Garrett Hardin's 'tragedy of the commons'. In a famous article in 1968, Hardin claimed that the commons was doomed to depletion because every user had an incentive to maximise what they could take out of it. Although the argument had been made before, it was seized upon by neo-liberal economists to justify privatisation. Yet the claim was always contested. Indeed, shortly before he died, Hardin confessed he should have called his article 'The tragedy of the *unmanaged* commons'. And this is what has been happening: more and more of the commons have been less managed, and thus prey to enclosure, privatisation and commodification.

Hitherto, there were social conventions and mechanisms that limited the tragedy of depletion. The commons are not, or should not be seen as, merely a set of public 'resources'. Ivan Illich made the tantalising remark that the environment as commons should be distinguished from the environment as resource, the former being for people's subsistence, the latter for the production of commodities.[3] He lamented the loss of the distinction in the English language.

Elinor Ostrom's rebuttal of Hardin – for which she received a Nobel Prize for Economics – was partly historical, partly normative. Her argument, made by many others as well, was that small communities of trust have often emerged to stop depletion of the commons. For such trust to hold, communities of social solidarity and empathy must be cherished, handed down from generation to generation. But the neo-liberal agenda has aimed to destroy such communities, as they stand against commodification, commercialisation and profit.

The Economist, a classically liberal magazine, defined rent seeking in a restrictive but useful way: '"Rent-seeking" is what economists call a special type of money-making, the sort made possible by political connections. This can range from outright graft to a lack of competition, poor regulation and the transfer of public assets to firms at bargain prices.'[4]

The last aspect is the concern of this chapter, extended to cover the transfer of public assets to individuals and interests as well as to firms, and the giving away of the commons to private owners, from which they can earn rental income. Democratic account-ability is among the victims.

THE LAUDERDALE PARADOX AND HARTWICK'S RULE

Relevant to this discussion of the commons are two funda-mental but neglected propositions – the Lauderdale Paradox and Hartwick's Rule of Inter-Generational Equity. The Laud-erdale Paradox, formulated in 1804 by the eighth Earl of Lauderdale, states that as private riches grow public wealth declines. He attributed this to 'contrived scarcity' created by concentrated private ownership of assets, most notably land and housing, leaving less to be shared by everyone else.

Hartwick's rule is about sustainability. In 1977, economist John Hartwick posited that, to assure inter-generational equity, a soci-ety must invest enough of the rental income from extraction and use of exhaustible (and thus scarce) natural assets so that future generations can benefit as much as the present generation.

The conventional argument used to justify rent is that if a person invests in an asset, such as a house, they are entitled to receive a 'financial return' to recoup their costs and a bit extra if they let others make use of it. Leaving aside whether the asset was acquired through 'hard work' or inheritance, this may seem reasonable. But the cost of acquiring or exploiting the asset is not the only factor. The return to the asset holder also depends on the asset's *scarcity*. Think of the humble truffle that grows in damp soil under certain trees. It tastes rather nice, and smells interesting, but generally speaking it does not cost much to find and dig up. Nevertheless, since demand exceeds supply, the price (and the financial return) has soared. In parts of northern Italy, finding a large truffle is a way to celebrity and fortune.

In terms that classical political economists would have understood, rental income derives from the scarcity of an asset. Scarcity may be natural, as in the case of the truffle, because demand outstrips nature's bounty or because there are physical constraints on production or exploitation. But in modern capitalism scarcity is more often contrived, because a minority possesses most or all of an asset, because rules make it hard to produce or sell, or because demand is deliberately stoked to outstrip supply. A law enacted in Tudor times to limit enclosures of common land described the methods of achieving contrived scarcity as 'engrossing' (monopolising ownership or control), 'regrating' (purchasing a commodity for resale) and 'forestalling' (withholding a commodity from the market in order to force up the price). These mechanisms are all in operation today.

There has always been tension between 'the commons' – that which is public and open to everyone to use – and 'commodification', which turns things into commodities for private ownership and money-making. To adopt Marx's terminology, the commons have use value, not exchange value (a market price), simply because it is not – and by definition cannot be – a commodity that can be bought, sold or commercialised. That elevation of use value over exchange value is integral to the commons.

This has been misunderstood by neoclassical economists who treat nature and its components as 'free' because they have no exchange value. They are only seen as contributing to growth and riches when they are commodified or ascribed a value as 'environmental services'.

Throughout history, powerful interests have sought to privatise, enclose and commodify the commons – whether land, other spaces, amenities or intellectual ideas – to contrive scarcity and create income-earning assets. To the extent that they succeed, enclosure and privatisation drive up rental income and proliferate its sources, increasing private riches while eroding public wealth, as the Lauderdale Paradox predicts.

Hartwick's rule – often abbreviated as 'invest resource rents' – requires that rents due to scarcity (initially applied to extraction of exhaustible resources) are invested to benefit future generations as much as the present. A sophisticated economic literature has evolved around this rule, which will not be discussed here. The main point is that society as a whole should obtain income from the use of natural resources, not only to compensate for negative 'externalities' such as pollution that are not reflected in the market price, but also to contribute to the welfare and living standards of all. This is key to the idea of sustainable development. As the World Bank concluded, 'The Hartwick rule holds that consumption can be maintained – the definition of sustainable development – if the rents from non-renewable resources are continuously invested rather than used for consumption.'[5]

Most governments have not even tried to do what Hartwick's rule implies. They have allowed corporations to grab the lion's share of rental income from commercial use of natural resources, with little or no obligation to pay for the external costs. And, as Chapter 3 showed, corporations have also gained rental income from subsidies and tax breaks that encourage them to increase resource depletion.

SPATIAL COMMONS: THE TRAGEDY OF ENCLOSURE

> 'The law locks up the man or woman
> Who steals the goose from off the common,
> But lets the greater felon loose,
> Who steals the common from off the goose.'
> Seventeenth century, anonymous

The spatial commons comprise all our natural resources – land, forests, oceans, rivers and lakes, minerals under the ground and wildlife above it, even the air we breathe. These are the commons of popular imagination. In England, their importance was first recognised formally in the Charter of the Forest of 1217, issued in the name of nine-year-old King Henry III as an integral part of Magna Carta.[6] Reissued in 1225, the Charter of the Forest was reaffirmed by Edward I in 1299, when he confirmed it and Magna Carta as common and statutory law.

The Charter of the Forest recognised the 'free' man's right to subsistence on the commons, along with the right to roam, to travel freely. It enshrined principles of 'subsistence, no enclosure, neighbourhood, travel and reparations'.[7] It was also the first feminist charter in asserting certain rights for widows, including the right to collect *estovars*, that is, any produce of the commons needed for subsistence. And it was the first ecological charter, seeking to preserve the reproductive commons and the right to common (work collaboratively) in a sustainable way. It declared against commercial encroachment of the commons, including the damming of waterways for private benefit, and in favour of reparations for past encroachments.

Nevertheless, in Britain and elsewhere, throughout the ages, all forms of the reproductive commons have been eroded by enclosure, privatisation and commodification measures guided by the state. Enclosure was pivotal to the emergence of industrial capitalism, forcing many rural inhabitants off the land into dependency on wage labour in the mills and factories. It continued through the nineteenth century, as subsistence rights were chipped away. But in the twentieth century, as the social democratic state evolved, the role of the commons in providing subsistence dwindled. The state took over the role of guaranteeing subsistence, leaving defenders of the commons unprepared for the onslaught of the neo-liberal era.

The destruction of the classical commons has taken on global proportions. Neo-liberal governments have used considerable sophistry to justify privatising not just 'the people's land' but the resources underneath or on it. One of the worst examples has been the plundering of the world's minerals for the electronics industry, often through confiscation or usurpation of native land, for mining with cheap, disposable labour power.

An egregious case concerns North Sea oil. Leaving aside the contentious issue of whether this is British or Scottish oil, in equity terms it should have been exploited for the benefit of the whole of society. The Hartwick rule should have been applied. Instead, there was a huge rental transfer to an elite. Unlike Norway, which set up a sovereign wealth fund with the proceeds of oil sales, the Thatcher government sold drilling areas at fire-sale prices to a few multinationals. They received further subsidies to help them expand production, with much of the profits flowing abroad. Ironically, much of North Sea production ended up in the hands of Chinese *state* corporations.

Another manifestation concerns fracking. Governments in Britain, as in other countries, lobbied by powerful interests, have given corporations ownership and usufruct rights to common land to earn rental income from extracting gas from shale rock. Nobody can deny the environmental and social costs. Yet landowners and local authorities have been promised subsidies to allow fracking on their land. And companies are being allowed to drill in parts of the country's national parks, precious wild spaces, despite a pledge by Energy Secretary Amber Rudd before the 2015 general election that they would be protected. 'We have agreed an outright ban on fracking in national parks [and] sites of special scientific interest', she said. Immediately after the election, the same minister announced that fracking would be allowed around and under them.[8]

Subsequently the Communities Minister was given the final say on fracking plans, removing local democratic control. Local authorities must now fast-track fracking applications, forcing them to cut corners. But if the minister deems the grounds for refusal inadequate, he can overrule the decision. And company appeals against refusal are to be determined by the minister, that is, on political, not technical grounds. As the Department of Communities put it, 'The Secretary of State hereby directs that he shall determine these appeals instead of an inspector.'

It is not just fracking. In 2015, the North York Moors National Park Authority narrowly gave the go-ahead for plans by a mining corporation, Sirius Minerals, to create one of the world's largest potash mines. This would involve drilling a 1.5km-deep shaft under the moors and a 37km-long tunnel to transport the deposits, with infrastructure within the park as well as outside it. Officials prepared a report that stated, 'The economic benefits ... and extent of the mitigation/compensation offered ... do not outweigh the extent of the harm,' and noted the park authority's 'statutory responsibility to conserve and enhance the North York Moors for the enjoyment of present and future generations.'[9] Strangely, they did not recommend rejection.

This may have been because there was local support for the £1.7 billion project, which Sirius claimed – on dubious assumptions – would create 1,000 jobs, boost exports and transform the economy of the depressed region. Local farmers and other landowners also stood to gain substantial royalties (rental income) for potash mined under their land. So perhaps it is not surprising that, despite pleas by conservation organisations, the government refused to call a public enquiry. The commercial juggernaut was allowed to plough on by the very authorities charged with safeguarding the commons on behalf of the public.

There are fifteen national parks in Great Britain, covering over 8 per cent of the land and recognised as 'protected areas' under the 1949 National Parks and Access to the Countryside Act. Yet, despite acknowledging the role of national parks in providing 'Britain's breathing space' in this overcrowded country, successive governments have cut funding to park authorities, pressurising them to sell land to pay for the upkeep of paths and forests. The Lake District, for instance, saw its annual budget slashed by 38 per cent between 2010 and 2015, obliging the park authority to sell prized plots in this iconic part of the national commons.

Similarly, the eight Royal Parks in London, which Queen Victoria gave to the nation in 1851, were intended as green spaces for the free use of all, rich and poor, constituting an integral part of the urban commons. Today, they are being commercialised. Between 2009 and 2014, the government cut funds for London's Royal Parks by a quarter and obliged them to raise 60 per cent of their income themselves. As a result, there is a growing practice of 'eventism', the renting out of parks for commercial events. Hyde Park's Winter Wonderland, Proms in the Park and rock concerts eat into quality space and the public's 'quiet enjoyment', blocking off large areas of the park not only during the events but after them as well, to allow the grass to recover. Once one form of commercialisation is allowed, others will follow.

Public parks, of which there are over 27,000 in the UK, are easy targets for privatisers preying on opportunities thrown up by the austerity narrative. But they are vital for healthy living in cities. Research has shown that living near a park improves health and a sense of well-being. It is part of a person's social income. All the ages of man and woman are found in a park – strolling lovers, playing children, joggers and walkers, the elderly out for a constitutional. All these activities are worth something, and are free! Only a pseudo-economistic calculus would give these uses a zero value. Yet the London Councils' Transport and Environment Committee has warned that budget cuts forced by the government threaten the piecemeal sale of London's parks to private firms, as councils are obliged to prioritise spending on the rising number of homeless and those requiring social care.

Another part of the spatial commons under threat is the time-honoured 'right to roam'. The Property Law Act of 1925 gives everyone right of access to 140,000 miles of recognised public footpaths. But the government has set a deadline of 2026 for all historic rights of way not already mapped to be included on an updated register. It will be a big challenge to identify and register these ancient rights of way in time, failing which they will be lost.

The commons are also being eroded and destroyed through privatisation of natural resources, a prime example being water. Privatisation enables commercial interests to restrict its supply (contrive scarcity), divert it to where profits are greatest and most assured and raise its price, thereby boosting rental income. And they can take short-term profits at the cost of creating long-term shortage. Most European countries have wisely kept water supply in the hands of public utilities. The UK experience of privatisation is unlikely to change their mind.

The argument for privatisation was that private companies would be more efficient than public utilities and would raise more money for investment in infrastructure, especially in replacing old (often Victorian-era) distribution pipes and improving storage facilities. Neither has proved to be true.[10]

Scottish Water, which remains a public utility, has invested more and charges consumers less than any of the ten companies in England, which have loaded themselves up with debt – partly to reduce tax bills – and used the money for generous dividends to shareholders (increasingly private equity groups) and huge bonuses for their executives. Thames Water, which supplies water to London, is owned by a private equity consortium and, despite steadily rising bills to customers, is so indebted that it has asked for government help for infrastructure improvements to overcome chronic supply and leakage problems. South West

Water charges are so high that the government pays the company to reduce household bills. And, ironically, *foreign* state capital is a major beneficiary of English water privatisation, with a heavy presence of sovereign wealth funds from China, Singapore, the Middle East and elsewhere.

The experience of water privatisation has been matched by the privatisation of Britain's railways. Fares have soared. So have profits, much diverted abroad. Two-thirds of Britain's rail operators are foreign companies, including state-owned railways from Germany, the Netherlands and France. Yet the companies require even more subsidy than the nationalised industry. In 1993, before privatisation, British Rail was paid £1.3 billion in subsidies. By 2006–07, the government was subsidising private operators to the tune of over £6.8 billion a year.[11]

Another, unappreciated erosion of the spatial commons is privatisation of the sky, particularly the night sky, giving corporations a means to increase income from using what is not theirs, by encroaching on our space. We are bombarded with commercial messaging on neon-lit billboards, seeking to condition our minds, and cannot avoid it without walking around with our eyes shut. To see the worst excesses, go to Warsaw, where the selling of knickers by 30-metre-square billboards on high-rise buildings might amuse at first sight, but is culturally impoverishing and a blight on the skyline. A similar point can be made about noise pollution in public spaces by commercial interests, such as 'muzak'.

The ultimate commodification of the commons, beyond all parody, occurred in 2015 in China. Chinese cities are on the frontier of rentier capitalism, spawning a rapidly growing plutocracy of billionaires as well as the world's largest precariat. They are also so heavily polluted with toxic smog that on many days of the year it is dangerous to breathe the air outside. Fresh air has become a scarce commodity, a situation happily exploited by an enterprising Canadian start-up, which bottles fresh mountain air from the Rockies to sell in the smog-affected cities of China. At $10 a bottle, market demand has far outstripped supply.

The commodification and privatisation of the commons is being shaped by an official vocabulary that is extending the sphere of rent seeking. The New Labour government began this by giving a commercial research company £100,000 to calculate the 'annual price of England's ecosystem',[12] a meaningless exercise. Sure enough, the company, having pocketed the money, concluded that 'some of the ecosystem may have an infinite value.' This did not deter the coalition government from setting up an 'independent, business-led' Ecosystem Markets Task Force, headed by Sir Ian Cheshire, chair of Kingfisher, a multinational retailer that owns the B&Q chain of DIY stores. In its final report in March 2013, the Task Force claimed to have identified 'substantial potential growth in nature-related markets – in the order of billions of pounds annually'.

The terms used by the Task Force indicate the intended commercialisation of the commons. Its report refers to 'natural capital', 'ecosystem services', 'green infrastructure' and 'asset classes' (aka habitats), all within an 'ecosystem market'. In responding to its recommendations, the government referred to landowners as 'providers of ecosystem services', who could presumably expect to be paid or subsidised for providing the 'services'. Meanwhile, the Task Force recommended reaching out to the ultimate rentiers, talking of 'harnessing City financial expertise to assess the ways that these blended revenue streams and securitisations enhance the return on investment of an environmental bond'.

The derivative of this Task Force, the Natural Capital Committee, is trying to put a value on all the nature in Britain. According to one definition, '"natural capital" refers to the living and non-living components of ecosystems – other than people and what they manufacture – that contribute to the generation of goods and services of value for people.'[13] But nature is not capital, unless turned to commercial use. To call it natural capital is to imply it is no longer part of the commons. Thus to call the world's mountains natural capital – as one member of the committee did[14] – is meaningless. Capital is about a relationship of production, about making profits. The committee is looking for ways of commodifying nature, without any democratic decision to do so or any system of accountability.

The depletion of the spatial commons is a global phenomenon. The war on the commons is an integral part of globalisation and resistance has been fragile. One laudable barrier is the United Nations world heritage site protection system, which has built up an impressive list of places considered to be of international importance. In 2014, the neo-liberal Australian government tried to delist 74,000 hectares of Tasmanian forest from protection to renew commercial logging. The UN Educational, Scientific and Cultural Organization (UNESCO), the watchdog for world heritage sites, said delisting would open the way for a rush of similar actions by other countries and refused this 'unacceptable precedent'. But world heritage sites are just one small portion of the global commons under threat.

There is a tendency to think of the commons as mainly rural.

But cities and towns are increasingly part of the contested terrain. Besides parks, think of all the streets and squares. Street-side trees are part of the commons. In Toronto, research concluded that living in a tree-lined street made people feel younger and more affluent and improved mental health.[15] But in Britain street trees are imperilled by lack of a government department or agency with designated responsibility for them, unlike government-owned woodlands, which are managed by the Forestry Commission. Under the austerity regime, local authorities are cutting back on spending to maintain, preserve and replant trees.

In Sheffield, budget cuts were followed in 2012 by a partial privatisation of tree care; the council entered a public–private partnership, signing a twenty-five-year private finance initiative (PFI) contract with a firm, Amey, to manage its roads, including the city's 36,000 street trees. To the dismay of residents, Amey immediately started to remove mature trees, felling 2,000 between 2012 and 2015. While Amey and the council claim the trees were dying, dangerous or obstructive, critics note that Amey was taking the cheapest, most profitable option, which minimised pruning costs and damage to pavements. More of the commons were lost.

More systemic is the privatisation and commercialisation of the urban commons – roads and squares, as well as whole areas of residential and non-residential public property. All over the world, cities' public places are being transferred from the sphere of the commons to private rentier capital, often as part of 'regeneration' or redevelopment plans.[16] Recall the protests in 2013 against the Turkish government's proposal to allow building of a shopping mall in Istanbul's Taksim Gezi Park, a recreational space.

In Britain, especially in London, encroachment on the urban commons by private, often foreign, capital has become endemic.[17] An emblematic example is Malaysia Square, built by a Malaysian consortium, which is at the centre of redevelopment of London's Battersea Power Station. The square is part of the 482-acre (195-hectare) Nine Elms site for 'high-security development', dubbed by one estate agent 'Singapore-on-Thames'. Thousands of foreign investors, mainly Asian, have bought the outrageously expensive apartments off plan, many with no intention of living there. Even before the apartments have been built, reselling has been rampant, generating a profitable secondary market. One agent said that investors were treating apartment pre-sales as 'currency trades' or 'currency speculation'.[18]

Malaysia Square is designed by a Danish architect, his first venture in the country, and is described, accompanied by futuristic photo-images, as

> a two-level urban canyon with integrated bridges and stairways that reference Malaysia's distinctive landscape and geology. The spaces will be clad with a wide variety of material finishes, including limestone, granite and marble, reminiscent of the caves found in the country's Gunung Mulu national park. At the centre of the amphitheatre, a fountain is planned, which will take the form of Malaysia's national flower.[19]

London is being turned into part of the global rentier economy, losing its distinctive character and shrinking the spaces that ordinary Londoners can use freely. Privatisation of the urban commons now has an informal acronym, POPS (privately owned public spaces), to signify the growing number of squares, gardens and parks that look public but are not.

In 2009, Boris Johnson, then London's mayor, bemoaned the 'corporatisation' of streets and public spaces that made Londoners feel like trespassers in their own city. Even his headquarters, City Hall, and its thirteen-acre site are owned by More London, an estate management company bought in 2013 by a Kuwaiti property corporation, St Martins, which owns swathes of prime London property. Newly created Granary Square near London's King's Cross Station, one of Europe's biggest open-air spaces, is a private estate. Yet, despite his fine words, the mayor extended privatisation and corporatisation to an unprecedented degree. His watch included the Nine Elms development and the proposed private Garden Bridge across the Thames, which will not be a public right of way and will close for corporate events. Bishops Square, which includes Spitalfields Market and historic streets in east London, was sold to JP Morgan asset management.

Elsewhere in Britain, privatised public zones include Brindleyplace in Birmingham, Gunwharf Quays in Portsmouth and Liverpool ONE, the latter owned by the Duke of Westminster's Grosvenor estate. Exeter's Princesshay is owned by property group Land Securities and the Crown Estate, which manages the monarch's property portfolio. While developers often claim they are creating new public spaces, for example by reclaiming derelict land, these areas are being reshaped by commercial interests to maximise rental income from property and retail outlets, not to increase the urban commons as zones of freedom.

The sanitisation of large swathes of cities and towns acts not just to erase local traditions and character in favour of 'corporate sterility', but erects a barrier to creativity and expression in the form of what are sometimes called street politics and street art. As the sociologist Saskia Sassen has emphasised, commercial mega-projects kill the urban tissue and de-urbanise city life.[20] It is disingenuous for politicians such as Johnson to say that the idea behind all developments in London is to 'put the village back into the city'. More important would be to put the city back into the city, the town back into the town.

Private owners of public space can prohibit or restrict what people can do – eating and drinking, cycling or skate-boarding, busking, snoozing, even taking photographs – and can deny access altogether if they choose. Inevitably, the privatisation restricts social and political activity. In 2011 (and subsequently), Occupy London protesters were prevented from demonstrating in front of the Stock Exchange in Paternoster Square because, as the court injunction stated, 'The protestors have no right to conduct a demonstration or protest on the Square, which is entirely private property'.[21] Paternoster Square, close to St Paul's Cathedral, is owned by Japan's Mitsubishi Estate, which is making a substantial rental income from properties there, including offices of investment banks Goldman Sachs, Merrill Lynch and Nomura Securities.

Much of the City of London is now in private hands and thus off limits for legitimate protest. Protest is banned outside City Hall, managed by More London. Elsewhere in London, a witness statement in support of another injunction barring protestors from the Broadgate Estate around Bishopsgate and Liverpool Street stated: 'There are no public rights over the common parts. The gates to the estate are ritually closed, once a year, to ensure that no such rights can arise by prescription.'[22]

The right to demonstrate and to strike, and to participate in public life in what the ancient Greeks called the *agora*, a central gathering place for citizens, is being taken away in the commodification of the commons. It is the ultimate phase of the neo-liberal project.

The final part of the urban commons is known as the 'allotment' in the UK and by a host of other evocative names in other countries. Allotments are small plots for city dwellers and others to grow vegetables and fruit for consumption by themselves, family and friends. They symbolise the historical continuity of the commons. Allotments have had a chequered history. At the time of the Speenhamland system, they were opposed by Thomas Malthus and Edmund Burke on the grounds that they would reduce labour supply to employers and slow capital accumulation. But gradually through the nineteenth century, sentiment changed.

Three Parliamentary Acts between 1887 and 1908 empowered local authorities to acquire land to turn into municipal allotments and, in rural areas, County Smallholdings Estate. In the twentieth century, attitudes fluctuated, as did the number of allotments. But in the era of rentier capitalism, the attack on them has been quietly relentless as councils have sold off allotment sites for private development. There are some 250,000 allotments in Britain today, against 1.3 million just after the Second World War, and the numbers are shrinking despite nearly 100,000 people on waiting lists for one. Sadly, the Olympic Park at Stratford was built over thousands of historic allotments granted to residents of east London after the war.

The County Smallholdings Estate has also been eroded, its sale encouraged by the Conservative government's rural White Paper in 1995. By 2015, the estate had been reduced by a third, as local councils implemented cuts in response to shrinking funds from central government.

Allotments are a metaphor for the commons[23] and offer a source of social income. When they are sold for 'development', private riches are increased at the cost of lower living standards and quality of life that are not recorded or recognised. Selling allotments may increase 'economic growth', but to the detriment of 'public wealth'.

SOCIAL COMMONS

What might be called the social commons include the facilities and amenities essential to normal living that are provided outside the private market, built over the generations and paid for through taxes and donations. They cover the many services of the 'welfare state' – child and elderly care, healthcare, social services, housing – as well as mail services, public transport and basic infrastructure such as roads, sewerage systems, flood defences and so on. Like the spatial commons, the social commons are under attack from the forces of privatisation and commodification.

Social housing is a prime example, in Britain and around the world. The UK's coalition government reinforced the original right-to-buy policy by increasing the discount, giving a further boost to council house sales. In 2014–15, 12,300 council properties in England were sold, while fewer than 2,000 were set to replace them. The decision by the incoming Conservative government to permit all 1.3 million housing association tenants to buy their homes, at the same enticing discount, is another step in the privatisation of the social commons that will contrive more scarcity and force more families into expensive, privately rented housing, increasing unearned rental income for landlords.

In addition, councils are to be forced to sell properties that are in the top third of those they own by value. Many councils say this will mean selling all the new council homes they build, a disincentive to building more. The income from the sales is supposed to help finance lower-value replacements. But, as a housing executive for the London Borough of Islington pointed out, 'All new council homes in inner London will have to be sold off. And what incentives will we have to build again?'[24] The stock of social housing – the social commons – is being deliberately run down.

Redevelopment sites sold to developers are shrinking the stock of housing for low-income households all over Britain. Again, London is extreme. Thus, the Heygate Estate in London's Elephant and Castle area, which once housed 3,000 low-income people, was demolished and sold to a property company to create 2,500 homes, of which only seventy-nine were social housing. Large parts of the property market have been handed to foreign investors. By 2015, sites for about 30,000 homes were owned by ten investors from China, Hong Kong, Malaysia, Australia, Singapore and Sweden.[25] Described as 'safe deposit boxes', they were rental income mechanisms. Most of the planned building was for luxury housing, well out of reach of the average Londoner. The Ministry of Defence hopes to sell its Hyde Park barracks, a 'super-prime' site, for luxury apartments. Twenty developers are interested, with backing from investors from Malaysia, China, Abu Dhabi and Dubai.

Meanwhile, the government has embarked on a massive sale

of public land for private housing, with apparently little analysis or oversight. A report by the Parliamentary Accounts Committee (PAC) on the sale of nearly 950 sites between 2011 and 2015, intended for 100,000 homes, revealed that the government did not know how much the land was sold for, whether it was sold below its market value or how many houses had actually been built.[26] As the report concluded, 'There is no means of knowing whether taxpayers are getting a good deal from the sale of their land.' Yet more sales of public land are in prospect, supposedly for building 150,000 homes between 2015 and 2020. The PAC expressed understandable concern that, in a rush to meet government targets, land would be sold at knock-down prices, enriching property developers at public expense.

Then there is the creeping privatisation of the National Health Service (NHS), the most popular part of the British social commons. Although privatisation started under Margaret Thatcher, the decisive changes were made in 2007 by the Blair government. The reforms ushered in privatisation by stealth, by inducing NHS hospitals to contract out services. We consider the political aspects of what happened in Chapter 7.

Here, we may just mention the outrageous scandal of private finance initiative (PFI) hospitals under deals signed by over 100 NHS hospital trusts in England. Although conceived by John Major's government, all but one of these PFI arrangements were made between 1997 and 2010 under New Labour, which wanted to shift the cost of projects off government borrowing requirements. By 2016, the trusts were paying £2 billion a year to private companies (a figure set to rise) for building and operating new hospitals and renovating old ones. While the deals financed

£11.8 billion of hospital building, the trusts will have to repay £79 billion over the twenty-five to thirty years the arrangements last, more than six times the building cost and far more than if the government had borrowed the money on their behalf. Just four firms will be paid £39 billion.[27] Meanwhile, one in three hospital trusts are in the red and all are struggling to provide services.

PFI contracts do not only apply to hospitals. Across Britain, they have been used to fund schools, streetlights, prisons, police stations and care homes, burdening central and local government with huge debts to financial capital estimated at a whopping £310 billion, more than five times the value of the assets created.[28] Much of the rental income from taxpayer-funded debt payments is going to investment funds based in tax havens. The biggest holders of PFI equity are Semperian, based in the tax haven of Jersey; Innisfree, the biggest investor in hospitals after the NHS, whose largest shareholder is Jersey-based Coutts & Co.; 3i Infrastructure, a Jersey-based subsidiary of 3i, a venture capital company; and Equitix, acquired in 2015 by Tetragon Financial Group, based in Guernsey, another tax haven.[29]

NHS privatisation has been accelerated by the Health and Social Care Act 2012, which basically abolished the government's responsibility to provide a national health service. There is now no legal guarantee to provide comprehensive health services, beyond emergency care and ambulances, while NHS contracts have been opened up to unlimited privatisation.[30] Private service contractors, often with links to those commissioning their services, are making large rental incomes, paid by an increasingly cash-strapped (tax-funded) NHS.

The main claim for privatisation is increased efficiency in

providing services. There is little evidence to support that claim. NHS reforms have introduced more layers of highly paid managers to impose more bureaucracy, supervise an increasingly precariatised workforce and award contracts to private companies more intent on profits and rent seeking than patient care. This may extend to outright dishonesty. The former head of the NHS Counter-Fraud Service, lambasting cuts in the service's budget and staffing, claimed fraud could be costing £1 billion a year.[31] Privatisation multiplies opportunities for fraud. To this should be added the (legal) profits of private firms and the handsome salaries and bonuses paid to their executives, all gained with taxpayers' money intended for medical services.

Other parts of the social commons tend to be overlooked. Mail services in Britain have been privatised, the new owners of the Royal Mail receiving a hefty subsidy in the process. The initial price of shares was pitched below market value, providing a £750 million windfall to their holders on flotation in 2013. Most of this went to large investors such as pension and hedge funds. Among the beneficiaries were the financial institutions appointed to advise the government on the selling price. Besides handsome payment for this advice, they were sold large bundles of shares at the price they themselves determined. They promptly sold their shares when the price rose, laughing all the way to the bank.

In 2015, the British regulator Ofcom charged Royal Mail with breach of competition laws in relation to its proposed charges to rival operators for bulk mail delivery services. It had earlier launched a 'fundamental review' to assess whether existing regulation needed strengthening to prevent abuse of the company's near-monopoly position, including excessive charges for letters and parcels. A public service was handed over to private interests – no one should be surprised if a private near-monopoly acts like one.

Now consider a basic part of the social commons, bus services, which have performed an important social function since their introduction early in the twentieth century. Publicly owned companies have provided subsidised services on less popular routes so that people in rural areas, or on low incomes, can travel for work or leisure. But in Britain, in the austerity era, these vital services are being lost. Between 2010 and 2015, about 2,000 bus services and routes disappeared thanks to funding cuts by government, according to the Campaign for Better Transport. Between 2009 and 2014, council spending on transport fell by 20 per cent, and in some areas by double that.[32]

By eroding the social commons, such cuts increase inequality. The young, the elderly and those on low incomes and in the precariat rely most on buses and are most hurt by higher fares, worse services or lack of a service altogether. There are ripple effects on other aspects of living, making the personal loss greater than loss of the bus service alone. For instance, the cuts may make it harder for benefit claimants to search for jobs or attend employment offices for obligatory appointments. Under the new regime, if they are just five minutes late they can be sanctioned and lose a month's benefits, including housing benefit. That may lead to more debt and loss of rented accommodation. Petty indignities feed into more inequality. Cutting the bus service is just part of a chain of deprivation.

Journalist John Harris wondered rhetorically 'why this carnage hardly intrudes on political debate'.[33] He attributed it to the exceptional flourishing of public transport in London, where the chattering classes mostly live, and the lack of glamour associated with the common bus. Perhaps it also reflects the lack of interest shown by the Labour opposition in issues that most concern the precariat. That may change as a result of swingeing cuts to Transport for London's operating budget announced in the government's 2015 Autumn Statement. By 2020, London will be the only major European city without a subsidised transport service, which will mean worse services and higher fares.

Not even the police have been protected from privatisation and commodification. The famous headquarters of the London Metropolitan Police, New Scotland Yard, has been sold to an Abu Dhabi investment fund, which plans to knock it down for luxury apartments, making a tidy profit. Cuts in police budgets have led to sales of police stations to fund essential equipment, reducing quick response capacity. Even more worrying is a new subsidy scheme, Met Patrol Plus, enabling London boroughs to buy police services by paying officers' salaries. For each officer they pay for, they get another free! Naturally, it is the richer boroughs, or their private development partners, which are opting to pay. Some rich residents have clubbed together to pay for extra policing of their residential areas. This is deplorably regressive.

Another example concerns employment and welfare services that used to be an integral part of the public domain. Privatisation of these services has created new sources of rental income, based on the treatment of unemployed, disabled or otherwise disadvantaged people as rent-bearing assets. This is not unique to Britain. Denmark, Germany, the Netherlands, Sweden, Australia and the USA are all increasingly contracting out such services to private providers.

In Britain, the main privatised employment programmes are the Work Programme, aimed at pushing the unemployed into jobs, and the Work Capability Assessment, which is supposed to determine whether a disabled person is fit for employment. Work Programme contracts that run to 2017, worth an estimated £3–5 billion, are supposed to be funded by the consequent benefit savings. Providers are paid according to the number of people they place in jobs. But these are services people are obliged to use in order to receive a benefit. The state is creating a captive market and generating rental income for selected commercial interests.

Even before the Work Programme in its present form was introduced by the coalition government, the deficiencies of private provision were clear from the experience of other countries. Payment systems give private providers incentives for creaming (focusing resources on the easiest to place), parking (ignoring the hardest to place) and gaming (claiming credit for jobs found by unemployed people themselves or fabricating evidence of sustained employment).

Even on official figures, the Work Programme is not working. The evidence suggests that an unemployed person is no more likely to find a job through the programme than searching themselves, and is no more likely to obtain one matching their qualifications. The service is earning its keep, from the government's viewpoint, not by putting people into jobs but by withdrawing benefits from more people for alleged breaches of a multiplicity of petty rules.

There are many other encroachments on the world's social commons. In Tokyo, the homeless have traditionally slept on public benches in parks and shopping arcades. Now the benches have been reshaped so that anyone trying to sleep on them will slip off. A London apartment block put spiked studs at the building entrance to prevent homeless people sitting or sleeping there. In 2014, in Fort Lauderdale, Florida, ninety-year-old Arnold Abbott was arrested and threatened with jail and a $500 fine for the heinous crime of attempting to feed the homeless. The mayor said the arrest was justified because feeding the homeless annoyed local property owners. Today, the action is a crime in over thirty US cities.

CIVIL COMMONS: THE COMMERCIALISATION OF JUSTICE

A third form of commons is the civil commons, aimed at providing universal justice, based on due process, equality before the law and the ability to defend oneself. The civil commons were enshrined in Magna Carta, with the clear and incisive Clauses 20, 38, 39 and 40 of the original Charter of Liberties of 1215. Clause 20 established the principle of proportionality in the punishment for a crime and the need for a fair trial. Clause 38 required witnesses; Clause 39 that the accused be judged by his equals. Clause 40 stated that all had the right to justice, which should not be denied or delayed. Every modern government has paid lip service to those commitments.

However, the civil commons encapsulated by those lofty principles, though nowhere fully implemented, has markedly shrunk in recent years. A market in judicial services has been opened up, weakening any notion of universal justice. In addition, many more actions today are deemed to be criminal than was the case thirty years ago. This is an international pattern. But the trend in the UK has been especially remarkable, with almost one new crime added to the statute books for every day New Labour was in office.

The primary sentiment seems to be that public order security must have precedence over dissident freedom. Youths on the street, eccentrics, racial minorities and the homeless are not just seen as undesirable but presumed to be actual or potential criminals. New Labour epitomised this mentality with the 1998 Crime and Disorder Act, which introduced ASBOs (Anti-Social Behaviour Orders). Children as young as ten can be barred from noisy games or congregating in groups; failure to comply with an ASBO attracts criminal penalties, which can include imprisonment.

Meanwhile, costs and delays in the justice system have risen remorselessly. In the USA, 95 per cent of defendants enter a plea bargain or plead guilty to a lesser offence rather than risk going to trial, because the legal costs are so high. In the UK, successive governments have increased court fees, while making legal aid harder to obtain.

Legal aid is a civil right. It is meant to ensure that everybody has the means to defend themselves (or take action to enforce their rights) and have legally qualified representatives to do so. This principle has been eroded. For practical reasons, legal proceedings cannot be completely free, as resources are limited and frivolous prosecutions and defences would wreck the system. But the trend has been to make the justice system more expensive and harder to access, deterring many from seeking redress for wrongs or defending themselves from unwarranted accusations.

In the UK, mandatory criminal court charges of up to £1,200 were introduced in 2015 for all those found guilty after a hearing or trial. The Parliamentary Justice Select Committee, reporting in late 2015, said the charge for contesting a case provided 'perverse incentives' to plead guilty (in which case the charge was about £150) and was 'grossly disproportionate' for minor offences. More than fifty magistrates resigned in protest and the Lord Chief Justice himself argued that 'the scale of court fees, together with the cost of legal assistance, is putting access to justice out of reach of most, imperilling a core principle of Magna Carta.'[34]

Magistrates were not allowed to use discretion in applying the charge, or relate it to ability to pay. To compound the inequity, those who could not pay were sent to prison. The government has now dropped the charge. But the direction in which the authorities wish to go remains the same, a reduction in access to justice and the civil commons for those most in need as a way of lowering the costs of the judicial system and indirectly helping to reduce taxes on higher-income groups.

CULTURAL COMMONS: DEPLETED BY STEALTH

What might be called the cultural commons includes 'the arts', sports, the mass media, public libraries, art galleries, museums, concert halls and public places for performances and other creative activities. All of these are being depleted.

A defining act of the Thatcher government was the sale of sports grounds attached to state schools, land that belonged to the public and was paid for by taxpayers. This not only deprived youngsters of accessible space to play sports, helping to keep them fit, healthy and off the streets, but extended opportunities for property developers to earn rental income from what had been the commons.

Public libraries have long been part of the social fabric, important for most social groups, but more so for those without much money to spend on books and space in which to read them. In Britain and elsewhere, libraries enable people without computers at home to access information and knowledge and to participate as digital citizens, as more government and private services move online. They also act as venues for the arts. Although UK local authorities have a statutory obligation to provide 'a comprehensive and efficient library service', budget cuts are forcing some libraries to close and others to restrict services and lay off staff. Of the over 4,500 libraries in Britain, 500 were said to be under threat in early 2016.

In August 2015, 400 gallery staff working at the National Gallery, one of the world's most important art collections, were outsourced to Securitas, a security company with no institutional knowledge of culture or art services. Following a lengthy strike, the transfer went ahead after the Public and Commercial Services Union negotiated certain conditions, including reinstatement of its representative, who had been sacked during the dispute. More than half the gallery trustees, appointed by the government, are from the world of finance and business, oriented to the rentier capitalism model in which public assets can be restructured and partially or wholly privatised. The trustees will have seen the institution's employees as just a cost, not as an integral part of a precious piece of the cultural commons.

The action was a form of enclosure. Those outsourced employees, many of whom have worked for the National Gallery for years, can now be shifted to jobs anywhere in the company, which has contracts guarding ports and airports, shops and offices. They have lost their occupational security and have probably joined the precariat. Meanwhile, on its website, Securitas claimed that outsourcing lowered costs precisely because private companies could pay lower wages: 'The view held by some that outsourcing is more expensive than running things in house is simply not so when private security companies are able to pay their staff a lower rate.'[35]

The ancient Greeks taught us the vital need for public theatre and the value of public participation in the great tragedies which, through their complex human dilemmas, developed empathy in the citizenry, reminding each generation not to be too moralistic and judgmental. Shared culture encourages community and solidarity. Participation in and access to culture and creativity stimulates the imagination and widens horizons. If the public space of the cultural commons is eroded, the learning and reinforcement of empathy is eroded, reducing critical faculties. Swingeing budget cuts in the name of austerity for regional theatres, museums and libraries are limiting access to the cultural commons. If commercialisation leads to entry charges or higher ticket prices, those on low incomes will be the first to drop their use of them.

Privatisation of the cultural commons is deliberate. It is accentuating the commercialisation of art, fostering easy entertainment rather than challenging, critical and even subversive creations, the essence of art throughout history. Art will become more of an 'industry', with decisions on funding dictated by whether or not something will yield profits and a financial rate of return. A business-oriented mindset will be reinforced.

The mass media are also part of the cultural commons. For

meaningful democracy, and to ensure all perspectives and groups are represented, publicly owned and accountable media are essential. But, as discussed later, those media are falling victim to commodifying forces and interests. In the UK, the BBC (British Broadcasting Corporation) has been a bulwark of the political and cultural commons, but it is being squeezed of funds and subjected to political pressure that compromises its independence. In its white paper on the BBC published in May 2016, the government proposed to appoint half its governing board members, including the chair and deputy chair. And it has been told to outsource more production and make its output more 'distinctive' and less competitive with rival private broadcasters – in other words, to stop making popular programmes.

For years the government has held down the TV licence fee, which provides the BBC's revenue. In 2010, the coalition government reduced funding for the BBC World Service, an arm of Britain's 'soft power'. This was later partially reversed after the 2015 Strategic Defence Review admitted it was a mistake. But, again without public consultation, the BBC was told that as from 2020 it would have to absorb the £650 million loss of revenue from free licences for the over-75s, introduced in 2001, which the government currently pays for.

This is a classic example of the micro-politics of privatisation – deliberately weakening a public service, then claiming that because it is performing badly the private sector could do the job better. After the BBC threatened to close two television channels, BBC2 and BBC4, and all local radio stations to fill the hole in its finances, the government agreed some mitigating measures. But the threat to BBC services remains.

The government is also considering privatisation of Channel 4, launched in 1982 with a statutory public service remit, though funded by advertising. If sold, that public service remit would be lost, and the political opinions of its new owners would prevail, as they do with the Sky network, owned by the Murdoch media empire.

Finally, a subtler part of the cultural commons is street art and performances of all kinds in public places. including busking and diverse, often creative graffiti, which flourishes in and helps to alleviate the concrete drabness of many cities. As privatisation and commercialisation of cities gather pace, these people's commons are under siege. A case in point concerns the mosaics created by Sir Eduardo Paolozzi for London's Tottenham Court Road underground station, which, apart from their aesthetic appeal, blocked 1,000 square metres of wall from being used for adverts. In 2015, the decorative arches over the escalators were dismantled as part of the station's redevelopment, prompting a public petition to save them. Transport for London now plans to reinstate one of the arches as well as the murals. The other three arches will be reconstructed and go on public display at Edinburgh University. But the episode showed the vigilance required to save the cultural commons.

INTELLECTUAL COMMONS

Ideas and information should be part of the intellectual commons, available to all. Tim Berners-Lee, inventor of the World Wide Web, wanted the web to be part of that. But, although it is nominally free of charge, it has become a powerful means of exploitation and commodification, notably through the spread of intellectual property rights.

Turning ideas into intellectual property rights results in contrived scarcity by limiting access to and use of information. Capturing information for privileged commercial use drives up the price, giving the rights holders extra income. Sometimes called 'cognitive capitalism', the intellectual property system is in reality a system of rentier capitalism, resting on the contrived scarcity of the intellectual commons.

Paul Mason claims that, although corporations seek to restrict the supply of information, it remains abundant, since 'information goods are freely replicable'.[36] If this were the case, open access campaigners would have nothing to complain about. Powerful institutions and regulations promote the commercial capture of information as intellectual property, making much of it neither available, nor free, nor legally replicable.

The educational commons consist of the facilities that enable people to learn. Education is a natural 'public good' since one person having more of it does not prevent another from having more of it as well. We can all gain from more education. But the commercialisation of the education 'industry' has turned more of what purports to be education into a commodity. If I have more than you, I am more competitive than you and thus can expect to earn more than you. Almost everything on education that appears in the mass media these days puts most emphasis on income and job effects.

Education is meant to be liberating, a process of self-discovery and the pursuit of truth, knowledge and creativity. It loses its integrity once it becomes a sphere of market forces, property rights and rent seeking. Today, the educational commons have been depleted. The focus on 'human capital' formation – preparation for jobs – has taken over.

State schools should be the rock on which the system is constructed. But budgets for state schools have been squeezed in many countries, while private schooling has been boosted by subsidies and grants. In the USA, some school boards face bankruptcy, having borrowed heavily to fund schools in the face of shrinking tax revenue. In the UK, state schools have been laying off staff and school buildings have been falling into disrepair. Meanwhile, successive British governments have expanded quasi-private academy schools (similar to US charter schools) and so-called free schools: publicly subsidised, privately run schools.

Academies and free schools have become a subsidised rent-seeking device. In 2015, the Griffin Schools Trust, a small academy schools chain, was shown to have paid more than £700,000 in two years to 'consulting' companies owned by the trust's two joint chief executives and about £100,000 to three other consultancies in which the trustees had a majority interest.[37] An investigation by *The Guardian* a year earlier revealed that the largest chain in the country, Academy Enterprise Trust (AET), had paid nearly £500,000 in three years to private business interests of its trustees and executives.

In another case, taxpayers are paying £468,000 a year for a 'free' primary school to rent its land and buildings from an investment fund, Legal and General Property. By contrast, state schools usually pay nothing for state-owned buildings. This payment, index-linked to inflation, is guaranteed for twenty-five years. The investment fund issued a press release saying its purchase of the school 'represents an attractive opportunity to access a long-term secure income stream, backed by the government'.[38]

Very few members of the Conservative government went to state schools, and it is not surprising that it is running down the state sector while channelling funds to private alternatives. But the Labour opposition has done little more than complain that the government's failure to invest in young people is 'holding the economy back'. What an alienated way of looking at it. Education should be mainly for developing knowledge and understanding. That is the foundational principle on which the public university was based.

Besides schools and universities, the educational commons should include the institutional means of joining and remaining in occupational communities, that is, micro-societies that give members the opportunity to belong to a sphere of work and personal development. In the past, these were the professional and craft guilds, whose name derives from *geld*, meaning an association of persons contributing to a common set of purposes. Throughout history, guilds have provided institutional resistance to commodification, even though they have also been prone to rent seeking.[39] With appropriate regulations, the model of living and working they have embodied should draw support from a wide political spectrum. The left should be drawn to their potential to protect members from exploitation; the right should welcome them as a means of protecting individuals and groups against a centralised state.

CONCLUSION

'What is a cynic? A man who knows the price
of everything and the value of nothing.'
Oscar Wilde, *Lady Windermere's Fan*

Privatisation of the commons and public assets is central to the ideology of neo-liberalism. It was given global impetus by structural adjustment and shock therapy programmes fostered by the IMF and the World Bank from the 1980s onwards. In 2015, it was the turn of Greece. As a condition of financial loans, its government was obliged to sell assets worth over €50 billion. Part of the proceeds was to go to foreign creditors, part to shore up Greek banks. Such enforced privatisation is a way of boosting private riches at the expense of public wealth. There was no reason to think selling off Greek islands to foreign plutocrats would boost national development or help ordinary Greeks.

The depletion of the commons more generally has been a hidden part of the austerity agenda. Selling off bits of the commons has been presented as a means of cutting public debt and is really a means of accommodating tax cuts. The British government plans to privatise many more of the commons, citing the need to reduce the national debt. But selling off public assets to pay down debt in the short term fails Hartwick's rule, depriving future generations of those assets. The Chancellor announced in July 2015 that the government was seeking 'billions of pounds' more from selling public assets. The government still owns land and buildings worth £300 billion that belong to all British citizens. Why should they be sold to rich individuals or corporations for turning into a source of profits? Why should they be sold to finance tax cuts and increase subsidies for the wealthy?

The winners are the buyers of public assets and those who pay lower taxes. They tend to be one and the same. The losers are the users of the commons, especially those on low incomes. This is not a free market economy; the winners are not gaining from hard work, but from acquiring public wealth that generations have nurtured and preserved. The plunder goes on.

The depletion of nature for profits in the name of 'growth' is the ultimate form of rent extraction. If a corporation uses exhaustible elements of nature – and in their natural state they are not 'resources' – short-term growth is increased at the expense of long-term sustainability. As this shows up only in the longer term, politicians mostly give the commons insignificant value and very low priority. If, in the name of 'austerity', they claim they must cut budget deficits to boost growth, they are unlikely to care about the most vital deficit, that arising from using up natural phenomena that cannot be regenerated.

Historically, the second half of the nineteenth century saw loss of faith in the enclosure of land, as the growing middle class of urban dwellers fretted about loss of recreational space. This prompted creation of the Commons Preservation Society, which evolved into the National Trust. And the 1876 Commons Act ruled that enclosure should take place only if there were public benefit. Sadly, this principle has never been applied to the urban commons. If it had, few of today's urban roads and squares would be in private hands.

The commons are our collective heritage. They cannot be abrogated legitimately unless we, the people, explicitly decide we wish it to be so. Privatising and commercialising the commons is a form of theft, a form of corruption intended to generate rental income for a few, from newly created 'property rights'. The loss of the commons most affects those who rely on it most.

As the final chapter suggests, it is they who have the most interest in leading a revolt against those trespassing on our collective heritage. We should go back to our constitutional roots. Magna Carta and the Charter of the Forest are charters of *reparations*, restoring rights to the commons usurped by powerful interests. We need a new reparations charter to restore the commons that are being snatched so sneakily and illegitimately away from us.

Chapter 6

LABOUR BROKERS: THE PRECARIAT BEARS THE STRAIN

Economic liberalisation, the pursuit of labour market flexibility and a technological revolution have brought profound changes in the nature of labour and work, a dismantling of the traditional firm and a shift of bargaining power from workers to capital. The result has been persistent insecurity for millions and worsening inequality. Yet most of these changes will never be reversed. Rather, we need to adjust to them, control their excesses and redistribute their gains and costs.

In the past three decades, a global labour market system has been taking shape; more people than ever are moving abroad to take jobs and firms find it easier and cheaper to relocate jobs. Furthermore, the internet makes it possible to outsource labour without workers moving physically. It is also blurring the boundaries between paid labour and unpaid work.

In the 'industrial time' regime that predominated for most of the twentieth century, life was measured in blocs of time, during the day and week, and over a lifetime. People did labour for a certain number of hours a day at a fixed workplace; they went to jobs perhaps five days a week with two days off. Life followed a pattern in which time in school was followed by forty to fifty years in jobs, then retirement.

These patterns are breaking down, in what could be called a 'tertiary time' regime.[1] One result, in rich countries at least, has been a rise in the amount of (unpaid) work that people have to do, relative to the amount of (paid) labour. This means that real hourly wage *rates* have fallen by more than the statistics show, as only paid labour time is measured officially.

Even on official statistics, the income gained from labour has been declining, not for everybody or for every group, but on average. Lower wages mean more rental income for employers. Meanwhile, the technological revolution has been generating *more* work, belying the Jeremiahs predicting mass unemployment due to robotics and automation.

RENTIER PLATFORMS: THE NEW LABOUR BROKERS

> 'Maybe it's a stupid comparison, but it's like fighting
> with print in medieval times. It's not a problem;
> it's just a new business model.'
> Elżbieta Bieńkowska, EU Commissioner
> for Industry and the Internal Market

Probably never in the history of capitalism has its core trend changed so fast. The labour process is being transformed in several ways simultaneously, with the technological disruption of traditional occupations, new labour regulations undermining professions, globalising labour transactions and competition, and the emergence of digital 'tasking' platforms. Bieńkowska was referring to bans or restrictions imposed by several European countries on Uber, the app-based taxi service and the most emblematic of the new platform corporations.

A combination of the smartphone, cashless payment systems and the growing precariat have propelled the growth of digital service platforms. The McKinsey Global Institute estimated that what it called 'online talent platforms' could add 2 per cent to global domestic product between 2015 and 2025, creating 72 million full-time equivalent jobs.[2] While the heroic assumptions involved mean that little faith should be put on that figure, it does indicate the scale of the developments.

Digital platforms work as online marketplaces, matching buyers and sellers. They make money from taking a cut of each transaction, though some offer or require additional services that they themselves provide, for a fee. For instance, Uber provides insurance cover for its drivers while they are taking a fare. Most platforms for services have two features: they deal in short-term tasks (assembling a flat-pack wardrobe, writing a newspaper article); and the people supplying the services use their own equipment and assets (cars, homes, tools).

Many platforms claim to be part of a new 'sharing economy' that is boosting efficiency and incomes through increased utilisation of underused assets. However, they are in fact expanding the scope of commodified labour and the amount of unpaid work-for-labour, as we will see. All bypass the firm as traditionally understood. They are creating 'platform capitalism'.

In a seminal book, *The Innovator's Dilemma*, Clayton Christensen argued that innovation was 'disruptive' if it had the potential to generate new products or services or to deliver them in radically new ways.[3] He and colleagues later claimed that the provision of services through digital platforms did not meet two criteria for disruptive innovation – that the innovation must target the low end of an existing market and mainly draw in non-consumers of existing options.[4] But digital platforms surely qualify as disruptive on both counts.

Uber, for example, has expanded the market for taxi services by offering cheap rides, drawing in users previously put off by high prices and lack of flexibility of traditional taxi services. By late 2015 Uber had over 1.1 million drivers and was operating in 351 cities in sixty-four countries.[5] Airbnb has created a casual rental market enabling people to let rooms in their homes on a short-term basis, as well as providing a platform for conventional bed-and-breakfast operators. In 2015, it had 1.5 million listings, ranging from spare beds to castles in 34,000 cities and over 190 countries, and had more rooms on its books than some of the world's largest hotel chains. On the retail side, one and a half million 'makers' sell jewellery, clothing and accessories through the online marketplace Etsy, giving small-scale artisans access to buyers all over the world.

Some platforms are in direct competition with older forms of service. These include Uber, its US rival Lyft and imitators elsewhere such as GrabTaxi, operating in Southeast Asia, Ola in India and Didi Kuaidi in China. BlaBlaCar, a French start-up originally called Covoiturage, is a car-sharing platform that enables drivers making long journeys to share the cost by 'selling' empty seats. BlaBlaCar does not compete with taxis, since its average trip is 200 miles (320 kilometres). However, it could be said to compete with coaches and trains. Its founder claims to be 'disrupting the mobility business'.

Other companies put buyers in touch with providers of services ranging from housecleaning (Handy), valet parking (Luxe), grocery deliveries (Instacart), drink deliveries (Drizly) and dog-sitting (BorrowMyDoggy). Deliveroo delivers meals to your door; TaskRabbit undertakes domestic tasks and errands; Thumbtack finds local professionals to supply services, from installing a kitchen to teaching yoga.

It is a misnomer to call this the 'sharing economy'. These digital platforms are rentier entities; they control the technological apparatus but, unlike great corporations of the past, they do not own the main means of production. Rather, they are labour brokers, often taking 20 per cent (sometimes more) from all transactions.

'Crowdwork' platforms also act as labour brokers, providing a digital labour exchange through which organisations ('requesters') post online tasks, split into small, sometimes micro tasks, which workers ('taskers') then bid for. The platforms charge 10 per cent or more per transaction. The pioneer in micro-tasking was Amazon Mechanical Turk (AMT), set up by Amazon in 2005, but there are now dozens of crowdwork platforms, among the biggest being Upwork, PeoplePerHour and CrowdFlower.

Clickworker, based in Germany, boasts 700,000 'clickworkers' in 136 countries and big-name clients such as Honda and PayPal. Lancers, a Japanese platform, had 420,000 registered workers in 2015 and the Japanese crowd-labour industry body aims to increase the number of crowdworkers to 10 million by 2018 and 20 million by 2023.[6]

The platforms have grown astonishingly rapidly. Founded in 2009, by 2015 Uber had established itself as easily the most valuable American company of its generation; its implied valuation of about

$65 billion in early 2016 was higher than that of 80 per cent of firms in the S&P 500 stock market index. Airbnb, after just seven years of existence, was valued at $25 billion in 2015, more than twice its value a year earlier, making it the second most valuable private company in Silicon Valley. However, for every platform that becomes a household name, dozens fizzle out or remain as 'micro' as they began, overall they are expanding phenomenally fast.

Globally, firms spent well over $3 billion in 2014 on payments to online platforms and the taskers working through them, according to a Staffing Industry Analysts report.[7] A common attitude was summed up by Bob Bahramipour, CEO of Gigwalk, which recruits taskers for brief projects in retail, merchandising and marketing. He told the Associated Press: 'You can hire 10,000 people for ten to fifteen minutes. When they're done, those 10,000 people just melt away.'[8]

HOW VENTURE CAPITAL SHAPES PLATFORM CAPITALISM

Uber is lauded as an exemplary 'platform'. When it arrives in a target city, it launches a packaged recruiting programme for drivers, usually offering incentives. Then it undercuts official taxi fares by operating a flexible, demand-based fare scheme; this lowers fares at times of slack demand and raises them when demand is strong so as to attract more drivers. Once established, Uber uses drivers to offer other services. Just as Google uses search-related advertising to generate income with which it enters other businesses, so Uber's plan is to offer 'transportation as reliable as running water, everywhere for everyone'.[9]

Thus it has branched out into delivery services, providing lunch delivery, cycle courier services and deliveries of household supplies in various US cities. It reaches out to retailers as well, offering same-day deliveries. While others such as Postmates and Shyp are in the same space, Uber has greater scale and financial clout. It can raise cash quickly from new city operations and has been able to tap investors for huge sums – more than $9 billion by the end of 2015 – with which to intimidate competitors.

This has enabled it to finance operational losses as it expands into new markets by undercutting actual and potential rivals. According to leaked documents the company prepared for investors, operational losses reached a staggering $1 billion in the first half of 2015.[10] Yet Uber more than doubled its cash holdings to over $4 billion, giving it a handy war chest for future expansion.

Private equity financing enables Uber to squash competition through predatory pricing, extracting greater rents as its near-monopoly strengthens. Other start-ups are also gaining near-monopoly positions with the help of venture capital. They are not competing in free markets.

The USA has led the way. Paradoxically, private investors and private companies, as opposed to publicly listed companies, were boosted by the US Jobs (Jumpstart Our Businesses) Act of 2012, which was supposed to encourage firms to go public and list on Wall Street. President Obama said at the time that public companies were desirable because they expanded more quickly, created more jobs and operated with 'greater oversight and greater transparency'. But, whereas previously private firms were required to publish detailed financial information once they had over 500 shareholders, the Act increased that to 2,000. As a result, many more companies can opt to stay private so as to keep control in the hands of a restricted group and avoid public scrutiny of their dealings.

The capital for digital platforms, even the largest of which have chosen to remain private, comes from a narrow circle of investors from mutual funds, private equity firms, hedge funds and sovereign wealth funds. It is a market reserved for the elite and plutocracy, a sort of closet capitalism. Making it even more so, investors often demand assurances that the company will indemnify them if it goes public at a lower valuation. This 'ratchet' arrangement grants them extra shares to compensate for any shortfall. They thereby receive a free insurance against risk, a special form of rent.

Uber's predatory pricing policy, to open up markets and marginalise or crush rivals, has depended on private equity capital prepared to weather short-term losses in order to gain more long-term profits. In its battle with Didi Kuaidi in China, Uber has not only tried to undercut its rival's fares, but has been poaching and attracting drivers through a complex array of subsidies and incentives amounting to up to 130 per cent of the fare in some cities.

In Shanghai, for instance, if a driver completes twenty-five rides a week, Uber adds 110 per cent of any fare between 7 a.m. and 10 a.m., 80 per cent at rush hours, 60 per cent at weekends and 40 per cent during normal working hours. If a driver completes fifty rides a week, the subsidy is increased by another 20 percentage points all round.[11]

Uber's tactics in China appear to be having some success. By mid-2015, the technology hub city of Chengdu was its biggest market in the world by number of trips and Uber's CEO Travis Kalanick has announced plans to expand to 100 Chinese cities by the end of 2016.

Still, Didi Kuaidi, which dominates China's app-based taxi hailing market, has the financial firepower to fight back, in the form of one of China's sovereign wealth funds and its e-commerce behemoths, Alibaba and Tencent. They can help Didi Kuaidi play the long game too. It is operating its own subsidy scheme, paying higher basic rates and bonuses for taking ten or more fares during peak periods. This is not competition based on quality of service. It is a surrogate war waged by big-player financial capital on both sides.

A similar battle is taking place in India between Uber and Ola Cabs, which has raised capital from investors including Russian billionaire Yuri Milner's DST Global investment company, Japanese technology company SoftBank and Didi Kuaidi itself. In late 2015, Uber was operating in twenty-two Indian cities with about 250,000 drivers, while Ola, operating in 102 cities, claimed even more.

In the first round of this predatory model, the taskers (in this case drivers) may be among the beneficiaries, receiving loyalty premiums. But this is likely to be short-lived once a platform has established monopoly control of the market (or possibly oligopoly control by several platforms that tacitly agree to divvy up the market). The earnings of Uber drivers have already been cut in cities where the company is successfully established.

TASKERS IN THE PRECARIAT

'Salaried employment in the traditional sense of the word
is a notion that is gradually dying and we need to prepare
ourselves for the change that is coming. Tomorrow I should
easily be able to earn enough to live on, doing real work but

> without drawing a fixed salary. Instead, I could be an Uber
> driver, rent my house out through Airbnb, provide my work
> skills on community platforms. And why not think about
> becoming a teacher or lecturer via these same platforms?'
>   Pierre Calmard, CEO, iProspect[12]

That is one sanguine view of what is happening, presented by someone who is most unlikely to be an Uber driver or an Airbnb host any time soon. There is a more worrying perspective.

The number of taskers is rising extraordinarily fast. The McKinsey Global Institute (MGI) has predicted that by 2025 200 million nominally unemployed or part-time employees will be making extra from doing tasks through online platforms.[13] But MGI is too optimistic in implying that those earnings will merely supplement a main source of income. A US survey in 2015, commissioned by Upwork and the misnamed Freelancers Union, found that 75 per cent of people who had 'freelanced' in the previous year relied wholly or mainly on that labour; only a quarter were 'moonlighters' with conventional jobs.[14]

Another study estimated that 16 per cent of the US workforce was doing temporary, 'gig' or contract work as their main job in 2015, nearly double the proportion twenty years earlier, and that growth of 'non-standard work arrangements' appeared to account for all net employment growth in the US economy since 2005.[15]

Digital platforms are building a new 'putting-out' system and eroding old forms of service delivery, just as the original putting-out system eroded medieval guilds. They are leveraging change in all sectors where they are penetrating, with underappreciated spill-over effects. For instance, in the USA, the rise of Uber has hit

Medallion Financial, which makes loans to yellow-cab taxi drivers to buy their licences ('medallions'). Medallion has lost more than half its market value, in spite of rising profits.[16] It may cease to be able to help people become conventional taxi drivers. If so, it will show how rentier corporations can restrict the supply of competitors indirectly as well as by direct competition.

THE ON-DEMAND CONCIERGE ECONOMY

Three categories of tasker can be identified. The first consists of those in the 'gig' – or, more cruelly, 'concierge' – economy, performing services such as taxi driving, cleaning, handiwork or delivery, commissioned through digital platforms.

The platforms are earning high rental incomes at their taskers' expense. Uber takes 20–30 per cent of each fare, plus a booking fee in some cases, and dictates fares and routes. Airbnb nets 9–15 per cent on every booking. TaskRabbit charges 30 per cent of the task fee (15 per cent for repeat bookings) and obliges the client to pay an extra 5 per cent for its insurance guarantee scheme. The revenues gained from these transaction fees far outweigh the cost of services provided by the platform – development of the technology, administering booking and payment systems and so on.

The platforms insist that taskers are not employees but independent contractors, so are not covered by labour laws, entitling them to certain benefits and safeguards, including, in the USA and elsewhere, the right to unionise. Uber goes to great lengths to justify the independent contractor label, describing drivers as part-time 'driver-partners' who choose to provide rides using the

Uber platform. TaskRabbit's support centre poses the rhetorical question 'Do Taskers work for TaskRabbit?' and gives its answer: 'No, they do not. Taskers are local entrepreneurs and independent contractors who work for themselves. TaskRabbit simply provides the platform for Clients and Taskers to meet. We vet and background-check all Taskers before allowing them onto the platform to ensure they are professional and reliable individuals.'

This is disingenuous. Most taskers are neither entrepreneurial nor independent; few will build a business based on queuing for iPhone buyers, as some are tasked to do. But it would be equally wrong to call them 'employees' in the classic sense of that term; they are not directly supervised, they own the main means of production and, in principle, they have control over their working time.

However, taskers are not self-employed either. They depend on the labour broker (the platform) to obtain tasks and are subject to rules, such as wearing a T-shirt with the company logo or accepting a certain number of tasks. Yet, like the self-employed, they bear most job-related costs, including transport, repairs and maintenance, and insurance for accidents and ill-health.

Court cases in the USA and UK, claiming that taskers are employees, highlight the inadequacy of the dichotomy of 'employee' and 'self-employed'.[17] This is a new form of labour and categories should be adjusted accordingly. 'Freelance' is a misnomer, as is 'independent worker',[18] since most taskers are not 'free' or completely independent. 'Dependent' contractor is more apt than 'independent'. But 'tasker', as in doing tasks, conveys the phenomenon more pithily.

A decision to classify Uber drivers and other taskers as employees would reduce the platforms' rental income by hugely increasing their operating costs. Indeed, it would destroy their business model. This is why Uber agreed a proposed $100 million out-of-court settlement in April 2016 in return for maintaining drivers' status as independent contractors. At the time of writing the settlement had still to be approved by a judge.

When US home cleaning platform Homejoy folded in 2015, the reason given was a series of lawsuits by taskers demanding to be classified as employees. However, the business model was fatally flawed for another reason.[19] Homejoy offered cheap household services, taking a 25 per cent cut on transactions, which meant very low pay for those doing the tasks. This attracted inexperienced or desperate (even homeless) people who did low-quality labour. Customers and taskers also had a financial incentive to arrange things off Homejoy's books, avoiding the middleman.

Some small US on-demand platforms have decided to treat their taskers as employees and are still going, including Shyp (shipping), Munchery (meal delivery) and Luxe (valet parking). Lawyers for Uber drivers and others seeking employee status argue that the platforms can afford to operate on slimmer margins, which would trim but not eliminate their rental income.

While it seems preferable to make taskers a separate category, some platforms do behave in key respects like employers, dictating terms, controlling quality and disciplining taskers deemed to fall below set standards. For instance, Uber requires drivers to accept at least 80 per cent of drive requests.[20] TaskRabbit has moved from a system in which taskers bid for posted tasks to one that assigns them to tasks at an hourly rate. They then have thirty minutes to accept or reject the task.

Those failing to accept a certain percentage of tasks within a certain period, or failing to respond within thirty minutes, can be 'de-activated', with re-activation requiring successful completion of a re-education quiz. Too many slips result in the tasker being removed from 'the community' altogether. Ironically, far from helping people with other jobs to earn extra income, the change has made this harder, because other commitments restrict availability for tasks. Taskers have to be on call, making their description as 'independent contractors' even more far-fetched. As one Facebook comment put it, 'Anyone left working for TR [TaskRabbit] is an indentured servant ... You are not growing your own business; you are growing TR as a business.'[21]

Taskers are also subject to control through customer ratings posted on their profile. For instance, Uber drivers must maintain at least a rating of 4.6 out of five 'stars'. This is a new form of sweating, a low-cost way of inducing self-exploitation. Ratings are not just a feedback mechanism; they are a means of monitoring and disciplining, without the need for a supervisor. The platform is part of the panopticon state in which surveillance is being automated. Ratings are pernicious, since they impose constant regulation with little transparency or accountability.

An Uber driver may be rated poorly for a slow journey due to heavy traffic, for refusing to break the speed limit or for a difference of opinion, perhaps on a matter of politics, sport or religion. The client may be in a bad mood, or be prejudiced against certain ethnic groups. The ratings take seconds, but may have drastic implications for the tasker, leading to loss of income and future opportunities. If several customers give a driver a low rating, he or she will be 'de-activated'. There is no due process, no means of appeal.[22]

The relationship is supposed to be symmetrical, in that customers can rate taskers and vice-versa. Thus Handy commented:

> Handy is a transparent platform that takes care of every need in the home. As part of that transparency, we offer a two-way rating system so independent professionals can offer feedback on how a job went and customers can do likewise. This incentivises excellence on both sides of the supply and demand equation, provides constructive feedback for professionals and customers, and opens up more lines of communication to ensure the best possible experience in the home.[23]

This claim of rating equality does not reflect the reality. The consequences of a sub-par rating for a tasker are much more severe than a poor rating would be for a customer.

Some Uber drivers have been de-activated without notice and forced to pay for a 'training class' approved by the platform in order to be re-activated. Some platforms do not de-activate but downgrade the tasker receiving sub-par ratings so that he or she comes lower down the listings when searches are made. This is a powerful control mechanism.

In an impressive show of erudition, Californian Judge Edward Chen cited French philosopher Michel Foucault in his 2015 ruling that Uber had a case to answer in a class action suit brought on behalf of drivers claiming they should be classified as employees. Remarking that ratings gave Uber a 'tremendous amount of control over the "manner and means" of its drivers' performance', he noted Foucault's words in *Discipline and Punish* that a 'state of conscious and permanent visibility assures the automatic functioning of power'.

As Judge Chen pointed out, ratings make the relationship between the platform and tasker look more like a conventional employment relationship. And, when de-activating or downgrading is done without notice or warning, it is equivalent to being fired. If US courts eventually rule that platforms like Uber or TaskRabbit are employers, ratings to de-activate or discipline taskers could fall foul of Title VII of the Civil Rights Act, which forbids discrimination on the basis of sex, race, colour, national origin or religion.

Another issue raised by this form of tasking is the erosion of professionalism, an undercurrent in rentier capitalism. Uber is again an exemplar, since it has attracted high-profile protests from taxi operators claiming unfair competition in just about every city it has entered. Depending on the regulations in force, Uber crafts its business model to try to ensure its drivers are not subject to the rules that apply to conventional taxis. In London, for instance, licensed cabbies must drive only authorised vehicles ('black cabs') and pass a 'knowledge' exam involving memorisation of almost every street in central London.

Cities wishing to protect traditional taxis have been hitting back, by classifying Uber and other app-based taxi services as conventional taxis or by devising regulations to constrain their operations. In London, however, the Competition and Markets Authority has attacked regulations proposed by Transport for London as anti-competitive, suggesting lower standards for black cabs instead. And Uber and others are finding ways to operate within the new rules or are operating on the old basis pending lengthy court appeals. The threat to professional standards remains.

Disputes about standards are bound to arise whenever amateurs provide a service that hitherto was the exclusive preserve of those with qualifications or membership of an occupational community. Hotel and bed-and-breakfast organisations have attacked Airbnb, saying its 'hosts' have an unfair advantage because they do not need to comply with fire regulations or pay taxes on overnight stays. In New York, Airbnb has been accused of encouraging illegal lets and landlordism.[24] Amateurism is a route for cheapening labour and increasing the rental income of the platforms.

Taskers fit in the precariat. They lack income security, labour security and an occupational trajectory. They must do a lot of work-for-labour, unremunerated, off formal workplaces. Uber among others has tried to give the impression that most of its drivers are earning extra money to supplement a regular income. It seems rather that, globally, millions of taskers are scrambling for odd jobs and are otherwise unemployed or doing low-paid activities. They are on-demand servants for the elite and salariat. The concierge economy is part of the Second Gilded Age.

TASKERS IN CLOUD LABOUR

The second group of taskers consists of those doing online tasks. Initially, this was dominated by low-level micro-tasks, epitomised by AMT. However, online tasking has moved upmarket to cover many forms of professional work, such as accountancy, legal research, medical diagnosis and design. Professional tasking platforms include Upwork, Freelancer.com and PeoplePerHour. In California, UpCounsel provides online lawyers and handles its taskers' finances and document management. UpCounsel's CEO sees it as the start of 'the virtualisation of professional services'.[25]

The numbers involved in cloud labour are already large and growing fast. In 2015, AMT claimed to have over half a million taskers available at any one time. Upwork, formed in 2014 through a merger of Elance and oDesk, had 9 million registered 'freelancers' on its site from 180 countries, connected to 3.6 million client businesses. Australia's Freelancer.com claims nearly 18 million users posting tasks or seeking them.

The business models behind micro-tasking and freelance platforms differ. Micro-tasking platforms are based on an extreme form of Taylorism – the division of labour into components in which the manager does the thinking, the labourer the doing. It is clouded (literally) in euphemisms, such as the term used to describe the units of work, HITs (Human Intelligence Tasks). Many pay a few pennies or cents apiece. You have to do a lot of HITs to make a little money! One survey in 2012 found that taskers for AMT in the USA had done on average over 9,000 tasks, and their Indian counterparts over 6,500.[26] The average age was thirty-three. These figures are indicative of how minute the tasks typically are.

Micro-taskers are probably the most exploited and most likely to self-exploit of all taskers. Tasks are usually allocated at a set rate per task, which is often extremely low. Tasks may turn out to be more complex or time-consuming than taskers were led to believe. And in practice they have no means of redress should the requester avoid paying by claiming, falsely, that the work was not of sufficient quality, or simply fail to pay. As Michael Bernstein, who leads a Stanford University project on crowd sourcing, put it, 'AMT is notoriously bad at ensuring high quality results, producing respect and fair wages for workers, and making it easy to author effective tasks.'[27]

Requesters and broker platforms often seem to forget that the tasks are being done by 'real people' with real needs and emotions. Lukas Biewald, CEO of CrowdFlower, which specialises in collecting, cleaning and labelling data, revealed his true attitude in a moment of hubris when telling an audience,

> Before the internet, it would be really difficult to find someone, sit them down for ten minutes and get them to work for you, and then fire them after those ten minutes. But with technology you can actually find them, pay them the tiny amount of money and then get rid of them when you don't want them any more.[28]

Even though a majority of taskers have been in rich countries so far, reflecting access to reliable internet connections, cloud labour is globalising. Pay rates reflect the fact that tasks can be done equally well by someone in Bangalore or Accra as in Boston or Amsterdam. In that respect among others, platforms are undermining the ability of workers to obtain decent wages.

ON-CALL EMPLOYEES

A third group of taskers consists of employees, with employment contracts, who are called upon only as the employer requires and paid accordingly. These taskers, on zero-hours, 'on-call' or 'if-and-when' contracts, or subject to flexible schedules, are only remunerated for the hours they work on the contracted tasks.

Time and money spent on work-related activities they must undertake in order to do those tasks – providing their own uniforms or means of transport, for example – often go unrecognised and unremunerated. So-called 'flexible' schedules oblige those on such contracts to be on permanent stand-by, unable to plan, not knowing if they will obtain paid labour or how much. Some are doubly exploited, forbidden to take other jobs in case that affects their availability. Although the UK government banned 'exclusivity clauses' in 2015, employers can easily circumvent the legislation, for instance by offering a guarantee of as little as one hour a week, or simply by reducing offered hours for people known to have another job.

By 2015, nearly a million people in the UK were on zero-hours or similar contracts, according to official figures, and over 1.3 million were in part-time jobs because they could not find full-time ones. More generally, a quarter of the UK labour force – about 7 million people – had their schedules regularly altered at short notice by their employer, according to a 2010 survey.[29] The same survey showed that employer-driven flexible scheduling increased significantly between 2005 and 2010 in eleven out of fifteen European countries for which there were data. The highest proportion, rather surprisingly, was in Germany (32 per cent), followed by France (28 per cent), Finland and the UK (24 per cent) and Ireland (23 per cent). In the USA, in 2015 10–16 per cent of those in jobs had irregular or on-call schedules and nearly 7 million were working part-time 'for economic reasons'.

OCCUPATIONAL DISMANTLING

Digital platforms and their legions of taskers are eroding notions of employee and employment, and the body of labour-related entitlements and protections built up during the twentieth century. They are also accentuating the dismantling of occupational communities. For hundreds of years, occupational guilds defined working life, setting standards, codes of ethics, means of training and sources of social protection. They stood against the market. The neo-liberal agenda aims to dismantle them, and the on-demand economy is both a consequence and an accelerator of that. The costs include the withering of occupational ethics and routes of social mobility through professions and crafts.

Taskers have the potential advantage of flexible working. But they are being used to undermine professional qualifications, further marginalising the time-honoured concept of the professional and craft community. This is what platform corporations want, and what neo-liberals have always wanted, because they depict all collective bodies as distorting the market and preventing market clearing.[30] The platforms are reducing the rental income gained by those inside occupational communities and transferring that to themselves, further reducing the returns to labour and work.

One of the least analysed aspects of the neo-liberal agenda has been the re-regulation of occupations, including all the great professions. Milton Friedman, an architect of the Chicago school of economics, wrote his first book (with Simon Kuznets) in 1945 on the medical professions, criticising their rent seeking through restricting the supply of doctors, imposing high standards, controlling fees and so on.

When the neo-liberals achieved domination of the economics profession and economic policymaking in the 1980s, they launched an onslaught on occupational self-regulation. This was not deregulation, but state re-regulation. There was a shift to state licensing, usually by boards linked to finance or competition ministries. The avowed intention was to protect consumers, not those inside the profession or craft. Trade unions were not the only labour bodies to be weakened.

Britain, particularly under New Labour, followed the same course of taking control of work practices from professions and putting it in the hands of the state, with emphasis on licensing and negative licensing (suspending or barring people from practising). Licensing has facilitated rent seeking by outsiders, lowering the capacity of professional and craft bodies to generate or retain rental income for themselves. Two examples illustrate the general trend.

The Legal Services Act 2007 removed control of legal activities from the Bar Council and other bodies and set up a state body, the Legal Services Board, with a non-lawyer as its chair. The law was dubbed the 'Tesco' Act, because it opened up the prospect of standardised services sold in supermarkets. It has accelerated the fragmentation of the legal profession into an elite, a salariat and an expanding precariat, including paralegals, with little prospect of upward mobility.

This has created space for the penetration of legal services by digital platforms, which will gain rental income. Partial Uberisation will follow, transferring rental income to those possessing assets, outside the legal profession. The ensuing dynamics of inequality cannot be predicted with certainty, but one outcome will be greater income differentiation within the profession.

Much the same has been happening to the medical professions since they have been subject to more state regulation. This began with the Thatcher government, which changed the payment system and rolled back doctors' autonomy. But the decisive changes came under Tony Blair, when reforms led to the widespread contracting out of hospital services.

Outsourcing is accelerating the de-professionalisation of services and weakening the rent-earning capacity of professionals. Some analysts have argued that automation will – and should – largely displace the professions.[31] For example, in 2014 48 million Americans used online software rather than professionals to do their tax returns, and the most popular US legal service is legalzoom.com, an online advice and do-it-yourself document-drafting service. eBay and PayPal process over 60 million disagreements each year using 'online dispute resolution' software that helps settle disputes without involving lawyers.

The prospect that professions will be dominated by automated near-equivalents should alarm us. The issue is not just loss of income for those in professions and crafts. Occupations have been vital communities and zones of rights throughout history, involving more than just delivery of a commodified service. They impart ethics, collegial empathy and a culture of learning and questioning of received wisdom. Machines and software cannot do this.

An automated service may implement the conventional wisdom more accurately and consistently. It will deliver the norm. A community of human professionals delivers services distributed around the norm. This allows for the historical reality that, in every professional service, today's conventional wisdom can become tomorrow's obsolescent practice. What might seem odd today often becomes a new norm tomorrow.

Whatever the impact of online labour contracting, professions are being fragmented. On one estimate, 'the connected work marketplace', including forms of freelancing, professional networking sites such as LinkedIn and remote work apps such as GoToMyPC, will reach $63 billion globally by 2020, up from $10 billion in 2014.[32] The UK freelancers' association IPSE estimated that by 2015 there were 1.88 million 'independent professionals' in the UK, up by more than a third since 2008. IPSE claimed there was a major shift from 'having a job' to 'working for clients'. To what extent it will displace those in full-time employment is a matter of conjecture, but the scope to do so is vast.

AUTOMATION AND HETEROMATION

While the technological revolution is disrupting occupations, it is worsening the distribution of income by extracting rental income from labour and work for the benefit of labour brokers. This is reducing the number and range of high-paying jobs, directly by increasing the division of labour into smaller, cheaper tasks and indirectly by weakening the bargaining position of those in competition with taskers.

The combination of digital technologies and platform capitalism is also affecting the character of work and labour. It is reducing the number of defined jobs by shifting to tasks done by people who are neither employees nor independent contractors. At the same time, it is increasing the number of activities counted as jobs in our misleading labour statistics. By being commodified – made into market transactions – some forms of work previously done privately (or not at all) are being turned into jobs, or tasks for others to do.

On-demand shopping, queuing, cleaning and so on boost phoney 'employment', pleasing politicians, but in reality are merely substituting hired servants for the same work as before. If people order shopping and delivery online, rather than do it themselves, the 'work' of shopping is converted into someone's 'labour' of shopping. The same goes for activities that hardly count as 'work', such as dog walking. This is another reason why the claim that technology is displacing labour is misleading. The concierge economy is generating more labour.

To complicate the picture further, digital platforms are increasing the amount of unpaid work that does not count as labour by creating forms of work previously not done at all and by converting some forms of paid labour into unpaid work. As a mass phenomenon, this is unique to the twenty-first century.

Taskers must do many forms of work, unpaid, that would have been paid as labour in an equivalent conventional job. For instance, task rabbits are paid for tasks, but not for all the extra work they do, such as buying, cleaning and maintaining tools. Uber drivers must spend time and money looking after their vehicle and pay for their own fuel.

Meanwhile, the new technologies are inducing additional work, captured by the ungainly term of 'heteromation'. This unpaid work generates rental income for those controlling the technologies. The classic example is the provision of personal information by online users that gives the technology companies free data for building and operating their money-making services. Users may also unwittingly be helping the companies more directly. Google's reCAPTCHA anti-bot security system, for example, instead of generating random letters and numbers, requires users to parse a scanned image of a machine-unreadable word from a book (for Google's book digitisation project) or a photographed image of a street name or traffic sign (from Street View imagery used on Google Maps).

The work may be regarded by those doing it as productive or personally rewarding – participation in social media, for example – but the distinctive character of heteromation is that the rentier gains from the work of others through the ability to 'insert human beings within technological systems in order to allow the system to operate in intended ways'.[33]

As the vice-president for Research of Gartner, a technology consultancy, aptly said in 2012, 'Facebook's nearly 1 billion users have become the largest unpaid workforce in history'.[34] By the end of 2015, the number of Facebook users had risen to 1.6 billion.

Unsolicited training is another form of unpaid work encouraged by the new technologies and growth of the precariat. Often in desperation, people take online courses in several subjects, induced to do so by adverts, sweeteners, encouragement or insistence by employment offices. This work is partly speculative; there is no guarantee it will lead to any income or employment. Nor is it necessarily beneficial in other respects; there are always opportunity costs in using time and money for one thing which could be used for something else.

There is also the financial cost and the likelihood of what economists call 'pig cycle' effects: a shortage of pigs (marketable skills) leads to price rises for pigs (wage or employment opportunities for those with the skills), which lead farmers to invest in more pigs, which leads to a glut of pigs and falling prices (wages and job opportunities). Unlike pigs, the skills may have become obsolete by the time they have been expensively obtained.

UNDERPAID LABOUR AND WORKFARE

A free labour market would be one in which all labour transactions were based on a freely agreed contract between a buyer and a seller of labour that specified a price (the wage) and the labour expected. However, there is always some uncertainty on both sides, and usually the person selling labour is more vulnerable than the buyer. Minimum wage laws introduced in many countries, including the UK in 1999 and Germany in 2014, are intended to protect workers whose bargaining position is weak.

While a minimum wage (and its new variant, a 'living wage') may set guidelines of decency, they do prevent a free market from operating. And the level of the minimum wage is arbitrary, mixing consideration of workers' needs and expectations with the level thought to promote employment. It is a blunt instrument that has less impact than either its advocates or its critics believe. In today's flexible labour system, employers can easily find ways of keeping wages down. UK firms have responded to the introduction of the 'living wage' in April 2016 by restricting overtime, cutting bonuses and ending free food and paid breaks.[35] With the spread of tasking, the effect of minimum wages will become even weaker.

Of course, the minimum wage is not the only instrument that prevents operation of a free market, although it is probably the only one that aims to raise wages. An equitable labour market would be one in which the bargaining strengths of buyers and sellers were roughly equal. Yet, in contrast to the stated justification for minimum wages, governments have been weakening the bargaining power of employees and trade unions.

Defenders of 'free market' capitalism justify curbing unions' bargaining strength on the grounds that they push wages above market-clearing and productivity-driven levels. Defenders of unions argue that without them employers can and do take advantage of workers' vulnerability to force wages below market-clearing levels and even below the cost of subsistence.

Governments have lowered wages by more indirect means as well. Thus they have allowed and encouraged the spread of unpaid or low-paid interns which, through substitution and threat effects, drives down the wages of others doing similar labour in regular jobs.[36] A more systemic intervention has been the use of tax credits, discussed in Chapter 3, which enable firms to pay very low wages. They are a recognition that the labour market does not work in the way textbooks say it should.

A third intervention is the creeping use of workfare, developed stealthily from a policy of obliging the unemployed to seek jobs incessantly to one that increasingly forces them into unpleasant jobs paying benefit-rate wages, or even doing labour for no pay at all. When a government resorts to such policies it should acknowledge that it is helping to depress wages at the lower end of the labour market.

The reach of a minimum wage and the potential effects of workfare should be considered in the context of the spread of 'little platoons'. According to official statistics, in the UK alone between 2000 and 2015 about 1.4 million extra 'micro firms' (defined as having between zero and nine employees) came into existence. Many, if not most, will have been formed by self-employed freelancers and 'independent contractors'. Average income from self-employment fell by 22 per cent between 2009 and 2014, at a time when official statistics indicated that nearly three-quarters of the recorded rise in employment consisted of self-employment. Many taskers would be buried in there somewhere.

Some claim the growth of taskers will reduce inequality.[37] This is unlikely. There is ample anecdotal evidence and reason for thinking that wage rates are being driven down, both for those doing the tasks and those in competition with them in conventional employment. To reinforce the point, in the USA one of the founders of CrowdFlower indiscreetly revealed that 'the firm sometimes paid workers $2 to $3 an hour, rather than the federal minimum wage of $7.25, or paid workers in points for various online reward programs and videogame credits.'[38] It will be hard to prevent that sort of outcome.

THE REAL SHARING ECONOMY

Describing rentier platforms as the sharing economy is misleading and mischievous, allowing platforms to claim they are merely facilitating neighbourly sharing rather than providing a commercial service. One genuine sharing online community is Couchsurfing, which enables travellers to find a bed for a night offered for free by other members of the community. But Couchsurfing has been marginalised by the big commercial ventures, notably Airbnb.

Rentier platforms are also feeding off the erosion of the social commons and commodifying some of its traditional forms. For instance, by offering cheap taxi rides they may reduce the numbers using subsidised public transport and accelerate the loss of public bus services.

The real sharing economy is exciting some analysts. Paul

Mason sees the emergence of commons-based peer production in the likes of Wikipedia, Linux, OpenStreetMap and Mozilla's Firefox. In Spain, arts and culture collectives La Tabacalera and Medialab-Prado are prime examples. While these have great potential, they involve a lot of work by unpaid activists and can be pushed out or marginalised by commercial ventures. Many will need state subsidies in order to survive.

THE FIFTH LIE OF RENTIER CAPITALISM

'Everyone can enjoy a life of luxurious leisure if the machine-produced wealth is shared, or most people can end up miserably poor if the machine-owners successfully lobby against wealth redistribution. So far, the trend seems to be toward the second option, with technology driving ever-increasing inequality.'
Stephen Hawking, October 2015

The platform capitalism taking shape is not a sharing economy. Nor is it wholly parasitic; it offers new and more efficient services, and it is commodifying spheres that were outside the market economy. But it is transformative, contrary to the contention of defenders of the old labour system, such as Lawrence Mishel, president of the Democrat-leaning Economic Policy Institute in Washington DC, who has dismissed its impact as 'trivial'.[39]

It is transformative directly, by generating tasking labour for millions, and indirectly, through its impact on traditional suppliers of invaded services. Even if a majority of taskers are doing tasks part-time, their numbers are growing rapidly, scaring competitors to make concessions.[40] Moreover, since Mishel used official revenue data to dismiss the impact as trivial, he undermines his claim by noting that 'failure to report income is very common among independent contractors'.

In one respect, the on-demand economy reverses a capitalist mantra. Instead of being owned by capitalists, the main means of production are 'owned' by the taskers – the precariat. The platforms maximise profits through ownership and control of the technological apparatus, protected by patents and other forms of intellectual property rights, and by the exploitation of labour through tasking and unpaid work. Labour brokers are rentiers, earning a lot for doing little, if we accept their claim that they are just providing technology to put clients in touch with 'independent contractors' of services. Thus, Uber and rival Lyft insist they are technology, not transport companies.

As platform-based tasking expands, it will be appreciated just how isolated the precariat is in this zone, in constant competition with one another. The atomisation drives down wages and transfers costs, risk and uncertainty onto the precariat. So far at least, taskers have had minimal means or opportunities to coalesce.[41]

The 'sharing economy' has a cultural dimension as well. When someone 'shares' a car, apartment or utensils for money, they convert zones of privacy and use value into alienated commodities with exchange value. It is an instance of the Lauderdale Paradox, in which commodification is an act of privatisation that contrives scarcity of space or time.

These forms of labour intensify the pressure to commodify all aspects of life. Intensifying self-exploitation is a sad way for the precariat to respond to adversity. It is how those experiencing falling wages and living standards cover up the decline, for a while.

In addition, governments will have fiscal problems due to the changing character of labour and work. The shift to taskers will reduce tax revenue through lower employee and employer contributions and will push more people below tax thresholds, for example by expanding part-time labour. In many countries, payroll and income taxes are lower for those classified as independent contractors. So, the shift may feed into the austerity agenda by increasing budget deficits and fuelling demands for further cuts in public spending on the spurious grounds that they are necessary.

Among unexplored implications are the ecological costs and benefits of platform capitalism. The proliferation of quasi-taxis may have an adverse ecological effect. Besides allowing taxis with a lower standard of emission control than official taxis, the likes of Uber may induce a shift from mass-transit transport – buses, trams, tubes and trains – that has lower pollution costs.

Then there are safety concerns. If Uber and others allow their 'independent contractors' to drive as much as they wish, some may drive more hours than are safe. Limiting hours may not solve that problem if drivers survive by combining driving with a 'day job'. Of course, for the brokers the more fares taken the better; they should be obliged to bear at least some of the costs of accidents.

Such issues have yet to be considered by politicians. But the systemic point is that incomes from labour and work are dropping for most people in and around the precariat, while rental income is mounting fast. And so we come to the fifth lie of rentier capitalism, the claim that work is the best route out of poverty. The army of taskers and the precariat in general stand testament to that lie.

Chapter 7

THE CORRUPTION OF DEMOCRACY

There is a murkier side to the growth of rentier capitalism: the institutionalised manipulation of democracy. There are too many related developments to put them aside as marginal. This chapter risks being dismissed by critics as fanciful and exaggerated. All one can say by way of introduction is that my initial reaction to such claims was one of scepticism. Not any more.

Rentier capitalism depends on the state: not just a complicit government, but a set of institutions that shape processes and outcomes, with people who act as its servants. At present, a tiny minority are thriving, while millions are struggling with stagnant incomes and growing insecurity. This imbalance surely would not be tolerated in a proper democracy.

The main reason for rentier capitalism gaining ground is that powerful rentiers have ways of capturing the state and commodifying politics, while politicians can use rental income to indulge in clientelistic practices that help them stay in office.[1] The rent extractors have an interest in funding pet politicians; the latter have an interest in satisfying the rentiers. The relentless rise in wealth concentration has increased the ability of the plutocracy to buy political influence and thereby further increase the concentration of economic power.[2]

The result is 'thinner' democracy, based on a disengaged citizenry, a decline in voting, collapsing political party membership and increasing domination by a global plutocracy. This chapter considers the reasons for political disengagement, which is breeding a weary cynicism that must be overcome.

Rentier capitalism is fundamentally fraudulent. The neo-liberal rhetoric has extolled the virtues of free markets. Yet neo-liberals have constructed the most unfree market system imaginable. How did they get away with it?

Politically, they have been helped by a supine end-of-era social democratic rump that failed to mount a constructive critique of globalisation or to articulate a strategy to arrest the march of the rentiers. Social democratic and labour parties failed to respond to the neo-liberal agenda, and then had little to say in response to the financial crisis.

In the space left by the tired social democrats, the global plutocracy has captured the state and has been commodifying politics – making it part of the market economy, dominated by media experts, lobbyists and consultants – while making democracy 'thinner', in the sense that most people now regard politics as a cynical game no longer worth joining. Thus the defeat of electoral reform in the UK enabled the winning party in the 2015 general election to gain a majority in Parliament with the support of just 24.3 per cent of the electorate.

The claim of this chapter is that rentier capitalism has been entrenched by the commodification of democracy. Public opinion has been shaped by a specific ideology, aided by well-funded media and political movements representing finance. The rentier state operates by conveying the impression that, in return for putting up with grotesque inequalities, enough of the electorate will gain through tax cuts and subsidies. This is coupled with what Michael Ross called the 'repression effect': rental income allows governments to construct more repressive apparatus to control the anger of the losers and keep democratic pressure at bay.[3]

THE MONT PELERIN SOCIETY

In 1947, a small group, mostly economists but with a sprinkling of philosophers and historians, met in the Swiss resort of Mont Pèlerin, overlooking Lake Geneva, to form the Mont Pelerin Society (MPS). Pledged to promote 'free markets' and oppose state intervention, over the years they refined the ideological foundations of what is now termed 'neo-liberalism'. The MPS is still thriving, although its founders have passed into the history books.

The MPS has had a huge and continuing influence, particularly since the 1970s. Among its early members were many who went on to hold high-level political and financial positions. They included Ludwig Erhard, who became Chancellor of West Germany; Luigi Einaudi, who became President of Italy; Václav Klaus, who became Prime Minister and later President of the Czech Republic; Arthur Burns, who became chairman of the US Federal Reserve; Roger Auboin, who became general manager of the Bank for International Settlements (BIS); and Marcel van Zeeland, a senior BIS official. Charles Koch, billionaire funder of libertarian and conservative causes and Republican politicians who espouse them, has been a member since 1970.

The MPS has always had close ties to financial capital; its inaugural conference was funded by Credit Suisse. And it has always been an exclusive club of ideologues; prospective members have to be nominated by two current members, demonstrate their commitment to the society's aims and be approved by a membership committee. From the original thirty-nine members, by 2012 the membership had grown to about 700.

Four MPS economists have been particularly influential in the spread of neo-liberalism. The society's originator was Friedrich Hayek, an Austrian invited to the London School of Economics in 1931 by Lionel Robbins, another founding MPS member.[4] Hayek later became a professor at the University of Chicago. In 1974 his views won a global audience when he received the Nobel Prize for Economics from the Bank of Sweden. He later publicly defended the murderous Pinochet regime in Chile (in a letter to *The Times* and subsequently) and, while Hayek was honorary president, the MPS even organised a meeting in Viña del Mar, the Chilean resort where Pinochet's 1973 coup was planned.

Margaret Thatcher (another Pinochet supporter) had admired Hayek since her student days. When she became Conservative Party leader in 1975, in a first meeting with her shadow Cabinet, she fished out Hayek's *The Constitution of Liberty* from her bag and slammed it down on the table, saying, '*This* is what we believe!' Hayek's views included hostility to the public sector, state-based social protection and progressive tax, which he called unjust and oppressive. In 1984, Thatcher arranged for Hayek to be given the rarely awarded Order of the Companion of Honour by the Queen. Meanwhile, Ronald Reagan listed Hayek as one of the three people who had most influenced him and invited him to the White House.

In 1991, George H. W. Bush awarded him the US Presidential Medal of Freedom. Truly, a prophet honoured in his lifetime.

The second highly influential MPS member, possibly even more so than Hayek, was Milton Friedman, who had been the youngest inaugural member of the society in 1947. Associated with monetarism – and with supporting Pinochet, Thatcher and Reagan – in 1976 he too went on to receive a Nobel Prize for Economics. He and Hayek were two of the eight original members who received the prize, the others being George Stigler, James Buchanan, Maurice Allais, Ronald Coase, Gary Becker and Vernon Smith.

The third influential economist was Ludwig von Mises, proponent of the nineteenth-century Austrian school of economics, which shaped neo-liberalism. One of its tenets was that value could be measured only by the market. So something without 'exchange value' had no value at all. This helps explain the contempt of neo-liberals for preserving the commons and protecting the environment. What is the value of a public park if it is never intended for sale? Dismissal of the value of the commons is part of the neo-liberal framing of a market society. At that first meeting of the MPS in 1947, von Mises stomped out of a session on income distribution, shouting, 'You are all a bunch of socialists!'

The fourth name, Arnold Harberger, also a University of Chicago professor, is less well known outside the world of economics, but his baneful influence should not be forgotten. In 1999, he boasted:

I think my number of ministers [of finance] is now crossing twenty-five, and I know my number of central bank presidents has already crossed a dozen. Right now the central bank presidents of Chile, Argentina and Israel were my students, and the immediate former central bank presidents in Argentina, Chile and Costa Rica were also my students.[5]

Many of his former students were in prominent positions in the lead-up to the financial crash in 2008, and by the time he spoke to the MPS conference in Lima in 2015 he could doubtless have embellished his boast. He and Friedman groomed Chile's 'Chicago boys' to help Pinochet put their neo-liberal model into effect after the coup. With Hayek and von Mises, they forged what became the hegemonic doctrine, known colloquially as the Chicago school of law and economics.

No fewer than seventeen winners of the Nobel Prize for Economics between 1980 and 2008 were from the University of Chicago or were educated there. The academic discipline of 'economics' became a creature of an ideological paradigm.[6] 'Business schools' partially displaced economics departments and critics of neo-liberalism found themselves disenfranchised. The pluralism that had characterised economics faculties was jettisoned in most universities around the world. Leading economics journals became bastions of the new orthodoxy; only academics publishing in those journals could expect tenure and promotion.

Encouraged by the MPS, some of the world's most powerful financiers and plutocrats have poured vast amounts of money into so-called 'think tanks' intended to spread libertarian and neo-liberal views. They include the Heritage Foundation, the Hoover Institution, the American Enterprise Institute and the Cato Institute in the USA, the Institute of Economic Affairs, the Centre for Policy Studies, the Adam Smith Institute and Civitas in the UK and the Australian Centre for Independent Studies in Sydney, set up by climate-change denier Maurice Newman. The names give the impression they are politically neutral and 'scientific'.

The most successful umbrella for such institutes has been the Atlas Network, founded in 1981 by Sir Antony Fisher, an ardent Hayek disciple. He had set up the Institute of Economic Affairs in 1955 and helped establish the Fraser Institute, the Manhattan Institute for Policy Research and the Pacific Research Institute in the 1970s, all promoting the MPS line. Atlas helped to finance many of the subsequent generation of think tanks, providing training and guidance. Its network now embraces more than 400 think tanks in eighty countries.

One revealing aspect of the MPS, and the think tanks funded by its members, is their role in promoting denial of human-induced climate change. Four out of five climate-change denial books have been linked to free-market think tanks through their authors or publishers.[7] Many of those think tanks are known to receive funding from fossil fuel interests; others probably have too, but refuse to reveal their donors.

Another feature of the MPS is the contradiction between its advocacy of free markets, verging on religious faith, and its defence of property rights, however acquired, which is not the same thing at all. A hereditary monarchy is hardly consistent with free markets, in which meritocracy and 'hard work' determine rewards. Yet Hayek himself, after meeting Queen Elizabeth II, gushed to friends afterwards, 'This is the happiest day of my life.'

CIRCUITS OF POWER

There has always been a connection between the Mont Pelerin Society and the Bilderberg Group, established in 1954 at a meeting in the Bilderberg hotel in the Netherlands with the aim of bolstering 'free market' capitalism. Its annual conferences in luxurious retreats bring together for private discussions the world's top 'movers and shakers', including Prime Ministers, central bank heads, chief executives of banks and multinationals, and key opinion formers in think tanks and the media. MPS members have participated in meetings of the group from the beginning.

A list of those who have attended Bilderberg events since the 1950s would read like a Who's Who of finance and politics, though participants are drawn only from Europe and North America. It in turn is linked through members in common to the US Council on Foreign Relations and to the Trilateral Commission, both based in Washington DC. Members or former members of the commission, set up by David Rockefeller and Zbigniew Brzezinski in 1973 to 'foster cooperation' between Europe, North America and the Asia-Pacific region, have taken top positions in government, industry and finance, at national and international levels, including successive heads of the World Bank.

Other circuits of the rich and powerful include the World Economic Forum in Davos and its offshoots, and a number of multinational corporations that link the elite around the world. These include BlackRock, the world's biggest asset manager, whose tentacles stretch across the globe; it has a stake in almost every listed company in the world and controls $4.5 trillion in assets, including corporate bonds, sovereign debt and commodities as well as shares. It has become a major lobbying force on both sides of the Atlantic, frequently meeting key politicians and policymakers to press its financial interests 'on behalf of investors'.

Then there is the Carlyle Group, built on military contracts, with links to the Saudi royal family.[8] Carlyle has become the world's largest private equity company, operating globally. It runs a portfolio of more than 200 companies employing over 675,000 people. The prominent politicians appointed to its board of directors have all been on the political right; they include former US President George H. W. Bush, former US Secretary of State Howard Baker, a former US Secretary of Defense, former British Prime Minister John Major, two former Thai Prime Ministers, and an ex-President of the Philippines.

Carlyle, BlackRock and other private equity firms have made clever use of structures that minimise tax obligations, notably by setting up what are called 'pass-through' entities that pass most of their earnings straight through to their owners, so avoiding corporation tax. 'Pass-through' structures now account for a quarter of all US firms. In a review of what it called the 'distorporation', *The Economist* concluded that it 'should be a matter of great debate … Alas, it is a debate the country is either blithely or studiously failing to take up.'[9] It is not that these firms are corrupt; they do not have to be. Their financial power gives them political power.

While these elite circuits do not constitute the parallel 'world government' of the conspiracy theorists, such gatherings are bound to reinforce a sort of elitist 'group-think' that supports the prevailing policy paradigm.

PARTY POLITICS: FROM VALUES TO INTERESTS

Democratic politics has also been reoriented to serve financial interests. Before considering how the global plutocracy is funding that reorientation, we should look at how political parties have evolved.

Historically, parties grew by representing specific class values. In Britain, in the eighteenth century, the Whigs evolved as radicals opposed to the Tories; in the nineteenth, the Liberals emerged in opposition to the Tories; in the twentieth, Labour displaced the Liberals. In each case, the parties rested on class foundations. The Tories represented the landed aristocracy and then business interests, a loose alliance of the affluent, whereas the Labour Party emerged to represent the industrial proletariat.

In other countries, two opposing parties typically predominated. In the USA, after a change of sides, the Democrats became the party of the left, the Republicans of the right. In Europe, the right was represented by Christian democratic parties, the left by social democratic or socialist parties. For three decades after 1945 the latter held sway and, even when conservatives or Christian democrats were in office, they operated social democratic policies.

With the onset of the Global Transformation, leftish parties went into retreat. Their old class basis crumbled, in part reflecting the success of social democratic policies that had shifted more of the population into middle-income groups, and thus to more conservative ways of thinking. The industrial proletariat, to whom labourism appealed, was rapidly shrinking.

This led to a hiatus and a long period of social democratic defeat, amid occasional victories. Eventually, the world's social democrats came up with a new vision, known as the Third Way. Early prominent adherents were Bill Clinton and Tony Blair, with British sociologist Anthony Giddens its leading theorist.[10] The Third Way accepted neo-liberal economics – free markets – but advocated policies to remedy adverse outcomes, with a focus on eradicating poverty, particularly child poverty.

Class was downplayed. Tony Blair even announced in 1999, 'The class war is over.' He and others were not opposed to inequality. 'We are intensely relaxed about people getting filthy rich,' said Peter Mandelson, New Labour's principal strategist, who served in the Blair government and became Business Secretary under Gordon Brown. He was referring largely to Labour's attitude to financiers in the City of London. Both he and Blair went on to become what they had been relaxed about.

For a few years, social democratic leaders tried to develop a Third Way agenda at a series of international meetings. Participants included Blair, Clinton, Gerhard Schröder of Germany, Dutch Prime Minister Wim Kok, Romano Prodi, President of the European Union and intermittently Prime Minister of Italy, Presidents Cardoso and Lula of Brazil, Ehud Barak of Israel, José Sócrates of Portugal and Göran Persson of Sweden, along with Juan Somavía, head of the International Labour Organization. Although the circus fizzled, the Third Way mantle was still being worn in the second decade of the twenty-first century by the likes of Matteo Renzi, Prime Minister of Italy and an admirer of Blair, and Manuel Valls, socialist Prime Minister of France.

To critics, it looked like talking left but walking right; it was mostly platitudinous. When New Labour left office after thirteen years, inequality was greater than when they entered it. It was a similar story elsewhere, for Third Wayers did nothing to halt the growth of rentier capitalism or the hegemony of finance. Indeed, the first significant act of the Blair government was to make the Bank of England independent, abdicating democratic control and handing this important instrument of economic policy over to financiers.

New Labour distanced itself from the trade unions that represented its old class base. Like most democratic parties elsewhere, it opted for labour market flexibility, which meant rolling back the labour-based securities unions had fought for over the previous century. As Blair was preparing his last speech as Prime Minister to the Trades Union Congress in 2006, he told an aide he was not sure who would be more pleased, the audience or himself. He was jeered during the speech, unimaginable at any time in the previous 100 years.

When Margaret Thatcher was asked what she regarded as her greatest achievement, she is said to have replied: 'New Labour'. Blair and Brown openly admired her. But, soon after the end of the Labour government, commentators wondered if the Labour landslide of 1997 was analogous to the Liberal landslide of 1906, after which the Liberals dwindled into insignificance.

In the USA, Bill Clinton's Third Way variant also opted for flexible labour markets that promised growing inequality and insecurity. The defining moment came in 1996 when he signed the Personal Responsibility and Work Opportunity Reconciliation Act to fulfil his 1992 campaign pledge to 'end welfare as we know it'. Drawn up by Republicans in Congress, the Act was based on welfare reforms introduced in Wisconsin by its Republican governor and was profoundly regressive, introducing time limits for entitlement to benefits and extending workfare – forcing people into poverty-wage jobs.

Meanwhile, Robert Rubin, Clinton's Treasury Secretary, was placating the bankers and setting up mechanisms that were to lead to the sub-prime crisis. Larry Summers was Deputy Treasury Secretary when in 1998 he phoned Brooksley Born, head of the Commodity Futures Trading Commission, to tell her not to propose regulating derivatives trading. He shouted, 'I have thirteen bankers in my office, and they say if you go forward with this you will cause the worst financial crisis since World War II.'[11] She backed down, with disastrous consequences.

The Third Way was the endgame of twentieth-century social democracy; it had surrendered to finance. 'Left' parties everywhere had abandoned traditional values for a crude utilitarianism in trying to appeal to 'the middle class', the 'aspirational middle' or, in its later guise, 'the squeezed middle'. In doing so they were competing with the right, which was much more comfortable in that zone.

What has happened on the right is equally fascinating. Its old class base also weakened in the early phase of globalisation and the early stages of rentier capitalism. Deindustrialisation meant a dwindling number of industrialists to fund and mobilise support. Moreover, all across the Western world, middle-income groups seemed to be shrinking as well.

In 2004, defining middle income as between 75 per cent and 125 per cent of national median income, only in Scandinavian countries did about half the population fit, whereas in the UK and USA that middle had decreased to about a third.[12] It was to shrink almost everywhere after 2008. Since the right could not rely on the middle to win elections, it needed to appeal both to the growing upper echelons, who were gaining from finance and other sources of rental income, and to those disaffected with a moribund left.

Two developments on the right have defined the post-crisis period. First, there has been a new burst of populist right-wing parties. This has reflected both the loss of appeal of traditional labourism among the emerging social groups, notably the precariat, and the impact of the financial crisis.

As the crisis was caused by finance, political parties representing its interests might have been expected to lose support. However, research covering over 800 elections in twenty rich countries between 1870 and 2014 has found that far-right parties have usually been the main beneficiaries of financial crises.[13] The rise of the far right also reflects slow economic growth, which tends to produce fragmentation of political parties and parliaments, accentuated by financial crises.[14] Of course, fractionalisation creates scope for new movements and political realignments on the left as well as the right. But this may take time.

Second, an emboldened centre-right has moved to entrench its advantage by becoming the representative of global finance and rentier capitalism, remaking economies and societies to serve their interests. Consider how that is being done in Britain.

The Conservatives won the general election in 2015 with about 37 per cent of the votes and the support of just 24 per cent of the total electorate. This produced an absolute majority in the House of Commons. Never before had a party secured such a low vote and gained a majority. Once in office, the Conservatives announced a series of changes that would strengthen their position, starting with the redrawing of constituency boundaries. On one calculation, if Labour and the Conservatives had exactly the same number of votes, Labour would be forty-six MPs behind.[15] The government has also decided to extend the franchise to previously disenfranchised expatriates living abroad for more than fifteen years, so enlarging the elderly electorate, a major part of the Conservative support base.

Meanwhile, the voter registration system in existence since 1918, allowing one individual in each household to register all eligible voters in it, has been replaced by a system requiring every voter to register individually. This measure, the implementation of which was accelerated by the government ahead of 2016 local elections, was expected to lead to a drop of 1.9 million registered voters according to the Electoral Commission and more according to the independent Smith Institute.[16]

The newly disenfranchised consist largely of the young, particularly students, ethnic minorities and those in inner cities, all groups with an above-average tendency to vote (if they vote) for leftist parties. The move reduced the number of potential voters for the 2016 mayoral election in London by half a million, and increased the total of unregistered voters, already 8 million, to nearly 10 million – 18 per cent of the eligible British electorate.[17] The new electoral register will also be used to redraw constituency boundaries, redistributing seats away from urban areas with high proportions of private rented housing and multiple occupancy towards suburban and rural areas that favour the Conservatives.

Another measure relates to the funding of political parties. At the same time as raising the ceiling for donations to political parties, the government has limited Labour's funding base. It has required trade unions to give their members an 'opt-in' choice for political funding that was previously automatic. As critics pointed out, it did not introduce a comparable rule for corporate political donations, requiring shareholders' explicit consent to 'opt in'. And the Chancellor cut so-called 'short money' payments used to support opposition parties. Labour lost nearly £1 million annually as a result.

Other aspects of democracy have been weakened too. Workers in important public services are now barred from strike action unless this has majority support in a ballot *and* the support of at least 40 per cent of all those eligible to vote. That sets a stricter standard than politicians apply to themselves. Half the MPs elected in 2015 would not have passed the tests set for potential strikers.

Under the new law, even if enough employees vote to strike, the union must name overseers, who must register with the police, so identifying themselves for retribution. And they must give the police fourteen days' notice of exactly what actions they plan to take, or risk being taken to court. This diminishes associational freedom. To top it off, the law will allow a firm to bring in agency workers to replace strikers, so undermining the impact of the strike. This is taking sides before the rights and wrongs of a dispute are known.

The many restrictions put on the right to strike, and the dwindling share of workers in unions, have reduced the scope for industrial action to a whimper. But in any case, the precariat's main antagonist is the state rather than employers. Many in the precariat do not expect, or even want, to spend years with one employer, and thus are unlikely to be keen on costly action to obtain minor improvements in working conditions in their current workplace.

Be that as it may, it is the thinning of the democratic crust of society that should be of primary concern, epitomised above all by the commodification of party politics.

THE GAME OF PLUTOCRATS

Democracy is usually understood as a competition of political values and ideas, with informed debate preceding voting. Whatever the electoral system – 'first-past-the-post', as in Britain or the USA, or some form of proportional representation related to share of the vote – the health of democracy depends on the scope for debate based on truthful information.

Yet political campaigns are increasingly narrowing that scope, using the power of modern communications technology to manipulate public opinion with simplistic, emotive and often untruthful messages and images. One could say that this has always been the case. But it is much greater today. Those who control the means of communication can sway elections, and politicians who have the most funds at their disposal can deploy the money to influence minds, set the agenda and dictate what is perceived to be reality. Never has it been truer than now that 'power is truth'.

Today's plutocracy, since it is dominated by rentiers, will favour candidates, agendas and media that promote their interests. Consider a few facts about Britain. No political party has won a general election since 1974 without the support of Rupert Murdoch and his media empire, which includes the Sky television channels, *The Sun*, Britain's biggest selling tabloid, and *The Times*, the establishment newspaper. Murdoch is not British; he does not live in Britain; several of his employees and their associates have been convicted of illegally hacking mobile phones and bribing police officers for information. Yet Murdoch is still given quasi-royal treatment by the country's politicians. Andy Coulson, former editor of the now defunct Murdoch-owned tabloid

News of the World, was hired by David Cameron, then opposition leader, as his press spokesman and went with Cameron to Downing Street, only to resign when charged (and later convicted) of phone hacking.[18] After Tony Blair became Labour leader in 1994, he travelled halfway round the world to Australia to assure Rupert Murdoch that Labour would be no threat to his interests.

In the USA, plutocratic influence over politics is exemplified by two sons of a billionaire who made his early wealth from building oil refineries in the Soviet Union and Nazi Germany.[19] In the mid-term elections in 2014, the Koch brothers poured over $300 million into the coffers of right-wing candidates. Nine in ten of their funded candidates won. In 2015, the brothers pledged to give $900 million to conservative causes in the 2016 elections, a third of this intended for the race for the White House.

A pragmatic claim in favour of electoral democracy is that citizens should be able to decide how the money they pay in taxes is spent. Of course, some citizens are not taxpayers because their incomes are below the tax threshold. And some are denied the right to vote, such as prisoners in the USA, Britain and some other countries. But a principle derived from Magna Carta is 'no taxation without representation', as the Boston Tea Party slogan went. Now, we have a modern inversion – representation without taxation.

The USA has again led the way. One means by which the plutocracy has dominated US politics is through the establishment of charitable foundations, now numbering over 100,000, that can channel untaxed money into political campaigns with minimal scrutiny.

Even more momentously, in 2010 the US Supreme Court, in

a controversial case known as Citizens United, ruled that non-persons have free-speech rights, removing restrictions on election spending by corporations and other organisations. This has led to an explosion of spending in support of political candidates by corporate-funded Political Action Committees (PACs). Citizens United, which brought the case, is a PAC funded by the Koch brothers, with the stated goals of 'limited government, freedom of enterprise, strong families, and national sovereignty and security'.

This undemocratic development has crystallised the commodification of politics. The situation in the UK has not gone as far, yet. However, Conservative Party campaigns are being funded by plutocrats and multinational financial and other corporations, most of which pay little or no tax in Britain. Before the 2015 general election, the annual Black and White Ball to raise funds for the Conservatives was organised by the wife of a hedge fund manager, described by the *Financial Times* as an 'unassuming master of the universe'. The fund, Caxton Associates, is registered in the US tax haven of Delaware.[20]

The 2016 event was sponsored by Shore Capital, an investment bank registered in the tax haven of Guernsey. The wife of its chairman, who has donated £500,000 to the Conservatives, also helped organise previous balls. In 2014, the ball was attended by guests with estimated wealth totalling over £22 billion. By 2015, twenty-seven of the fifty-nine wealthiest hedge fund managers on the *Sunday Times* Rich List had donated a total of over £19 million to the Conservatives. Michael Farmer, a hedge fund manager who has given over £6.5 million, was made co-treasurer of the party and given a peerage.[21]

Even more disquieting is the growing financial role of foreign plutocrats, often with questionable backgrounds. In one small but symbolic example, at the Conservatives 2014 summer fund-raising ball the wife of Putin's ex-deputy finance minister, Vladimir Chernukhin, successfully bid £160,000 for a tennis match with David Cameron and then London Mayor Boris Johnson, and the auctioneer threw in the party co-chair as ball boy.

The Conservative Party has also set up a Leader's Group of donors who give at least £50,000 a year, enabling an international super-rich group of financiers and industrialists to have regular dinners with the Prime Minister and the Chancellor. Members have acknowledged that policies are discussed and developed at these gatherings.

This is political funding by and for an elite, denying the roughly equal access to funds that is needed for a fair democracy. The scope for corruption, overt or tacit, is clear. In 2013, after receiving millions in donations from hedge fund managers, the Chancellor scrapped a stamp duty reserve tax on investment funds which cut the taxes paid by hedge funds by an estimated £147 million. Similarly, attendance at dinners of the Leader's Group by heads of companies involved in North Sea oil was followed by new tax cuts and subsidies for the sector.

'GOLDMANSACHISM'

The financial crash that threatened the global economy in 2007–08 was due largely to recklessness by financiers in the big financial institutions. Yet executives of those firms continue to move into senior government positions that make economic policy nationally and internationally. Many of the top spots have been taken by people from just one Wall Street institution, investment bank Goldman Sachs, once dubbed by *Rolling Stone* magazine 'the vampire squid'.[22]

These unelected technocrats are running the global economy. Mario Draghi, ex-Goldman Sachs and president of the European Central Bank, instituted the policy of quantitative easing that has enriched the rentiers and has called for more powers for the un-elected ECB to force countries to undertake structural reforms in return for aid. He can act without having to obtain democratic consent. Indeed, according to polls, the country whose popula-tion was required to contribute most to QE, Germany, was vehe-mently opposed to the policy. Whether his critics were correct or not, this illustrates how undemocratic European economic policy has become. The proposed creation of a Eurozone finance minis-try, which the ECB supports, would make things worse.[23]

In the mid-1990s, Mario Monti, ex-Goldman Sachs, became an unelected EU Commissioner responsible for the internal market and then competition policy; he subsequently became the unelected Prime Minister of Italy. When eventually he had to go before the Italian electorate, he received a derisory vote.

In the USA, a series of Goldman Sachs executives moved into top government posts. Robert Rubin, Treasury Secretary between 1995 and 1999, was described by Bill Clinton as 'the greatest Secretary of the Treasury since Alexander Hamilton'. After the 2008 crash, Clinton admitted Rubin had been wrong in recom-mending against regulating derivatives, a factor in the crash, and also a major source of income for Goldman Sachs.[24]

In 2006, Henry Paulson, Goldman Sachs's CEO, was appointed

Treasury Secretary. In 2007, he described the US economy as 'very healthy', and in July 2008 said the USA had a 'safe banking system'. However, in a speech that November, he said:

> We are working through a severe financial crisis caused by many factors, including government inaction and mistaken actions, outdated US and global financial regulatory systems, and by the excessive risk-taking of financial institutions. This combination of factors led to a critical stage this fall when the entire US financial system was at risk. This should never happen again. The United States must lead global financial reform efforts, and we must start by getting our own house in order.

In short, the former CEO of Goldman Sachs, who was in charge of economic policy, had been spectacularly wrong. But he was not required to resign; he stayed in office until 2009.

The Canadian Governor of the Bank of England, Mark Carney, was also previously employed by Goldman Sachs. William Dudley, chair of the Federal Reserve Bank of New York, is another Goldman Sachs alumnus. In Britain, Jim O'Neill, former Goldman Sachs chief economist, was ennobled and made a Treasury minister in 2015. O'Neill predicted before the financial crash that millions were about to enter the world's affluent middle class. Months later, millions more had joined the precariat instead, many with unsustainable debt.

Goldman Sachs represents an interest – finance capital. Those trained and working in it espouse and serve that interest. And while it appears omnipresent in global economic policymaking, other financial institutions also have alumni in key positions. In

2015, French President François Hollande nominated François Villeroy de Galhau, a former executive of commercial bank BNP Paribas, as governor of France's central bank. Nearly 150 of France's most distinguished economists issued a public protest, arguing that 'grave conflicts of interest' cast doubt on his ability to act 'with full independence'. He was appointed nevertheless.

Goldman Sachs and other financial firms were the main beneficiaries of the re-privatisation of Lloyds Bank that the British government had rescued after the crash. They have also been main beneficiaries of bank bailouts and quantitative easing policies, often devised by their own people inside and outside government and central banks.

This inevitably leads to questionable behaviour. In the midst of the 2008 crisis, Goldman Sachs and Morgan Stanley, major broker-dealers, were allowed to become bank holding companies, giving them access to government liquidity to keep them afloat. It was later revealed that Goldman Sachs had drafted a proposed press release to be put out by the New York Federal Reserve, Wall Street's bank regulator.[25] Although the Goldman draft was never released, the episode indicated the unhealthy relationship between regulator and regulated.

In 2014, a disgruntled staffer leaked records showing that the New York Fed had been remarkably lenient in investigating a dubious transaction by Goldman Sachs involving the merger of two oil companies, in one of which the bank had a financial interest (and a Goldman banker had a personal stake). Another staffer revealed that a Fed official had passed confidential information to a banker in the firm.

Wall Street aspirants allegedly take a job at the Fed in the hope of moving later to the private sector, where the pay is higher than the paltry $225,000 they receive at the Fed. The *Financial Times* identified at least forty profiles on the LinkedIn professional network that list both the New York Fed and Goldman Sachs on their resumes. The revolving door of finance and government, particularly involving a single investment bank, is just one aspect of the hegemony of financial capital in policymaking. Thus Hillary Clinton was dogged throughout her presidential campaign by accusations that she would be soft on the banks, after it emerged that she had been paid $600,000 by Goldman Sachs for 'speaking fees'.

'POWER IS TRUTH': THE WITHERING OF CIVICS, THE POWER OF METAPHOR

It may seem a long way from the world of financial political manipulation to education, but the links between the rentier economy and education, and the loss of respect for the enlightenment values of education, should be raising more concern.

In a telling British example, in 2007 the *Financial Times* sent a prominent correspondent to visit a state secondary school in Tower Hamlets, in London's East End, one of hundreds of schools encouraged by New Labour to form 'school–business partnerships'. This school had formed a partnership with an American investment bank; a bank executive chaired the school's governing body and bank staff helped in classes and mentored pupils. The headmistress claimed that for a school–business partnership to work, it was necessary to have a 'shared culture'. The correspondent was so moved by the school's ethos that he broke down in tears, or so he claimed.[26] A few months later, that bank went spectacularly bankrupt after gambling with the money of millions of people, precipitating the world's financial crash and ruining many lives. The name of the bank? Lehman Brothers.

This type of partnership is just one way in which state educational systems are being used to promote an ideology rather than critical social thinking. Across the world, schooling and university learning is being commodified; increasingly, the main preoccupation is preparation for obtaining jobs and earning money. At university level, the shift from government grants to student loans has further pressured students to focus on the income-earning potential of the courses they choose.

One outcome has been the marginalisation of cultural, artistic and philosophical learning. Many students emerge from formal education with scant knowledge of public policy, civics, history, culture and art. They are not so much un-educated as dis-educated, more easily influenced by the glib and the superficial. That increases the potential power of the media and of charismatic politicians armed with well-honed phrases and images.

Presentation of news and public issues in the mainstream press, television and radio has increasingly become 'infotainment'. Commercial broadcasters tilt current affairs coverage to reflect and amplify the views and prejudices of their owners, or of a target political or social group, as Fox News and right-wing talk radio do in appealing to conservatives and evangelicals in the USA. Online, news is filtered so that people with particular views or orientations can receive only stories supportive of those views. Amazon, Facebook, Google and others use browsing history to identify users' preferences and give them 'what they want' to read, see and hear, so opposing views go unseen and prejudices are entrenched.

Politicians have always used similes and metaphors to attract electors. But modern communications and lack of reasoned debate make simple messages more powerful today. A tweet that goes viral can be based on a lie but be powerfully effective. In a single week of campaigning in the primaries to become the Republican nominee for US president, Donald Trump (slogan: 'Make America Great Again') averaged one 'misstatement' every five minutes, according to calculations by *Politico* magazine, which chronicled his stump speeches and press conferences.[27]

British readers may recall Conservative billboards before the 2015 general election showing a miniaturised Ed Miliband, the Labour Party leader, pasted in the jacket pocket of the leader of the Scottish National Party. There was no evidence that Miliband was 'in the pocket' of the SNP; indeed, his party was fighting it in Scotland (a battle it lost dismally, emerging with just one MP out of fifty-nine) and Miliband had opposed its bid for independence during the 2014 referendum campaign.

As a hired strategist gleefully claimed afterwards, the misleading advert helped the Conservatives win. It symbolised the state of democratic politics. Large amounts of money went on a slick advertising campaign that was about images and metaphors, not policies and arguments for and against them.

POLITICAL CONSULTANTS: WIZARDS AND SNAKE-OIL SALESMEN

These days, elections are increasingly run by consultancy firms using sophisticated selling techniques. The more those techniques are refined, the more democracy is commodified and the ethos of democracy as traditionally understood denied. Political consultancy has become a multinational industry. There is an International Association of Political Consultants, as well as European, British and American Associations.

When Australian Lynton Crosby was hired to sell the Conservatives to the British electorate, four features stood out. He was not British, was paid a huge sum, had previously been a lobbyist for the tobacco industry and was able to insist on 'complete authority' over the campaign. What does that say about the state of *British* democracy?

Crosby has been successful with right-wing campaigns. Americans David Axelrod and Jim Messina have been more eclectic, selling their services to various politicians, including Barack Obama. In 2010, Axelrod was paid handsomely to advise Yulia Tymoshenko in her unsuccessful bid for the presidency of Ukraine. She ended up in jail after losing to Viktor Yanukovych, a convicted thug, who had languished in the polls until another American, Republican Party strategist Paul Manafort (later to be employed by Donald Trump), was hired by his oligarch backers. Yanukovych was stopped from making speeches or appearing on television. He won, only to be chased out of the country for corruption in 2014.

Axelrod subsequently advised Mario Monti in his failed attempt to be elected Prime Minister of Italy; Monti gained 10.5 per cent of the vote with his paid help. In 2014, Axelrod was hired by Ed Miliband as strategist for Labour's ill-fated campaign. Paid £225,000, he visited London three times, misspelled Miliband's name in a tweet and advised him to 'follow his North star', whatever that meant.

Meanwhile, Jim Messina was hired by the Conservatives to work with Crosby and his Australian sidekick, Mark Textor. According to the Electoral Commission, Messina's firm was paid £370,000. Crosby's firm was paid £2.4 million and Crosby was knighted in the 2016 New Year's honours. Thus the election campaign was orchestrated by a bunch of foreign mercenaries.

Messina went back to Washington DC to work on Hillary Clinton's presidential bid, only to be hired again in Britain, this time by the Remain camp for the June 2016 referendum on EU membership. Meanwhile, the Leave campaign hired another American advisor, Gerry Gunster, a veteran organiser of US ballot wins, including successful moves to block local taxes on sugary drinks. Politics has been commodified, with foreign salesmen shaping the products and competing to sell them.

In addition to the use of political strategists, all three main British parties have received pro bono consultancy services, including staff secondments, from multinational consultancies, notably PwC and KPMG. While the consultancies insist they do not draft policy, this assistance clearly benefits them (and their clients) in terms of policy information and networking.

LOBBYISTS AS LEECHES

There have always been shadowy characters trying to persuade politicians that their interest is the public's interest. But, in recent years, lobbying has become a huge and profitable industry. Multinational corporations have devoted a vast amount of money to the dark arts of lobbying. In 2012, American corporations accounted for over three-quarters of the $3.3 billion officially spent on lobbying in Washington DC.[28]

That is an underestimate; it does not include company employees in 'corporate communications' or 'government relations', whose job consists of lobbying for policies that favour the corporation and its commercial interests. Companies also use professional lobbying firms and fund academics willing to provide supposedly independent legitimation for their claims.

The business of lobbying is about increasing income and guarding one's patch; it has little to do with expanding production.[29] Many lobbyists can boast that they have crafted legislation, often to gain extra rental income for their industry or corporation. In 2013, it was discovered that a Congressional Bill to regulate the financial sector was drafted by Citicorp lobbyists.[30] Lee Drutman found that the more companies lobbied, the lower the tax rate they ended up paying.[31]

Of course, this subversion of democratic politics is not confined to America. According to the Corporate Europe Observatory, there are at least 30,000 lobbyists in Brussels, nearly matching the number of European Commission staff. These lobbyists, mostly representing corporate interests, with huge budgets, influence by some estimates three-quarters of EU legislation.[32] They fill a void of political engagement by ordinary Europeans. And it is striking that not only is genuine civil society underrepresented, but American firms are much more prominent than European ones.

Rentiers tend to mount more determined lobbying campaigns than their opponents, since they have individually more to gain or lose. Losers from strengthened intellectual property 'rights', for example, may not understand what is involved and the individual loss may be small or unknown. The corporations that gain from patents and brands have the upper hand because the stakes are so much greater.

Corporations and the wealthy also have more means of lobbying. In the UK, making matters even more one-sided, legislation in 2014 severely restricted the lobbying ability of non-governmental organisations, charities and trade unions, but not corporations. The Lobbying Act blocks them from spending more than £20,000 (£10,000 in Wales, Scotland and Northern Ireland) during an election campaign on issues that might affect the outcome. This restricts their ability to speak out on policy ahead of elections – for instance, to oppose the plan to repeal Britain's Human Rights Act.

Meanwhile, companies can pay cash for access to senior politicians. There is now a 'business day' at the annual Conservative Party conference when lobbyists and corporate executives can pay £2,500 to have private conversations with ministers, including those dealing with financial or procurement issues. Labour and the Liberal Democrats hold similar events, although they charge half as much and cannot offer ministers in office. This is yet another example of commercialised democracy.

The term 'crony capitalism' describes the blending of commercial interests with political power. The transition of party donors into senior government posts is a classic example. The many dubious cases in Britain include John Nash, a venture capitalist with commercial interests in education and healthcare (and a board member of the right-wing think tank Centre for Policy Studies). Having donated generously to the Conservatives, he was given a peerage and appointed Schools Minister in 2013. It would be hard to pretend there is no conflict of interest. Similarly, Lord Sainsbury, former chair of the eponymous supermarket chain, who has donated millions of pounds to the Labour Party, was appointed Science Minister in the New Labour government. These are just two examples of crony capitalism.

PRIVATISATION AND POLITICAL REVOLVING DOORS

Privatisation of public services is rife with potential for corruption and rent seeking. Successive governments have allowed ministers and advisors to move between political posts and private firms gaining from government policies. Britain's National Health Service (NHS) exemplifies this revolving door, although it is by no means unique.

Although NHS privatisation began under Margaret Thatcher, the decisive changes were made by the Blair government while Alan Milburn was Secretary of State for Health. Milburn and his then advisor, Simon Stevens, co-authored NHS Plan 2000, the reform that ushered in market-style commissioning, the contracting out of services by NHS hospitals in England and an expansion of the disastrous Private Finance Initiative described in Chapter 5.

In 2001, Stevens became Blair's personal advisor on healthcare and in 2004 he moved from his Downing Street job to become an executive in UnitedHealth Group, the USA's largest healthcare insurer and a provider of private health services. UnitedHealth had recently won its first NHS contract; it subsequently became one of the biggest suppliers of back-office services to NHS hospitals and family doctors. In 2014, the coalition government appointed Stevens to run NHS England, by then in the throes of a fresh round of privatisation initiated by Andrew Lansley, Health Secretary between 2010 and 2012.

While Stevens was lobbying for privatised health services at UnitedHealth, the firm was the subject of a class action lawsuit brought by the American Medical Association for underpaying doctors and overcharging patients; it subsequently paid $350 million to settle the case. In 2006, the US Securities and Exchange Commission pursued UnitedHealth's chief executive for illegal backdating of stock options, as a result of which he was forced to resign and repay $468 million in partial settlement. Nevertheless, the firm paid him a 'golden handshake' of nearly $1 billion, the largest in US corporate history. More recently, Optum, a subsidiary of UnitedHealth, has been accused by the US government of claiming for looking after people in hospices who were not terminally ill.

In 2015, NHS England announced a new list of approved private suppliers, a list dominated by outsourcing giant Capita; the 'big four' management consultants PwC, Ernst and Young, McKinsey and KPMG; and Optum. They all became members of the Commissioning Support Industry Group, described as 'a low-profile body that affords them regular access to senior NHS officials overseeing the creation of the new market in commissioning services'. Capita won a four-year contract from NHS England worth £1 billion to be the sole provider of administrative services for GPs, opticians and dentists, even though it had previously failed to deliver adequate services to some local NHS trusts.[33]

There is no suggestion that Stevens was involved in any of the illegal activities that have dogged UnitedHealth, but he nevertheless stayed loyally employed at vice-president level during and after the scandals. When appointed NHS chief, he had substantial shares in UnitedHealth; it was not unreasonable to question the propriety of his appointment.[34]

Now consider two health ministers, Alan Milburn (Labour) and Andrew Lansley (Conservative). As Health Secretary, Milburn extended NHS privatisation and, after he left office, both his private secretary and his media advisor went to big jobs in UnitedHealth. Milburn himself became advisor to Bridgepoint Capital, a venture capital company that finances private firms supplying services to the NHS.

In 2013, PwC, the world's biggest accountancy and consultancy firm, hired Milburn to chair its UK Health Industry Oversight Board, whose aim is to expand PwC's lucrative NHS consultancy business.[35] Clearly, the involvement of PwC and other consultancies opens the way for political influence by their other clients interested in NHS contracts of all kinds, from data collection to insurance. And there are conflicts of interest. In 2013, two ex-PwC employees were among the seven directors of Monitor, the health services regulator; the previous year, Monitor paid £3 million for PwC services. PwC, like other accountancy firms, also advises clients, including healthcare companies, on tax-avoidance strategies.

So much for Milburn. Andrew Lansley, Health Secretary from 2010 to 2012, accelerated NHS privatisation with the Health and Social Care Act 2012. He left Parliament in 2015, was made a life peer in the dissolution honours and has since taken advisory roles with private companies doing business with the NHS. These roles include advising corporate clients of US-based management consultancy Bain & Company on 'innovation in healthcare';

advising Swiss pharmaceutical firm Roche, a beneficiary of the cancer drugs fund Lansley set up in 2010 to pay for medicines considered too expensive by the NHS; and advising US private equity giant Blackstone, with $91 billion under management, on investing in the health sector.[36] Clearly underemployed, he also works for his wife's public relations firm.

As Health Secretary, Lansley privatised the NHS helpline, renamed NHS 111, which was put out to contract. It has been subject to a deluge of criticism for poor delivery. The firm winning most NHS 111 contracts, Harmoni, was bought by Care UK, whose former chairman, John Nash, made substantial donations to the Conservatives and to Lansley's personal office when he was shadow Health Secretary.[37] Care UK's owner is Bridgepoint Capital, which employs Alan Milburn; its director of healthcare is Jim Easton, a former member of the NHS National Commissioning Board, now called NHS England, which awarded NHS 111 contracts.

There have been other examples of revolving doors linked to the continuing privatisation of public services. One New Labour minister for defence procurement went on to join the board of a major defence contractor. Other former ministers have joined banks and educational firms profiting from contracts with the public sector. Even if the individuals concerned are not corrupt, this is institutional corruption.

COMMODIFICATION OF THE MEDIA

It is important for democracy for a broad cross-section of views to be represented in newspapers, TV and radio. We routinely condemn countries in which the rulers allow only their opinions to be transmitted. Is the current state of affairs in 'free market' societies much better? In the USA, just six corporations own 90 per cent of the media.[38]

If most of the media are owned by corporations and plutocrats, is it likely that a balanced plurality of views will be presented? While media magnates have existed since the birth of newspapers, the twentieth century saw a flourishing of independent print journalism and the creation of public broadcasters with, in the BBC's case, a mandate of political impartiality. However, as noted earlier, the BBC is under attack, while the ideological lopsidedness of the privately owned media is now extreme. After the election in 2015, the Chancellor met Rupert Murdoch twice 'off the record' just before cutting the BBC's funding by forcing it to bear the cost of free TV licences for over-75s; Treasury officials met senior executives from Murdoch's company four times.[39] Through 21st Century Fox, Murdoch has a controlling stake in Sky UK, the satellite broadcaster, which would benefit from a weakened BBC.

Murdoch, an Australian-born naturalised American, has never hidden his intention to influence British politics. When Labour leader Neil Kinnock lost the general election in April 1992, the now notorious headline in *The Sun* was 'It's The Sun wot won it'; the newspaper had run relentless attacks on Kinnock and the Labour Party, culminating in an equally famous headline on election day itself: 'If Kinnock wins today will the last person to leave Britain please turn out the lights.'

Viscount Rothermere owns the *Daily Mail*, the *Mail on Sunday*, the London free newspaper *Metro*, many regional newspapers and a chunk of ITN (Independent Television News). A billionaire who inherited his wealth, he has 'non-dom' tax status and owns his media business through a complex structure of offshore holdings and trusts that has enabled him to pay almost no UK tax on his income, investments or wealth. He is a keen supporter of the Conservatives. His great-grandfather, who set up the *Daily Mail* in 1896, was made the first Viscount; he used the newspaper to support fascism in the 1920s and 1930s, and in 1939 wrote a letter congratulating Hitler, whom he had met, on his invasion of Czechoslovakia.

The Barclay brothers, billionaire supporters of the Conservatives, own the *Daily Telegraph*, *Sunday Telegraph* and *Tatler* magazine. Another media baron is Russian-born Evgeny Lebedev, owner of *The Independent* and the London *Evening Standard*. His wealth comes from his father and co-owner, a former KGB agent turned banker dubbed 'The spy who came in for the gold', who did remarkably well out of the collapse of the Soviet Union.

These gentlemen dominating the media hardly represent ordinary British citizens. The wealth of Rothermere and Lebedev is not remotely due to 'hard work' in 'free markets'. National newspapers owned by trusts and public companies, which include *The Guardian*, *The Observer* and the *Daily Mirror*, have a smaller circulation and less ability to survive losses. And there is no counterweight to Murdoch's Sky. Thus, the question should be whether the commercialised media distort democracy. For example, take coverage of three political issues – climate change, welfare and migration.

Even though there is a consensus among climate scientists that human activities are changing the climate to a dangerous degree, the *Mail*, *Express*, *Times*, *Sun* and *Telegraph* titles all continue to run opinion columns and leaders by sceptics, who are mainly on the political right. US media are worse culprits; even liberal newspapers interpret 'balanced' coverage as requiring reporting of, thus giving respectability to, the views of climate change deniers.

Similarly, for years, the right-wing media have given prominence to stories about migrants, using terms like 'invasion', 'flood' and 'hordes'. This has led to people vastly overestimating the share of the migrant population in Britain, which feeds a right-wing political agenda, further exacerbated by highlighting examples (often exaggerated for effect) of migrant involvement in crime, welfare abuse or bad behaviour. 'Afghan couple who have nine children and receive £5,000 a month in benefits have asked for free IVF treatment after arriving in Austria (and the wife is 44)' ran a typical headline designed to raise readers' hackles on MailOnline, the most viewed English-language news site in the world.[40]

More generally, the right-wing media seize on stories of welfare abuse, again giving the impression that abuse is extensive. Hard evidence shows that fraud is minuscule. But many voters have been convinced that it is a deep-seated problem, again playing to a right-wing narrative. In late 2015, Adam Perkins, a lecturer in neurobiology at King's College London, published a book claiming that state benefits made generations dependent and workshy.[41] Other academics pointed to the lack of evidence to back his claim (and the existence of other studies showing no widespread dependency). Still, the book was seized upon by the popular press. The *Daily Star*, a downmarket tabloid that is part of the Express stable owned by billionaire Richard Desmond, headlined its story: 'Benefits turns [*sic*] slobs into thugs claims new book', adding, 'Britain's benefits culture has turned generations into workshy and dysfunctional slobs.'

If most of the media are controlled by an elite, if they are linked to a dominant political party and set of interests, if that party is funded by the plutocracy and if lobbyists are well-funded foot soldiers for the same interests, we need to ask how political change can be brought about.

CONCLUSION

With the mainstream media controlled by rentiers and their representatives, with political parties unduly influenced by them and with the rife indulgence in what has been called agnotology (the deliberate fostering of ignorance or doubt), the widespread disillusionment with conventional politics should not be surprising. One symptom of the malaise was the political emergence of Donald Trump, a caricature of a 21st-century populist, playing on prejudice, offering superficial analysis and a simplistic set of policies, yet still able to draw the support of millions of Americans. He inherited his plutocratic status, squandered a lot of money in bad business decisions and yet rails against the elite in his pursuit of the American presidency. His type could emerge almost anywhere.

The corruption of democracy is considerable. If governments are funded by people who gain from tax havens, can we really believe decisive action will be taken to control them? The Panama Papers, leaked as this book was nearing completion, revealed that no fewer than seventy-two former or current heads of state or government had benefited from tax havens. They showed how hypocritical and complicit the political mainstream has become.

Chapter 8

RENT ASUNDER: THE PRECARIAT'S REVOLT

'Capitalism based on rent-seeking is not just unfair,
but also bad for long-term growth.'
The Economist, 15 March 2014

The Economist's liberal instincts are in this instance correct. Yet global capitalism is increasingly based on rent seeking, with minimal opposition from politicians, economists and mainstream media. And, with the laudable exception of its stance on intellectual property, *The Economist* has usually been on the side of the rent seekers and those serving their cause. Rentiers and those paid to be their servants have done very well over the past three decades. But the system is economically unjustifiable, morally unjust and inherently unstable.

Suddenly, political lethargy seems reprehensible. The inequality has become obscene; too many people are suffering from chronic insecurity. Revolt is coming, in many forms. The first round was proudly 'leaderless', as figures in the Occupy movement kept on saying. They were primitive rebels, mould-breaking in intent, but ultimately breaking nothing. The energy fizzled and eventually died. Or did it?

What started with the Arab Spring went on into the Occupy movement and its tented occupations of squares and parks in cities and towns in many countries. Those occupations brought together diverse groups. They were not in vain. Gradually, the defiant activists drifted away. But the indignation fed into more coherent, more sustainable movements, epitomised by the *indignados* and others in Italy, Greece, Spain and Portugal.

These were still the collective actions of primitive rebels, knowing what they were against but not knowing what they wanted instead. But they helped forge a common identity, producing an understanding that there were millions of people in similar circumstances, with similar needs and aspirations. This is a necessary stage in forging effective opposition to the dominant economic structures that are being supported by mainstream political parties and the institutions they serve.

By 2014, it was evident that 'days of protest' had served their purpose and were using up social energies to diminishing effect. It was also evident that the widespread refusal to engage in formal party politics and elections was just what the representatives of rentier capitalism would want. Leading social democrats, as well as their opponents, were prone to dismiss the growing precariat as 'post-political'. This was to confuse the dismissal of politicians as 'all the same' with a rejection of politics per se.

Other critics, mostly of a Marxist persuasion, dismissed the idea that a precariat could become a coherent group able to achieve political change. Reaching back to nineteenth-century ways of thinking, they envisage a socialist revolution led by a unified 'working class'. It will not happen. Those who insist on nineteenth-century solutions to 21st-century problems do progressive politics no good at all.

Inequality and insecurity are now so extreme, and so class-based, that if there is to be a counter-movement it must be led by the group – the precariat – that is most disadvantaged by rentier capitalism. A group identity must be forged and used to mobilise energies and vision or there will be no coherent movement for change. The pitchforks the plutocrats fear will not be raised in sufficient numbers to induce concessions. In the remainder of this chapter, it will be assumed that new progressive politics will emanate from the precariat.

The politics of resistance to rentier capitalism are clear. The revolt will not come from the plutocracy, the elite or the salariat. They all gain from forms of rent. Today, perhaps a third of the revenue of the German salariat comes in the form of shares and profit-related pay. It may be even more for the American salariat. Company pension funds also depend on financial investments. If the precariat's wages fall, profits and dividends are likely to rise. Thus the salariat does not have the same material interest, and it is folly to imagine a 'united working class' or that a party platform oriented to 'the middle class' will serve the aspirations of the precariat.

The 'proficians' – consultants or freelancers with technical skills, working on 'projects' under contract – also gain from subsidies, tax breaks and the like. They are unlikely to have similar material interests, and welcome rent-seeking opportunities. But with their life of insecurity, they should be sympathetic to the realities faced by the precariat. They are potential allies.

The proletariat is too enfeebled and atavistic, pining for a real or imagined past and hanging on to the labourist traditions of social democratic parties. It is easy prey for populists and neo-fascist politicians, playing on racism and xenophobia.

Only the precariat has the potential, in terms of size, growth and structured disadvantage, to articulate a progressive response to rentier capitalism and its corruption. The lumpen-precariat, the underclass, does not have the agency to act, although some in it might join protests, as they did in 2011. Literally, as beggars, they cannot afford to be choosers.

So, the revolt must be led by the precariat and those around them. But, to have a chance of success, it must have three features: a sense of unity around commonly held beliefs; a sustainable understanding of the flaws, inequities and unsustainability of existing arrangements; and a reasonably clear vision of feasible goals.

Although there are other matters on which to revolt, here we will concentrate on what is required to achieve Keynes's 'euthanasia of the rentier', in the context of an irretrievable breakdown in the twentieth-century income distribution system. Politicians should be more honest. If they believe in free markets and an open economy, as they claim, they should recognise that the Great Convergence traced in Chapter 1 will continue, that average real wages will continue to stagnate and that wages for the precariat in the industrialised world will continue to fall.

Of course, efforts should be made to raise productivity and skills. But no individual country can presume to do better than others pursuing the same ends. It is disingenuous if not dishonest to urge everyone to do the same thing and imagine that all will gain.

Those benefiting from rentier capitalism are likely to want to keep wages down in their own country, since they are not confronted by the Fordist dilemma. Henry Ford in the 1920s famously realised that to make profits from mass production of his little black cars, workers had to have enough money to buy them.

Today, the manufacturers or service producers wish to minimise labour costs. Their main markets are often elsewhere.

To curb the adverse distributional effects of a rentier economy, a new distribution system must be constructed in which wage earners and others receive part of the income accruing to rent and profits. Wages by themselves will not sustain living standards. In the twentieth century, it made sense to focus on wage bargaining. That will not work now. The struggle must be to build a new system. While wages will continue to stagnate, innovative ways must be found to limit and share rental income and to share profits. Otherwise inequality will continue to grow, with ugly social and political consequences.

THE JUST REVOLT

> 'The chief penalty of refusing to participate in
> politics is being ruled by someone worse.'
> Plato, *The Republic*

Protest comes in many forms. The right to associate freely has been whittled away in many countries, as has the right to strike. These forms of protest traditionally acted as safety valves for society and for the economy. Today they are enfeebled.

A challenge for the precariat is to find appropriate *forms* of organisation. What collective bodies can be vehicles for a renewal of progressive politics? Historically, the great associational – or congregational – bodies that have nurtured opposition to an oppressive, regressive state have included the churches, guilds, craft unions, industrial unions and political parties.

Churches and their non-Christian equivalents are scarcely ideal in today's more secular societies. But they could play a useful role in deflating the moralistic posturing that is used to justify the coercion and sanctions that underpin today's utilitarian politics, and in opposing the evil sects that are thriving in a world of seemingly endless war. In these respects, they could be valuable allies against the state.

Occupational guilds, which had nurtured countercultures for hundreds of years, were displaced by the unions in the nineteenth and twentieth centuries. And labour unions bulldozed the craft unions that had also stood against the market in preserving the values of work over the dictates of labour. Resurrecting occupational bodies would help in producing communities opposed to neo-liberalism and the rentier practices that it fosters. But they too could play only a secondary role.

One modern form of congregational body is the 'non-governmental organisation', the NGO. Some have subversive energy, exposing damaging trends. But while some keep progressive thinking alive, too many are co-opted and made a managerial part of the state.

As for politics, the corruption of old progressive parties due to the loss of a class base suggests three possibilities. Some hold that, as there is little difference between the main parties, we should not engage with any of them. Others believe that the best way forward is to enter existing parties and aim to change them. And others call for new parties or a realignment of party divisions.

I will consider the arguments for each option by reiterating an amicable debate held in 2015 with Polish intellectual, activist and publisher Slawomir Sierakowski of the Krytyka Polityczna (Political Critique) network.

FROM NO POLITICS TO PRECARIAT POLITICS

'Precari invisibili – Rompiamo il silenzio'*
Placard worn in Bologna's social strike, November 2014

The social strike (*sciopero sociale*) is an Italian phenomenon in which many thousands take to the streets in days of protest. It recognises that the old labour strike is ephemeral in a global economy in which the state and finance are the primary antagonists.

Antonio Gramsci's chilling aphorism that the old is dying but the new is yet to be born seems apt to the present, when the Global Transformation – the construction of a *global* market system – has broken down old systems of regulation, social protection and redistribution, but new systems have yet to be built. Five crises are rolled into one – fiscal, financial, distributional, existential and ecological. Should any of us now stand aside from engaging in the struggle for a better future?

In confronting crises, the revival of progressive politics goes through several phases. The first is when the old paradigm has collapsed as a progressive strategy. One could say it has done its work, or that its failings brought it down. Thus 'labourism', the dominant discourse of the twentieth century, was an advance on previous ways of thinking of society. But it ceased to be an attractive way of looking at the future many years ago.

Old 'left' parties have tried to appeal to what they see as the middle class. But they entered crowded territory and have been dragged to the right to compete with libertarian and

---

* 'The invisible precariat – We are breaking the silence'.

populist parties. Sierakowski argues that, as there is little difference between mainstream parties, we should abstain from politics altogether. In his view, 'social-democratic economic policy within a single state is practically impossible'.[1]

This is neither proven nor easy to define. Old social democratic policies may be inappropriate for the twenty-first century. That does not mean progressive politics are impossible. The rejectionist position risks leading to cynicism – nothing can be done, so let us do nothing. And it begs the question: what should be progressive politics today? Unless we can define what is wanted, we cannot fairly say that political action is or is not feasible.

The Third Way and New Labour did not try to confront the constraints to a progressive strategy thrown up by neoliberalism and the interests gaining from globalisation. They did not confront growing inequality and even had the temerity to boast about it, as a way of appealing to the affluent and powerful. Their agenda was not only misconceived but unsustainable, because fewer and fewer could be bothered to support them.[2]

However, if there is a perception that there is no choice – or 'the illusion of choice' – then it is up to the progressive imagination to present a new direction and strategy. Czesław Miłosz, the Polish poet and writer who won the Nobel Prize for Literature in 1980, saw even enlightened minds enslaved by 1950s communist ideology preaching that there was no alternative. Once it was clear there was one, the game was up. Neo-liberals, and the interests that thrive under rentier capitalism, also want us to think there is no alternative to existing structures and inequalities. We play into their hands if we ourselves say there are no choices and use that as a rationale for not joining political parties. We must assert that there is and always will be a realistic and desirable alternative.

Sierakowski and others believe it is impossible to transform existing parties from within. What happens to the British Labour Party will be an interesting test. Jeremy Corbyn's victory in the leadership election in September 2015, based largely on his appeal to the precariat, was mould-breaking; it put an end to New Labour as a realistic project. But infighting may dissipate energies and lead to electoral wilderness. As with all social democratic parties, Labour is trapped by its history.

Parties ossify, and once they cease to be driven by class values easily become vehicles for corruption and nepotism. For example, prominent members of Spain's Socialist Party as well as politicians from the conservative People's Party have been implicated in corruption scandals. In France, it is the same. In Britain, former Labour and Conservative ministers have also been caught in financial scandals.

The 'professional politician' has become the norm, losing touch with the values and class aspirations that drove the party in its early days. The children of one generation of leaders are groomed for succession. This has happened in American politics – think of the Bushes, Kennedys and Cuomos – and in Britain, where offspring of former senior politicians – such as Stephen Kinnock, son of Neil (former Labour leader), and Nick Hurd, son of Douglas (former Conservative Foreign Secretary) – have been slotted into safe parliamentary seats. Dynastic politics also characterised Pasok (the Panhellenic Socialist Movement) in Greece, which imploded once Syriza emerged as a credible alternative.

Sierakowski's second argument for rejecting party politics is that parties no longer encourage critical debate and that they are 'as good at dumbing down the public as are most television pro-grammes'. Yet this is a generic challenge. Our commodified edu-cational system means that even higher-level education denies many people a culturally enriching experience that stimulates critical thinking. But there is no reason why progressives cannot struggle to overcome all forms of dumbing down – in the media, political parties and education.

Political parties in Poland have suffered particularly in this regard; this can be attributed to the brevity of its democratic era and the hegemony of shock therapy in the 1990s, when, as noted ear-lier, billions of dollars and euros were showered on the country to ensure the neo-liberal model succeeded. Solidarność (Solidarity), the trade union that became a political movement that brought down the communist regime, was unable to reach the emerging precariat. Subsequently, there was little to choose between the main parties, both profoundly neo-liberal and conservative, al-though the Law and Justice Party, which won the general election in 2015, became virulently nationalistic and xenophobic.

Once parties degenerate into rent-seeking entities, they must be killed off, not resurrected. That leaves the third option, estab-lishing new parties or political realignment. This may be the most promising route for overcoming the interests and imagery of neo-liberalism. It offers the prospect of a new movement to represent the emerging groups and the enlightenment values of progres-sives through the ages, encapsulated in the great trinity of *liberté*, *egalité* and *fraternité*. Here we can incorporate the perspective of the precariat.

The emergence in 2013 of Beppe Grillo and his MoVimento

5 Stelle (M5S) in Italy was a forerunner. It briefly struck a chord with the precariat, especially when Grillo derided establishment politicians as 'dead men walking'. But its incoherent mix of populism and neo-liberalism failed to break the mould. It was followed by other movements, in the form of Sinistra, Ecologia, Libertà (SEL) in Italy, Podemos ('We can') in Spain, Syriza in Greece, and incipient parties elsewhere, such as Alternativet in Denmark, Razem in Poland and Left Bloc in Portugal. In a way, the revived Scottish nationalist and the Catalan independence movements were part of this.

In general, a progressive shift will come only after a lurch to the right by the old left results in mass desertion by its supporters and revulsion within the emerging mass class. This is what is happening. The old progressives are stuck in tired agendas, while pandering to the interests of the elite. Their vocabulary reveals little understanding of contemporary realities, including the insecurities, anxieties and aspirations of the emerging class. As the *indignados* slogan put it, 'Our dreams do not fit into your ballot box'. Or, as another put it more subversively, 'The worst thing would be to return to the old normal'.

It is true that the initial phase of reaction consists of widespread psychological detachment from party politics and a shift of energies to symbolic days of protest. These dissipate frustration but do little to advance new progressive politics. It is what happens after that phase that matters.

The precariat's mood has been one of derision towards politicians in general and mounting anger towards the plutocracy, financiers and the elite. This is not apathy. It has fed into the actions of primitive rebels. But Sierskowski has little faith in our ability to turn this into something more, claiming that 'we are reluctant to become engaged, animated, or active, feeding our reluctance with a sense of shame, both crippling and near universal [leading to] an overwhelming paralysis of action'.

Who is this 'we'? Between 2011 and 2015, there were over 800 mass demonstrations in cities around the world, more than in any comparable period in history. There is a lot of energy out there. Moreover, new parties and movements have emerged, whether we like them or not. In Spain, Podemos went in two months from non-existence to winning seven seats in the European Parliament. In the general election of December 2015, it ran the socialists close for second place and gained seventy-nine seats in Parliament. In Greece, Syriza went from nothing to becoming the government in a very short time, while in the UK general election in 2015 the Scottish National Party went from six to fifty-six MPs, winning almost all the parliamentary seats in Scotland.

Regional independence movements are commonly seen as a resurgence of nationalism, which brings a lot of baggage. But embedded in them is hostility to centres of global finance. Scottish resentment was directed most towards 'the City of London', the heart of world finance. Scotland and northern parts of England have been hardest hit by the British Disease described in Chapter 1 – the domination of politics by financial interests, leading to an overvalued exchange rate that decimates industrial production and employment.

Similarly, in Spain, Catalonian independence movements epitomise the motivation of precariat-style mobilisation, which is hostility to the most relevant centre of global finance, in their case Madrid, and a desire to recreate sustainable communities of security and creativity. It is more about an exciting vibrancy than nationalism.

Meanwhile, ominously, neo-fascist populist parties have sprung up all over Europe. That in itself should persuade others to re-engage, by supporting movements promoting reforms that would erode the populists' support base. That will mean avoiding populism and developing a transformative strategy.

Sierakowski claims there has been no political action because people have succumbed to the neo-liberal trap of 'individualisation' and because 'people will not risk their own careers if they are not sure that others will do the same'. This overlooks the fact that most in the precariat do not have careers to risk! The precariat has nothing to lose but its insecurity. Thus it can forge an identity of relative deprivation, a consciousness that historically has usually prompted collective action.

As with scientific revolutions, a new progressive movement comes only when the old paradigm has been discredited and when a new, albeit embryonic, paradigm is ready to take its place. This is where we are today. An alternative paradigm must be articulated and disseminated before success can be achieved. And the movement to achieve it must emanate from the emerging mass class, although there will be a need for cross-class alliances on specific issues.

Pierre Bourdieu, writing in 1997, doubted that the precariat could be mobilised, due to a loss of faith in a positive future. That pessimism can be attributed to the times. The 1990s saw the zenith of neo-liberalism. Old-style social democracy was dying; state socialism was discredited; the IMF and World Bank were in charge; and neo-liberals were setting the agenda almost everywhere.

The precariat was just taking shape. Its members had not

reached the crucial stage in the development of a class-for-itself, that of 'recognition', associated with mass awareness of class consciousness. That was to come after the financial crash of 2008, when governments rescued the banks, whose opportunistic profiteering had been the main cause, and when 'austerity' turned out to be a front for giving more to rentiers at the expense of everyone else. The Arab Spring and Occupy movement triggered a global realisation that 'we' were a subject, a class in the making.

This is a necessary step in the reinvention of progressive politics. It is understandable that, at such a moment, old parties are rejected as unfit for purpose. But detachment may allow the neoliberal state to recover its poise and confidence. The difference between twentieth-century social democracy and today's emerging politics is that, whereas the proletariat's primary antagonist was the employer, the precariat's is the state, representing the interests of global finance and rentiers. For the precariat, employers come and go in a global market system in which the firm is increasingly a commodity.

In any progressive movement, first comes the 'primitive rebel' phase of resisting regressive and oppressive changes. Then comes the 'recognition' phase, as more people realise they have much in common and sense they are becoming a class. Later there is a struggle for 'representation', to have their interests represented inside the institutions of the state. The final phase is a struggle for 'redistribution', to equalise access to the key assets of their society.

By 2015, the precariat was fighting for representation and was beginning the struggle for redistribution. In some countries, as mentioned earlier, representatives of the precariat have formed new parties. Although they may fail to achieve what their adherents hope, they are breaking the mould of old systems. This is a necessary condition for re-inventing the future and giving people hope of a Good Society that transcends endless consumerism and pervasive insecurity.

Disaffection with old parties is shown by the steady decline in voting, especially by youth and the precariat in general. Over a third of the US electorate does not vote in presidential elections, and in most democracies winning parties have been gaining little more than a third of the votes cast. When even flawed but well-meaning options become available, such as Bernie Sanders in the USA, a surge of enthusiasm occurs. Timid establishment types will not succeed, but bolder souls should take heart. Energies can be turned into re-engagement.

RIGHTS AS DEMANDS

'They don't call it class warfare until we fight back.'
Occupy Wall Street poster

Rights always begin as class-based demands, made against the state. They succeed in becoming rights when a sufficiently strong and committed mass of people with like-minded concerns and interests force the state to accede to them. They become rights initially as concessions to pacify the emerging class.

This is the main lesson of Magna Carta, not its specific contents, however revolutionary for the time some of them were. The Charter of Liberties, forced on King John on 15 June 1215, was a class-based set of demands for the restitution and restoration of customary rights and practices. John and his entourage had built up an oppressive system of rent extraction, encroaching on the commons and taxing the feudal nobility to fill his coffers. In the end, it induced revolt by the barons.

By the time the Charter of Liberties became Magna Carta in 1217, it had been joined by the Charter of the Forest, a set of rights for the common man and, for the first time, to a minor but significant extent, woman. Again, it was mainly about restoring customs and the commons. And again it turned demands into rights. Revolt, against encroachment by the rentier class, was the spur. Today, those who then rebelled against the state are lionised for advancing freedom and equality. Yet they did so in violation of 'the law' because they believed the rules and procedures laid down by the monarch were unjust.

We could say revolt is equally justified now. The levers of power are concentrated in the hands of a rentier minority, the structures are suffocating and a growing minority is bearing the burden of inequality without means of redress. The revolt should aim to achieve Keynes's desired 'euthanasia of the rentier', weakening mechanisms that produce rental income. But there is something more.

The failing distribution system and emerging class structure have produced inequalities of particular relevance to the precariat. A century ago, progressives linked to the proletariat hoped to gain control of the 'means of production'. Today that would excite humour and puzzlement. The means of production are not the assets over which the redistributive struggle should take place. For the precariat, the assets of most value are those essential to a decent life in modern society – income security, time, quality space, uncommodified education, financial knowledge and financial capital.[3] Policies should be judged by whether or not they would reduce the unequal distribution of these key assets.

The reforms proposed in what follows would move the economy towards a new income distribution system, starting with changes that would help achieve the euthanasia of the rentier and going on to advocate two pillars for building a distribution system that would reduce inequality and insecurity while promoting more ecologically sustainable growth.

TOWARDS THE 'EUTHANASIA OF THE RENTIER'

Recall the architecture of rentier capitalism described in Chapter 2. The legitimacy of the intellectual property system depends on striking an acceptable balance between providing incentives for innovation and ensuring public access to information and the products of research. That balance has been upended in favour of the rentier, with intellectual property now a prime source of rental income at the expense of the public interest.

The trend to ever-stronger intellectual property protection must be reversed. Patents should only be granted for significant inventions, and protection terms should be shortened. The ownership of patents granted on inventions that derive from publicly funded research should be shared with the institution concerned, which should be entitled to insist on licensing the patent to others on reasonable terms. This would improve access to new drugs that are now prohibitively expensive. Governments should make full use of the flexibilities written into the WTO's TRIPS agreement, which include compulsory licensing in the public interest. And there should be more emphasis on other ways of incentivising research and innovation, such as public prizes, public procurement practices and tax arrangements.

The copyright regime also requires tipping the balance away from the rentiers towards the public interest, by shortening protection terms (fifty years from date of creation for literary works is ample) and expanding 'fair use', 'personal use' and other exceptions. Open access – for instance through creative commons licensing – should be the norm for publicly funded work.

Similar proposals have come from several respected organisations advocating reform of the intellectual property system.[4] They would reduce but not end rent extraction from intellectual property. So this and other rental income should be subject to a levy that would go into a sovereign wealth fund, as discussed later, for distribution to all citizens.

Given the anti-free-market orientation of the intellectual property regime, it should be relatively easy to mobilise a coalition to oppose its extraordinary rent-seeking apparatus. Libertarians on the right and progressives on the left should be united in a common cause, even though they come to it from different perspectives.

The coalition should also unite against trade and investment accords, which have been vehicles for extending neo-liberal hegemony around the world, favouring rentiers of all kinds. In particular, the Investor–State Dispute Settlement process is secretive, undemocratic and inequitable. It should be radically reformed or abolished. Already some developing countries are refusing to put ISDS clauses in investment agreements. The

European Commission, faced with opposition to ISDS in the projected Transatlantic Trade and Investment Partnership with the USA, felt impelled to come up with an alternative, which was little better. The unfairness of the ISDS, and the threat it poses to public services and the commons, have mobilised popular opposition throughout Europe and North America.

More generally, there needs to be a concerted effort to end the subsidies and selective tax breaks for rentiers that are the bane of the modern state. They are regressive, distortionary, costly and inconsistent with the free markets the neo-liberals claim to support. The precariat should take the lead in mobilising opposition, with support from across the political spectrum. Every political party should pledge to promote a National Commission for the Monitoring and Elimination of Subsidies.

Finally, rentiers must be prevented from buying politicians and political parties to do their bidding. There should be tougher rules, strictly enforced, on lobbying and revolving doors. All countries should cap election spending and provide state funding for political parties that reach a threshold of support. In addition, parties should only be allowed to raise money from membership subscriptions and individual donations. Companies, institutions and other 'non-persons' should be barred from funding parties and politicians. In the USA, the Citizens United ruling must be overturned. And only individuals eligible to vote should be allowed to make political donations. Foreign oligarchs should have no role in a nation's democratic politics. That these remarkably reasonable reforms probably require a revolt merely testifies to the grim dystopia we face. The slogan everywhere should be: 'No representation without taxation!'

MAKING WORK PAY: REGULATE LABOUR BROKERS

As argued elsewhere,[5] and subject to the reforms outlined in this chapter, the labour market should be made into a 'free market', with the price – the wage – determined by bargaining and contract, according to the perceived value to the buyer and seller. However, for that to work, the bargaining positions of the parties must be roughly equal. Tax credits should be phased out, as they are distortionary and, to some extent at least, a source of rental income for employers. But they should go only when something better is introduced. Meanwhile, the trend towards workfare should be reversed. It is coercive, distorts the labour market, lowers reservation wages and is paternalistic and illiberal. Progressives must have the courage to oppose it. Similarly, the trend towards behaviour testing and sanctions against claimants distorts the labour market, is regressive and offends principles of social justice. It is class politics at its moralistic worst.

Many politicians and commentators claim to have faith in a statutory minimum wage, and in a higher variant known as the 'living wage'. While useful for setting standards, these scarcely affect the precariat. Since their introduction in Britain, average real wages have stagnated and social income has fallen; fewer workers have access to non-wage enterprise benefits or contributory state benefits, while the growth of unstable jobs and practices, such as zero-hours contracts and tasking, has increased the ratio of unpaid work to paid labour.

Predictably, the obligation to pay a 'living wage' (actually just a higher minimum) from April 2016 has led UK employers to introduce more flexible working and cut overtime, bonuses and perks, which will leave many employees little better off.[6] A higher minimum wage will also lead to more automation of service jobs, as indicated in the USA.[7] Something stronger is needed.

Wages and returns to labour are diminishing. But online labour brokers are making huge rentier incomes. Although they do not yet account for anything like a majority of labour relationships, their growth and potential for driving down wages and working conditions make it essential to give them priority attention.

What should be done? It is important to accept that the on-demand economy is here to stay; there is no going back to earlier employment relations. Unions and activists should not repeat the reaction to labour flexibility policies in the 1980s and 1990s, when unions refused to negotiate and simply resisted, eventually conceding on more unfavourable terms. Had they negotiated for a new social compact when they had sufficient strength to do so, insisting on basic security for all in return for flexibility, there would be much less insecurity for those performing labour today.

The on-demand economy requires new forms of regulation and social protection to redress the growing imbalances and inequities. These should start with something basic. Every period in which labour and work has been transformed has led to an overhaul of statistics used to represent reality. This matters, because statistics orient public debate and policy thinking. Crowd labour, new forms of labour triangulation and growth of the precariat make current official statistics even more unfit for purpose. Most taskers are neither 'employees' nor 'self-employed', while the popular term of 'freelancer' is inappropriate since they lack the freedoms associated with being an independent seller of services.

Where taskers are contractors working primarily for one

company and required to comply with its rules and standards, there is a case for calling them employees, as the California appeals court decided in the case of FedEx drivers. But any distinction between contractors and employees will be arbitrary. Instead of trying to shoehorn tasking into the dichotomous classification of contractor or employee, taskers should form a separate category.

This is one reason for strengthening taskers' collective bargaining capacities. Tasker associations should be set up, as separate entities or within occupational bodies. Certainly, the emergence of taskers will intensify friction between groups of workers; there is not and never has been a 'unified working class'. The divergence of interests is why a 'collaborative' bargaining system is needed, for bargaining between complementary or substitute occupational groups, not just between employers and employees.[8]

On one side are employers, requesters and labour brokers; on the other, employees, taskers and freelancers. Why should only employees be covered by the protections built up in the twentieth century? Anybody doing any kind of work should have the same rights and entitlements.

Online brokers avoid paying payroll taxes for taskers and do not provide non-wage benefits that employees are supposed to receive, including equipment needed to do their job, paid holidays, company pension contributions and, in the USA, medical insurance. In return for their intermediary role, the brokers typically take 20 per cent of earnings. They are free-riding on the public, since taskers fallen on hard times will need state benefits that the brokers do not pay for.

For that reason among others, there should be a levy (tax) of, say, 20 per cent of their earnings from labour broking, or a levy paid for each tasker they contract. Brokers should also provide insurance cover, including accident insurance, for taskers while on jobs contracted through their platforms. If this is a 'sharing economy', as its advocates claim, costs as well as benefits should be shared.

As an emerging 'profession', labour brokers should be registered and required to join an association that develops ethical codes and monitors their conduct. In the UK, work has started on a consumer trust mark for online platforms, including labour brokers, intended to promote good practice for handling consumer complaints. Minimum requirements will be set by the Skoll Centre for Social Entrepreneurship at Oxford University's Said Business School, working in collaboration with Sharing Economy UK. This trade body, created in March 2015 by twenty-eight online businesses, includes Airbnb, car-hire service Zipcar and cleaner-booking platform Hassle.com.

A consumer trust mark is seen by the platforms as a way of encouraging people to use their services. But if standards can be set for consumers they should also be set for the treatment of taskers. Codes of ethics and good practice should be drawn up, with tasker involvement. These should include written contracts between broker and tasker, a right for taskers to know and correct information held on them by the broker, a ban on blacklisting taskers who complain or sue for compensation, and due process restraints on use of customer ratings. Brokers should also ensure that taskers are paid promptly for contracted tasks.

One exploitative practice requires a special response. Some platforms, such as Innocentive (research problem solving for corporations) and Tongal (a video makers' network), pay modest prizes to taskers who submit commercially viable ideas. This enables firms to buy ideas at a fraction of their value as revenue-generating intellectual property. Regulations should ensure that taskers (and employees) receive a fair share of any continuing income stream from their ideas.[9]

To protect taskers, and raise their income, several other reforms are essential. Occupational licensing must be rolled back. Licensing is the form of state regulation promoted in the neoliberal era instead of guild regulation. In the USA, over 1,000 occupations are now subject to licensing, most unnecessarily. The insurance industry dominates licensing, transferring risks, uncertainty and costs onto workers, and enabling licensing boards to block or punish people, usually without due process. Labour brokers and the precariat should be united in wishing to see less licensing. It is a means of restricting the right to practise forms of work, and thus of lowering the income of many competent people, while licensing boards gain rental income by charging often steep licensing fees.

Licensing should be limited to occupations that involve externalities and dangers, as in the case of surgeons and architects. Otherwise, collective self-regulation should be revived. And there should be more reliance on accreditation, that is, membership of an association that testifies to competence or experience. Under an accreditation system, anybody can practise a particular form of work and customers can choose whether to use an accredited or non-accredited professional. For all professions, an international accreditation system should be constructed, with standardised rules.

Taskers on zero-hours contracts, on call or subject to 'flexible' schedules set by the firm should be compensated for the inconvenience and insecurity, for instance through 'stand-by bonuses' as in Germany, or given a base salary or retainer. They should also be allowed to do work for other employers. All task-ers should have the right to decline tasks demanded with less than twenty-four hours' notice, without loss of pay or opportunity, to allow them to gain more control of their lives.

Taskers should have a right to legal advice on contracts and disputes, paid partly by contributions from labour brokers. Taskers should be required to make a partial payment, to discourage frivolous actions, but access to legal advice would encourage both sides to make agreements transparent and standardised as far as possible.

To achieve these reforms will require a struggle. It will not happen otherwise. The precariat's vulnerability today is a threat to all to-morrow. When sweating spreads to taskers, the threat to wages and working conditions of those outside the precariat grows. Wages will fall drastically unless a countervailing strategy is implemented.

BUILD DEMOCRATIC SOVEREIGN WEALTH FUNDS

Now we come to the first of two pillars for a new distribution system that would also help achieve the 'euthanasia of the rentier'. This is the sovereign wealth fund, a national fund built up from the proceeds of economic activity, which is ideal for pooling and redistributing rental income. Such funds have a long pedigree, although most have been captured and distorted by elites, so far.

By 2016, there were nearly eighty state capital funds, with assets totalling $7.2 trillion, more than is managed by all the world's hedge funds and private equity funds combined. Although the majority of sovereign wealth funds have drawn on profits from oil resources, they can be fed from any source a government chooses. Typically, however, state-owned investment funds are financed by foreign earnings and they invest globally, rather than in their own country.

In most cases up to now, the funds' objectives have been determined by financiers and elites oriented to rent extraction. They are used to insulate government budgets from fluctuations, help monetary authorities manage excess liquidity, invest in infrastructure and build up national savings. But there is no need for those to be the only or even the main objectives. Considerable redistribution could be achieved by putting a share of profits and rental incomes into a fund for reducing inequality and economic insecurity. That means wresting control of these funds from the elite and instituting democratic governance.

Every country should set up a democratic sovereign capital fund, fed from a share of rental income, including at least 10 per cent of profits from exploitation of natural resources, along the lines of the Alaska Permanent Fund or the Norwegian Government Pension Fund Global (GPFG), the biggest sovereign wealth fund in the world.

In the 1970s, Britain and Norway chose different paths for North Sea oil exploration and production. Norway retained national ownership of its oil reserves, rented out its fields to the oil companies and put part of the profits into a national fund. It decided that the value of the capital should be preserved for future generations, introducing a rule allowing the government to spend no more than 4 per cent of the returns on investment each year. Another rule was that the fund could invest only in foreign assets.

Thus Norway became a rentier state, but the income was set to benefit all Norwegians, including future generations. It built in respect for the Hartwick Rule of inter-generational equity. It is also overseen by a Council of Ethics that decides whether the fund should exclude certain companies from its investments.

The Economist has described the Norwegian fund as 'perhaps the most impressive example of long-term thinking by any Western government'.[10] Today, every Norwegian is technically a krone millionaire, which in plain English is economically secure. By contrast, Britain opted for privatisation of its North Sea oil reserves. It distributed the immediate gains in tax cuts for the rich and in welfare payments arising from high unemployment linked to the strong currency and the resultant deindustrialisation then devastating British manufacturing.

According to PricewaterhouseCoopers, had the UK used tax receipts from its oil and gas fields to build up a wealth fund, it could now have a fund with £450 billion of assets, bigger than those of Kuwait, Qatar and Russia combined.[11] The ultimate irony is that privatisation has enabled Chinese state enterprises to own a significant stake in UK oil fields, channelling profits to a nominally communist superpower. One doubts that is what Thatcher and Nigel Lawson, her Chancellor, intended. But the outcome stemmed from their ideological decision.

That error should not be repeated with fracking – the extraction of gas and oil from shale rock. These resources belong to the people. If fracking is permitted to continue, part of those profits should go into a sovereign wealth fund.

Contributions from exploitation of a country's natural resources should be supplemented by a levy on all other forms of rental income, including royalties and fees from intellectual property and the rental income gained by online labour brokers and other platforms. For example, if Uber takes 20 per cent of each taxi fare, then 20 per cent of that should go into the fund.

There are other innovative ways of financing such funds. Thus, bailing out banks may have been justified to avoid economic collapse and mass bankruptcy. But there is no moral justification for using public money to boost the incomes of bankers and other financiers, especially as the mess was largely due to their negligence and rapaciousness. Instead of taking a temporary stake in failing banks and then selling them once profitable, governments could have enabled a sovereign wealth fund to take permanent stakes, with the returns going to the fund for the benefit of the public. If any institution is deemed too big to fail, the implicit moral hazards justify a substantial public stake.

Tony Atkinson has advocated a sovereign wealth fund that would increase the net worth of the state by taking stakes in companies and property. This would not amount to nationalisation, but would derive a public benefit from minority shareholdings in high-tech, financial and resource-intensive sectors.

In addition, most subsidies covered in Chapter 3 should be ended, with some of the money freed up going into the sovereign wealth fund. Another source of funding should come via monetary policy. Quantitative easing channelled billions into financial markets, to relatively little positive effect. Had the money been directed into sovereign wealth funds, they could have been effective vehicles for redistributive and growth purposes.

There is one vital extra dimension. Fund governance should be transparent and democratic, with an independent board and clear terms of reference. The Norwegian Fund has rules that are relatively democratic, as does France's Strategic Investment Fund, set up in 2008. But most current sovereign wealth funds remain opaque and secretive.

Sovereign wealth funds are by no stretch some wild socialist enterprise. Most have conservative roots. Back in the 1860s, the Texas Permanent School Fund took control of about half of the state's land and the mineral rights that were still in the public domain.[12] In 1953, the fund added coastal 'submerged lands' after they were relinquished by the federal government. It was an unheralded rescue of the commons. Today, the fund distributes over $800 million to state schools, operating alongside a $17.5 billion Permanent University Fund, which owns over 2 million acres and uses the proceeds to support the state's public university system.

Another fund with conservative roots is the Permanent Wyoming Mineral Trust Fund, which has assets of over $7 billion, gained from mineral extraction. This fund was used to eliminate state income taxes, which might be regarded as a misuse but shows the power of such a fund.

Once set up, most funds have proved popular. When President Obama tried to privatise the Tennessee Valley Authority, the legendary public company that produces electricity and manages the Tennessee River system, local Republicans, worried about higher prices and loss of state revenue, blocked the proposal. Similarly, Alaskan citizens have defended the Alaska Permanent Fund, set up in 1976 by a Republican governor to distribute a portion of oil revenues, against corporate and even Republican efforts to have it partly or wholly privatised.

A sovereign wealth fund has advantages over company

profit-sharing schemes that are often advocated as a means of reducing inequality, notably by Hillary Clinton in her campaign for the US presidency. Some economists advocate incentives to companies to institute profit sharing, including tax breaks and preference in awarding government contracts.[13] But such schemes would actually be regressive and distortionary. By definition, they favour employees, insiders, rather than the precariat, and in practice they benefit the elite and salariat more than the lower-paid. Sovereign wealth funds have much more redistributive potential.

CONSTRUCT A BASIC INCOME

Wealth funds must be coupled with a way of distributing the proceeds to citizens. The optimal solution would be to build up a 'social dividend' system, providing every legal resident with a modest but growing basic income, partly paid out of the fund. This would have desirable and emancipatory properties. It would reduce income insecurity and increase the incentive to take paid work, overcoming the poverty trap inherent in existing means-tested schemes. And it would encourage people to shift to more unpaid care and ecologically valuable work reviving the commons.

A basic income should be the second pillar of a 21st-century income distribution system. Over the ages, many distinguished economists, philosophers, sociologists, psychologists, theologians and political figures have proposed it in some form. The Basic Income European Network (BIEN), set up in 1986 to promote research and advocacy, later evolved into the Basic Income Earth

Network to reflect a growing global membership.[14] And since the crash of 2008 many more people, across the political spectrum, have come to see a basic income as essential to combat rising inequality and insecurity. It should be regarded as part of a package of reforms, not a panacea; by itself it would be less effective than if combined with supportive institutional changes.

Existing social assistance schemes are costly, administratively inefficient, inequitable and ineffectual in reducing insecurity and inequality. Nearly a century of research has demonstrated time and again that targeting and means testing do not work as intended. Still, moralistic politicians continue tightening conditions, making schemes more selective and punitive and stigmatising some of society's most vulnerable people. Workfare is inevitably down the road, dressed up shamelessly as 'reintegrating' people into society. Meanwhile, poverty traps and precarity traps remove the incentive for those receiving meagre benefits to take low-wage casual jobs. Nobody in the salariat or elite would step out of bed if they faced a marginal income tax rate of 80 per cent. Yet that is what politicians demand of the precariat. The hypocrisy is breathtaking. With a basic income as the base, the poverty trap would be removed.

The basic income or social dividend would be paid, individually, as a modest monthly sum (not in the form of lump-sum capital grants, which invite ill-judged, 'weakness-of-will' spending splurges). The income would go to every legal resident, with a minimum residency requirement for non-citizens of, say, two years. As such, it would not, strictly speaking, be a 'citizenship income'. Crucially, it should be unconditional in behavioural terms, paid regardless of family status, work status or age, although the payment could be smaller for children.

For efficiency and solidaristic reasons, a basic income should be universal, with higher tax on higher incomes to claw it back from the rich. Most advocates propose basic income as an alternative to existing social protection systems. It might be more politically feasible to build up a basic income system in parallel with or in addition to other schemes, while gradually phasing out means-tested and behaviour-tested schemes and distortionary tax credits and regressive subsidies. In either case, the standard objections have been refuted repeatedly, so are restated only briefly here.[15]

Critics claim a basic income would be giving 'something for nothing'. Yet the elite and the salariat receive a lot of something for nothing, in the form of inherited wealth as well as from rising asset values and government subsidies for which they have done no work.

In 1797, Thomas Paine argued that a payment should be made to 'every person, rich or poor', as a kind of ground rent on land, which properly was 'the common property of the human race', and as a repayment of debt, since the wealthy had acquired their riches 'by living in society' and thus owed 'on every principle of justice, of gratitude, and of civilisation, a part of the accumulation back again to society from whence the whole came'.[16]

Such a payment could be described as a social dividend, a modest return (or inheritance) on the collective investment and efforts of the many generations who built the collective wealth on which we depend. It could be paid for largely by capturing rental income, without deterring investment, innovation or sustainable growth. By contrast with tax credits, a basic income would reinforce people's bargaining strength vis-à-vis employers and authority figures of all sorts. It would advance real freedom.

A less convincing but popular argument for basic income is that automation and robotics are going to lead to the mass displacement of labour and mass unemployment. As argued in Chapter 1, there is no reason to think there will be a shortage of *work* for decades to come. Every society has a vast array of unmet needs. However, a basic income would be beneficial in tilting human activity towards forms of work that are not labour and enabling many to have greater control of their time.

The rationale for basic income is partly a matter of social justice and partly a need to reduce the dangerous growth of inequality and insecurity. There are also instrumental reasons. People who have basic security tend to be healthier and more resilient.[17] And they are more productive, cooperative, tolerant and altruistic. These are a formidable set of arguments for moving in the direction of basic income.

BASIC INCOME PILOTS: QE FOR REAL PEOPLE

The 2008 crash, the perception that the global economy is facing secular stagnation, and fears, however misplaced, that the technological revolution is creating a future of labour displacement, have led to growing calls for basic income pilot schemes of one sort or another; some have been carried out. Before considering them, it is worth commenting on one misguided approach and one great missed opportunity.

The misguided proposal is that stagnation justifies 'helicopter money', an image first suggested by Milton Friedman in which central banks would print money and throw it out of a helicopter for people to spend. In early 2016, this idea was garnering increasing interest, including from Mario Draghi, head of the European Central Bank. Martin Wolf of the *Financial Times* concluded that central banks should 'be given the power to send money, ideally to every citizen'.[18] But the main objection to 'helicopter money' is that it would leave economic policy in the hands of bankers rather than democratically accountable bodies.

The missed opportunity was a big one. Recall that in 2015 the European Central Bank (ECB) began a 'quantitative easing' programme that pumped into financial markets the equivalent of 10 per cent of Eurozone GDP. Just beforehand, Jean-Claude Juncker, the new President of the European Commission, announced with much fanfare an 'investment plan for Europe' aimed at pump-priming €315 billion in infrastructural investment. Neither programme confronted the three crises facing the European Union – slow growth, growing inequality and dangerous populist reactions to migration.

As even the OECD has admitted, inequality is an impediment to growth. It constrains and distorts aggregate demand; it tends to raise government budget deficits, because the rich more easily avoid and evade taxes and the poor do not earn enough to pay them; and it enlarges current account deficits, as the rich spend disproportionately on imported goods and services. Inequality is also a cause of migration from south and east Europe to north and west.

Many EU countries need more migration, since birth rates are below reproduction rates and populations are ageing. Yet, while the poorest areas are drained of human skills and energies, migration to richer parts of Europe is inducing xenophobia and populist neo-fascism.

A way of addressing all three issues – inadequate demand, inequality and migration – would have been for the ECB and the European Commission to channel some of the funds earmarked for QE and infrastructure to low-income regions with high out-migration in the form of EU dividends (basic income). While raising aggregate demand may be desirable, it should be done in a way most likely to stimulate local investment and demand for local goods and services. QE does not do that; direct transfers to people would.

Monthly payments, guaranteed for two years, could be provided to every man, woman and child in, say, four areas on a pilot basis. Payments would be made only to those living in the area. So, while people would still be free to move away, the payments would encourage them to stay. Many areas of heavy out-migration in Eastern Europe have average incomes hovering around €400 a month. If every resident were given half that each month, there would be three positive effects – less out-migration, more growth and less intra-EU inequality.

Unlike QE, such transfers would not reduce pressure on governments to cut budget deficits, if that were considered important. It would also be consistent with a moral migration policy, ameliorating conditions that induce impoverished Romanians and Bulgarians, for example, to go to places where anti-migration sentiment is dragging governments in illiberal directions.

Why did the ECB not do something like this? The answer is probably because the policy choice was left to unelected bankers.

The lost opportunity was replicated in the USA and UK. The $4.5 trillion in QE by the US Federal Reserve was enough to have given $56,000 to every household in the country.[19] Instead, it fostered new asset bubbles and more inequality. Similarly, had the UK's £375 billion of QE been diverted to pay a basic income, everyone legally resident in Britain could have received about £50 a week for two years.[20] Inequality would have been reduced, economic security improved, growth boosted. Instead, asset bubbles, debt, homelessness and food banks have grown. As spending cuts mount, politicians and financial elites should not be surprised when the anger turns on them.

An alternative approach is needed. A pilot basic income scheme would give policymakers a good opportunity to see if and how it would work. In 2016, pilots were being planned in nineteen Dutch municipalities, led by the city of Utrecht, and in Finland, where the government put aside funds (initially €20 million) for a pilot to last two years. On the other side of the Atlantic, the provincial government in Ontario, Canada, is planning a basic income experiment, and the provinces of Quebec and Alberta have indicated interest.

There are also private initiatives that show up the timidity of politicians. In California, Sam Altman, president of Y Combinator, a start-up 'accelerator', has committed funds to a five-year basic income experiment. GiveDirectly, a charity that channels money directly from online donors to recipients, has moved from giving random individuals a basic income to more community-oriented experiments in Africa. In Germany, a crowdfunding scheme selects individuals by lottery to receive a basic income for a year. The challenge is to make these experiments into genuine basic income pilots in which everybody in a community is given an equal amount, not just selected individuals. Community effects matter, as basic income pilots in India and Namibia and the 1970s Mincome basic income experiment in Canada have demonstrated.

Some schemes have emerged by accident rather than design. In Cherokee, North Carolina, a small town in the eponymous Native American reservation, the tribal council decided in 1996 to distribute half the profits of its casino each year to all tribal members. This creamed off surplus rental income and, after starting modestly, as of 2015 paid each person $10,000 a year.[21] Research tracking children over the years found, among other benefits, that recipients did better at school than non-recipients and were much less likely to drift into criminality.

In two pilots in Madhya Pradesh, India, conducted between 2009 and 2013, everyone in nine villages – over 6,000 men, women and children – received a small monthly basic income, and their experience was monitored by comparison with a greater number in thirteen otherwise similar villages.[22] The recipients were more likely to improve sanitation and came to have better nutrition, health and healthcare. Children went to school more regularly and performed better. Adults increased their work and productivity. The relatively disadvantaged, such as women, the disabled and the elderly, benefited most. And the basic income had a liberating, emancipatory effect out of all proportion to its monetary value.

While we cannot be sure that what works in one place will work elsewhere, there is no evidence from any of the pilots done so far to support claims that a modest basic income would induce laziness or irresponsible behaviour. On the contrary, evidence gathered by psychologists and others indicates that giving people basic security fosters altruism, cooperation and tolerance, precisely what is needed to head off growing neo-fascist populism.

Some believe that more basic income pilots are unnecessary, since the evidence is overwhelming. However, the challenge is to win political legitimacy for moving in that direction. Pilots can show how a basic income would work and identify procedural obstacles and difficulties that would need to be tackled for optimal implementation.

One related proposal is a 'participation income', long advocated by Tony Atkinson, which would be paid only if a person did some form of work, or 'made a contribution'. His specific proposal is that people should be required to undertake a portfolio of activities for thirty-five hours a week.[23] This would be administratively costly and generate the same inequities as workfare schemes, including sanctions and wrongful denial of payment. What would happen if somebody could not find thirty-five hours of legitimised activity? The scheme would also force those with least skills and schooling to take onerous, low-paying activities, which would have a distortionary effect on the labour market, depressing wages for others doing similar labour.

Rather than forced 'participation', which at best is paternalistic and patronising, we should demonstrate belief in freedom. And in fact all the pilots and experiments so far have shown that most people learn to use their time well.

The ideal would be to construct a multi-tiered social protection system with a basic income at its base made up of three components. The first would be a modest social dividend, paid to every individual legally resident, with children receiving perhaps half as much as adults. This would be supplemented by needs-based payments, set by additional costs of living, for disability, frailty, old age and so on. The third component would be a 'stabilisation grant', which would rise in recessions and fall in booms, acting as a counter-cyclical measure.

To stop governments manipulating the system for political ends, the basic income should be supervised by an independent commission, its members nominated (and approved democratically) for a single five-year term and charged, like the Bank of England's Monetary Policy Committee, with adjusting the levels of all three components according to democratically determined criteria.

There could be just one condition for receiving the basic income – a moral (not legally binding) commitment to vote in general elections and to attend one public political meeting a year. The hope would be to encourage voter registration and avoid the thinning of democracy that is afflicting almost every country.

CONCLUSION

A tragedy of the years following the financial crash of 2008 was that those who had pushed for the policies and regulations that caused the crisis were able to retrench and renew the growth of rentier capitalism. This was at the cost of growing inequality and insecurity, against a backdrop of an interminable war mentality, anomic terrorism and an unprecedented surge of refugees. Meanwhile, proponents of austerity increasingly resemble medieval quacks. If the blood-letting of public spending cuts does not reduce debt and stagnation, bleed some more. Without a new income distribution system, a dark age threatens.

We need to achieve Keynes's euthanasia of the rentier. But without more public pressure – let us persist in calling it revolt – the rent extractors will continue to thrive, while more of those who rely on 'hard work' will face declining living standards. It may be a cliché, but we cannot expect poachers to become gamekeepers, the elite to turn protectors of the precariat.

The rent seeking unleashed by neo-liberalism has created a profoundly corrupt economic system. A progressive response is overdue. Today we are in dangerous times because mainstream parties of the left are in intellectual paralysis, their leaderships wedded to utilitarianism, trying to appeal to an alliance of their perception of the middle class and proletariat. In their weakness, they are allowing the baser elements of centre-right parties to go unchallenged. Healthy democracies need morally and intellectually strong combatants.

Party politics is at its strongest when parties represent class interests and aspirations, and when they eschew utilitarianism. As precariat parties take shape, this will become clearer. The precariat must build its own future, not expect old structures to do so. And it cannot succeed solely through engaging in political parties. A revival of the march to real freedom and equality can only be gained through collective action, creating communities and networks of subversion as well as consolidation. The most exciting aspect of contemporary movements is that such networks are taking shape very quickly. The forward march will soon be resumed.

There is one aspect on which we should all unite. The commons are the bedrock of the distribution system. If they are depleted, privatised or commodified, people's social income suffers, along with the joy in life. The commons belong to all of us; nobody should be allowed to monopolise or deplete them. We need to restore all aspects of the commons, including the rivers and lakes, the land and the sea, our natural resources and the social and intellectual commons.

No country should be obliged by bankers or financial agencies to sell its national assets and heritage through enforced privatisations designed to raise funds to pay foreign creditors. Greece's humiliation in this respect should be a rallying cry. To tell a sovereign country that it must sell its ports, railways and airports to foreign capital, and consider selling its islands and great monuments, is ideological hegemony at its most hubristic.

Everywhere, the commons as a political subject must be rescued from marginalisation, so that people can appreciate its value and the roles it has played in history. A sustained campaign is needed to restore and revive the commons. Fortunately, there is an ideal opportunity. The first commons charter, the Charter of the Forest, marks its 800th anniversary in 2017, having been issued in November 1217, alongside Magna Carta.

This would be an ideal year to launch a campaign for the restoration of the commons. The public parks, libraries, museums, public paths, roads, squares, night-time sky and the wildlife that share the commons with us should be decommodified, rescued as a source of public wealth, not one of private enrichment.

The Charter's greatest achievement was to set a framework for defending common rights – local communities, usufruct, reproduction, resource restoration and nature preservation rights. Throughout British history – and in other countries where similar principles were embedded in laws and practices – the Charter quietly acted as a moral break on commerce. It was a defence of common rights against private property rights. Weakened during the twentieth century, with more enclosure and commercial intrusion, it has been battered in the austerity era. It is time for a fightback.

ENDNOTES

CHAPTER 1

1 *An Economy for the 1%*, Oxfam Briefing Paper 210, January 2016.

2 J. M. Keynes, *The General Theory of Employment, Interest and Money* (Palgrave Macmillan, 1936), Chapter 24.

3 A. B. Atkinson, *Inequality: What can be done?* (Cambridge, MA, and London: Harvard University Press, 2015); T. Piketty, *Capital in the Twenty-First Century* (Boston: Harvard University Press, 2014).

4 Some use a more restrictive definition to mean an economy where more is collected in rent than in taxes, the rent comes from foreign sources, only an elite gain from rent seeking and the government is the main rent collector. See H. Beblawi, 'The rentier state in the Arab world', in G. Lucciani (ed.), *The Arab State* (London: Routledge, 1990), pp. 85–98.

5 For an interpretation, see G. Standing, *Work after Globalization: Building Occupational Citizenship* (Cheltenham: Edward Elgar, 2009).

6 This stability was known as Kaldor's Law after the economist who explained it. N. Kaldor, 'A model of economic growth', *Economic Journal*, 67 (268), 1957: 591–624.

7 M. Jacques, 'It's not the Chinese economy that's on life support', *The Guardian*, 14 September 2015.

8 Charles Goodhart, former member of the Bank of England's rate-setting committee, and Manoj Pradhan have subscribed to this view. Morgan Stanley, *Can Demographics Reverse Three Multi-Decade Trends?* (London: Morgan Stanley, 2015).

9 J. Kynge and J. Wheatley, 'Emerging markets: Redrawing the world map', *Financial Times*, 3 August 2015.

10 G. Standing, *The Precariat: The New Dangerous Class* (London: Bloomsbury, 2011).

11 J. Anderlini, 'China to become one of world's biggest overseas investors by 2020', *Financial Times*, 25 June 2015.

12 J. Kynge, 'State-owned Chinese groups' acquisitions in Europe raise concern', *Financial Times*, 29 February 2016.

13 'Flow dynamics', *The Economist*, 19 September 2015, p. 73.

14 G. Tett, 'The credit bubble, the bears and the central bankers', *Financial Times*, 1 October 2015.

15 B. Bernanke, 'Monetary policy and the housing bubble', Speech to the Annual Meeting of the American Economic Association, 2010; IMF, 'The changing housing cycle and

the implications for monetary policy', in *World Economic Outlook: Housing and the Business Cycle* (IMF, 2008).

16 H. A. Simon, 'The corporation: Will it be managed by machines?', in M. L. Anshen and G. L. Bach (eds), *Management and the Corporations* (New York: McGraw-Hill, 1985), pp. 17–55.

17 P. Mason, *Postcapitalism* (London: Allen Lane, 2015).

18 Among others, see M. Ford, *The Rise of the Robots* (New York: Basic Books, 2015); N. Srnicek and A. Williams, *Inventing the Future: Postcapitalism and a World Without Work* (London: Verso, 2015); G. Pratt, 'Is a Cambrian explosion coming to robotics?', *Journal of Economic Perspectives*, 29 (3), Summer 2015: 51–60; J. Rifkin, *The End of Work: The Decline of the Global Labor Force and the Dawn of the Post-Market Era* (Kirkwood: Putnam Publishing Group, 1995); M. Snyder, 'Robots and computers could take half our jobs within the next 20 years', *Economic Collapse*, 30 September 2013; R. B. Freeman, 'Who owns the robots rules the world', *IZA World of Labor*, 2014. Paul Mason, for example, stated bluntly that IT 'has reduced the need for work'.

19 C. B. Frey and M. A. Osborne, *The Future of Employment: How Susceptible Are Jobs to Computerisation?* (Oxford: University of Oxford, 17 September 2013), mimeo.

20 L. Elliott, 'Robots threaten 15m UK jobs, says Bank of England's chief economist', *The Guardian*, 12 November 2015.

21 J. Bessen, 'The automation paradox', *The Atlantic*, 19 January 2016.

22 The growing merger of physical, digital and biological technologies has been dubbed the Fourth Industrial Revolution. K. Schwab, *The Fourth Industrial Revolution* (Geneva: World Economic Forum, 2016).

23 L. Karabarbounis and B. Neiman, 'The global decline of the labor share', *Quarterly Journal of Economics*, 129 (1), 2014: 61–103.

24 R. Dobbs, T. Koller, S. Ramaswamy, J. Woetzel, J. Manyika, R. Krishnan and N. Andreula, *Playing to Win: The New Global Competition for Corporate Profits* (New York: McKinsey Global Institute, September 2015).

25 One US study suggests that the whole of the decline in the labour share is due to a rise in the capital share of intellectual property, in which the intellectual property owners have captured all the resulting productivity gains. D. Koh, R. Santaeulàlia-Llopis and Y. Zheng, *Labor Share Decline and Intellectual Property Products Capital*, mimeo, 29 February 2016.

26 D. Power, G. Epstein and M. Abrena, 'Trends in the Rentier Income Share in OECD Countries, 1960–2000', Political Economy Research Institute Work Paper 58A (Amherst: University of Massachusetts, 2003).

27 Ibid., Fig. IV.1.1.

28 E. Goldberg, E. Wibbels and E. Mvukiyehe, 'Lessons from strange cases: Democracy, development, and the resource curse in the US states', *Comparative Political Studies*, 41, (2008): 477–514.

29 A. Jayadev and G. Epstein, 'The Correlates of Rentier Returns in OECD Countries', Political Economy Research Institute Work Paper 58A (Amherst: University of Massachusetts, 2007).

30 G. Krippner, *What is Financialization?* (Department of Sociology, University of Wisconsin, 2005), mimeo.

31 C. Roxburgh et al., *Global Capital Markets: Entering a New Era* (New York: McKinsey Global Institute, 2009), p. 9.

32 The hypothesis that financial innovation leads to Ponzi finance is associated with

Minsky. H. P. Minsky, *Stabilizing an Unstable Economy* (New Haven, CT: Yale University Press, 1986).

33 B. Milanović, *The Haves and the Have-Nots* (New York: Basic Books, 2011).

34 R. Fuentes-Nieva, 'Who is the richest man in history? The answer might surprise you', Oxfamblogs.org, 2015.

35 Atkinson, 2015, op. cit., p. 182.

36 A. B. Krueger, *The Great Utility of the Great Gatsby Curve* (2015); R. Chetty, N. Hendren, P. Kline, E. Saez and N. Turner, 'Is the United States still a land of opportunity? Recent trends in intergenerational mobility', *American Economic Review, Papers and Proceedings 2014*, 104 (5): 141–7.

37 Standing, 2011, op. cit.; G. Standing, *A Precariat Charter: From Denizens to Citizens* (London: Bloomsbury, 2014).

38 M. Bitler and H. Hoynes, 'Heterogeneity in the impact of economic cycles and the Great Recession: Effects within and across the income distribution', *American Economic Review, Papers and Proceedings 2015*, 105 (5): 154–60.

39 L. Michel, J. Bernstein and S. Allegretti, *The State of Working America 2006/2007* (New York: Cornell University Press, 2007).

40 E. Brynjolfsson and A. McAfee, *The Second Machine Age* (New York: W. Norton, 2014).

41 T. Krebs and M. Scheffel, 'Macroeconomic evaluation of labour market reform in Germany', *IMF Economic Review*, 2013.

42 L. Elliott, 'UK wage growth stifled by tepid investment and low-skilled migration', *The Guardian*, 23 September 2015.

43 'The tax-free recovery', *The Economist*, 20 September 2014, p. 33.

44 A. J. Cherlin, *Labor's Love Lost: The Rise and Fall of the Working-Class Family in America* (New York: Russell Sage, 2015), p. 61.

45 J. Furman and P. Orszag, 'A Firm-Level Perspective on the Role of Rents in the Rise in Inequality', paper presented at 'A Just Society' centennial event in honour of Joseph Stiglitz, Columbia University, 16 October 2015.

46 An analysis by *The Economist* found that two-thirds of the 900 US economic sectors it looked at had become more concentrated between 1997 and 2012. It estimated that the dominant firms gained 'exceptional profits' over and above what would be 'normal' in a more competitive market, of some $300 billion a year – equivalent to 1.7 per cent of GDP. 'Too much of a good thing', *The Economist*, 26 March 2016.

47 J. Furman, *Global Lessons for Inclusive Growth* (Washington DC: US Council of Economic Advisers, 2014).

48 D. Corbae and P. D'Erasmo, *A Quantitative Model of Banking Industry Dynamics*, mimeo, March 2013.

49 For example, Chris Huhne and Vince Cable, former Liberal Democrat ministers in the British coalition government, cited in C. Huhne, 'Gloomy, but right', *Prospect*, October 2015, pp. 72–4.

50 M. Wolf, 'Helicopter drops might not be far away', *Financial Times*, 23 February 2016.

51 Standing, 2014, op. cit.

52 J. Tanndal and D. Waldenstrom, *Does Financial Deregulation Boost Top Incomes? Evidence from the Big Bang*, Centre for Economic Policy Research, DP11094, February 2016.

53 K. Cooper, 'Emerging market loans threaten British banks', *Sunday Times*, 4 October 2015, p. 2.

54 A. Haldane, 'A radical prescription', *Prospect*, October 2015, pp. 36–8.
55 J. Kay, *Other People's Money: Masters of the Universe or Servants of the People?* (London: Profile Books, 2015); W. Hutton, *How Good We Can Be* (London: Little, Brown, 2015).
56 'The other deficit', *The Economist*, 17 October 2015, p. 38.
57 R. Gordon, *The Rise and Fall of American Growth* (Princeton: Princeton University Press, 2016).

CHAPTER 2

1   D. McClintick, 'How Harvard lost Russia', *Institutional Investor*, 27 February 2006.
2   'The new age of crony capitalism', *The Economist*, 15 March 2014, pp. 9, 53–4; 'The party winds down', *The Economist*, 7 May 2016, pp. 46–8.
3   M. Lupu, K. Mayer, J. Tait and A. J. Trippe (eds), *Current Challenges in Patent Information Retrieval* (Heidelberg: Springer-Verlag, 2011), p. v.
4   Letter to Isaac McPherson, 13 August 1813. A public good is one that can be consumed or used by one person without affecting its consumption or use by others; it is available to all.
5   'A question of utility', *The Economist*, 8 August 2015.
6   M. Mazzucato, *The Entrepreneurial State: Debunking Public vs Private Sector Myths* (London: Anthem Press, 2013).
7   M. Boldrin and D. Levine, *Against Intellectual Property* (Cambridge: Cambridge University Press, 2008).
8   OECD, *Enquiries into Intellectual Property's Economic Impact: Chapter 1 – Synthesis Report*, DSTI/ICCP(2014)17/CHAP1/FINAL, August 2015.
9   Boldrin and Levine, 2008, op. cit.
10 J. De Ruyck, 'Finding the right balance between IP and access to science', Intellectual Property Watch, 3 August 2015.
11 Boldrin and Levine, 2008, op. cit.
12 For instance, A. Johns, *Piracy: The Intellectual Property Wars from Gutenberg to Gates* (Chicago: University of Chicago Press, 2010).
13 M. Boldrin and D. Levine, 'The Case Against Patents', Federal Reserve Bank of St Louis Working Paper 2012-035A, 2012, p. 7.
14 'Zombie patents', *The Economist*, 21 June 2014, p. 70.
15 For example, K. Lybecker, 'The sticking point that shouldn't be: The role of pharmaceutical patents in the TPP negotiations', IP Watchdog, 3 August 2015.
16 'The price of failure', *The Economist*, 29 November 2014.
17 J. Stiglitz, 'Don't trade away our health', *International New York Times*, 31 January 2015.
18 Boldrin and Levine, 2008, op. cit.
19 D. Baker, *Bigger than the Social Security Crisis: Wasteful Spending on Prescription Drugs* (Washington DC: CEPR, 2005).
20 G. Velásquez, *The Grant of Patents and the Exorbitant Cost of 'Lifesaving' Drugs*, South Views No. 121, 12 November 2015.
21 J. Parker, *Indigenous Innovation Remains Key Feature of New Development Policies*, US China Business Council, 12 November 2013.
22 A. Schotter and M. Teagarden, 'Protecting intellectual property in China', *MIT Sloan Management Review*, 17 June 2014.
23 E. Roth, J. Seong and J. Woetzel, 'Gauging the strength of Chinese Innovation', *McKinsey Quarterly*, October 2015; E. Tse, *China's Disruptors: How Alibaba, Xiaomi,*

Tencent and Other Companies Are Changing the Rules of Business (London: Portfolio Penguin, 2015).

24 Thomson Reuters, *China's IQ (Innovation Quotient): Trends in Patenting and the Globalization of Chinese Innovation* (Thomson Reuters, 2014).

25 WIPO, *World Intellectual Property Report 2015: Breakthrough Innovation and Economic Growth* (Geneva: World Intellectual Property Organization, 2015).

26 J. Band and J. Gerafi, *Profitability of Copyright-Intensive Industries*, Policybandwidth, 2013.

27 L. Menand, 'Crooner in rights spat', *New Yorker*, 20 October 2014.

28 P. Baldwin, *The Copyright Wars: Three Centuries of Trans-Atlantic Battle* (Princeton: Princeton University Press, 2014.)

29 'Academics want you to read their work for free', *The Atlantic*, 26 January 2016.

30 'Do not enclose the cultural commons', *Financial Times*, 19 April 2009.

31 WIPO, *World Intellectual Property Report: Brands – Reputation and Image in the Global Market Place* (Geneva: World Intellectual Property Organization, 2013).

32 *BrandZ Top 100 Most Valuable Global Brands 2015* (Millward Brown, 2015).

33 Ian McClure suggests that intangible assets have risen from 20 per cent to 80 per cent of US corporate value since 1975. I. McClure, *From a Patent Market for Lemons to a Marketplace for Patents: Benchmarking Intellectual Property in its Evolution to Asset Class Status*, mimeo, May 2015.

34 K. Tienhaara, 'Resisting the "law of greed"', greenagenda.org.au, September 2015.

35 'Free exchange: Game of zones', *The Economist*, 21 March 2015, p. 65.

36 C. Shepard, 'The secret US trade agreement that will make income inequality worse', care2.com, 15 February 2015.

37 D. Autor, D. Dorn and G. Hansen, 'Untangling trade and technology: Evidence from local labour markets', *Economic Journal*, 125 (584), 2015: 621–46.

38 'Trade minister must listen to medical specialists on TPP', Scoop.co.nz, 15 July 2015.

39 J. Capaldo, 'The Trans-Atlantic Trade and Investment Partnership: European Disintegration, Unemployment and Instability', Global Development and Environment Institute Working Paper 14-03, October 2014; J. K. Sundaram, 'Some Real Costs of the Trans-Pacific Partnership: Lost Jobs, Lower Incomes, Rising Inequality', GDAE Policy Brief 16-01 (Global Development and Environment Institute, Tufts University, February 2016).

40 *The Economist*, 21 March 2015, op. cit.

41 'E. Morozov, 'What happens when policy is made by corporations?', *The Observer*, 12 July 2015, p. 29. He cited a report by the Progressive Policy Institute, a neo-liberal outfit that promotes US economic interests, and the Lisbon Council, based in Brussels, whose donors include US technology companies Google, HP, IBM and Oracle. The Council's co-founder and former director was put in charge of the European Commission's European Policy Strategy Centre. The two bodies have been lobbying to have the EC reform its data protection laws for the benefit of US firms, classic rent seeking.

42 D. Novy, 'Attention David Cameron: Time to stop the scaremongers from strangling TTIP', theconversation.com, 5 October 2014.

43 Tienhaara, 2015, op. cit.; Corporate Europe Observatory et al., 'The zombie ISDS', February 2016.

44 D. Quijones, 'Spain gets bitter costly foretaste of its beloved trade pacts', Wolf Street, 13 August 2015.

45 A. G. Arauz, *Ecuador's Experience with International Investment Arbitration* (Geneva: South Centre Investment Policy Brief No. 5, August 2015).

46 'Halt to trade talks urged amid fears over secret talks', *The Guardian*, 5 May 2015, p. 22.

47 Autor, Dorn and Hansen, 2015, op. cit.

48 Novy, 2014, op. cit.

49 F. Lavopa, *Crisis, Emergency Measures and the Failure of the ISDS System: The Case of Argentina*, South Centre Investment Policy Brief No. 2, July 2015.

50 Tienhaara, 2015, op. cit.

51 C. Provost and M. Kennard, 'The obscure legal system that lets corporations sue countries', *The Guardian*, 10 June 2015.

52 P. Mason, *Postcapitalism: A Guide to Our Future* (London: Allen Lane, 2015).

53 G. Alperovitz, 'Distributing our technological inheritance', *Technology Review*, 97 (7), 1994: 30–36; G. Alperovitz, 'Does Mark Zuckerberg really deserve all that money?', AlterNet, 9 March 2012.

54 G. Van Harten, M. C. Porterfield and K. P. Gallagher, *Investment Provisions in Trade and Investment Treaties: The Need for Reform*, Global Economic Governance Initiative Policy Brief 5 (Boston University, September 2015).

CHAPTER 3

1   ILO, *Tackling youth employment challenges: An overview of possible actions and policy considerations* (Geneva: ILO, 2011).

2   The British government's plan to charge big companies an apprenticeship levy also invites moral hazards. Companies will obtain vouchers to pay apprentice-training providers, who can exchange them for cash from the government. Business lobbies and unions warned that the levy could encourage companies to rebadge existing training schemes as 'apprenticeships' so as to use the vouchers.

3   S. Evenett and J. Fritz, *Throwing Sand in the Wheels: How Foreign Trade Distortions Slowed LDC Export-Led Growth* (Centre for Economic Policy Research, 2015).

4   UK capital gains tax rates were cut in the 2016 Budget from 28 per cent to 20 per cent for higher-rate taxpayers and from 18 per cent to 10 per cent for basic-rate taxpayers, levied on profits over £11,100 from asset sales. The change will benefit a tiny minority of the ultra-wealthy.

5   J. Ungoed-Thomas, 'Zero tax bill for big six', *Sunday Times*, 31 January 2016, p. 1.

6   S. Bowers, 'UK tax policy dictated by companies not ministers says leading Treasury expert', *The Guardian*, 28 June 2015.

7   José Antonio Ocampo, member of the Independent Commission for the Reform of International Corporate Taxation, cited in V. Houlder, 'Call to reform "outdated" global corporate tax regime', *Financial Times*, 5 October 2015.

8   M. Sumption and K. Hooper, *Selling Visas and Citizenship: Policy Questions from the Global Boom in Investor Immigration* (Migration Policy Institute, October 2014).

9   J. Tyson, 'Reforming Tax Expenditures in Italy: What, Why, and How?', IMF Working Paper 14/7, January 2014.

10 W. Quigley, 'Ten examples of welfare for the rich and corporations', billquigley.wordpress.com, 13 January 2014.

11 L. Story, 'As companies seek tax deals, governments pay high price', *New York Times*, 1 December 2012.

12 A. Young, 'Tax dodge: Apple, Pfizer among top companies that added nearly $90B to their offshore cash hoards through tax inversion in 2014', *International Business Times*, 4 March 2015.

13 J. Doukas, 'Unintended consequences of the ECB's quantitative easing programme could undermine Europe's recovery', Europpblog, 22 June 2015.

14 Quigley, 2014, op. cit.

15 T. deHaven, *Corporate Welfare in the Federal Budget*, Cato Institute, Policy Analysis No. 703, 25 July 2012.

16 R. Wood, '20 really stupid things in the US tax code', *Forbes*, 16 December 2014.

17 K. Barnham, *The Burning Answer: A User's Guide to the Solar Revolution* (London: Weidenfeld & Nicolson, 2014).

18 K. Farnsworth, 'The British Corporate Welfare State: Public Provision for Private Businesses', SPERI Paper No. 24 (University of Sheffield, 2015).

19 J. Ferguson, 'Prepare for tax hikes', *MoneyWeek*, 11 March 2015.

20 M. L. Crandall-Hollick, *The Earned Income Tax Credit (EITC): An Economic Analysis* (Washington DC: Congressional Research Service, 1 February 2016).

21 *New Zealand Herald*, 26 August 2015.

22 A. Darling, 'Why I'm backing Liz Kendall for Labour leader', *The Observer*, 19 July 2015, p. 25.

23 R. Paul, *Investigating the Relationship Between Tax Credits and Wages Offered by Employers*, Civitas, February 2016.

24 'From the people, for the people', *The Economist*, 9 May 2015. In 2016 there were signs of waning enthusiasm for peer-to-peer lenders and the US Treasury issued a white paper calling for tougher oversight.

25 L. Browning, 'Too big to tax: Settlements are tax write-offs for banks', *Newsweek*, 27 October 2014.

26 G. Claeys, Z. Darvas., A. Leandro and T. Walsh, *The effects of ultra-loose monetary policies on inequality*, Bruegel Policy Contribution, Issue 2015/09, June 2015.

27 M. Beraja, A. Fuster, E. Hurst and J. Vavra, 'Regional heterogeneity and monetary policy', Brookings Institution Working Paper, 2015; Claeys et al., 2015, op. cit.

28 Studies cited in F. Giugliano, 'Rich economies question faith in power of lower exchange rates', *Financial Times*, 8 March 2015.

29 R. Reich, 'How Goldman Sachs profited from the Greek debt crisis', *The Nation*, 15 July 2015; W. Cohen and R. Reich, 'Debate: Is Goldman Sachs partly to blame for Greece's debt crisis?', *The Nation*, 3 August 2015.

30 D. Gayle, 'Foreign criminals use London housing market to launder billions of pounds', *The Guardian*, 26 July 2015. In 2016 the government announced plans to create a register of the true owners of as many as 100,000 offshore companies investing in British property.

31 H. Osborne, 'Generation Rent: The housing ladder starts to collapse for the under 40s', *The Guardian*, 22 July 2015, pp. 1–2.

32 D. Pegg, 'Private landlords given £14bn tax breaks in 2012–13', *The Guardian*, 27 May 2015.

33 M. Rognlie, *Deciphering the fall and rise in the net capital share*, Brookings Papers on Economic Activity, March 2015.

CHAPTER 4

1 'The never-ending story', *The Economist*, 20 November 2015, p. 13.

2 C. Reinhart and K. Rogoff, 'Growth in a Time of Debt', NBER Working Paper No. 15639 (Cambridge, MA: National Bureau of Economic Research, 2010).

3 T. Herndon, M. Ash and R. Pollin, *Does high public debt consistently stifle economic growth? A critique of Reinhart and Rogoff* (Amherst: Political Economy Research Institute, University of Massachusetts, 2013).

4 A. Pescatori, D. Sandri and J. Simon, 'Debt and Growth: Is There a Magic Threshold?', IMF Working Paper WP/14/34, February 2014.

5 For example, D. Igan, D. Leigh, J. Simon and P. Topalova, 'Dealing with household debt', in S. Claessens, M. Ayhen Kose, L. Laeven and F. Valencia (eds), *Financial Crises: Causes, Consequences, and Policy Responses* (Washington DC: IMF, 2014); A. Mian and A. Sufi, *House of Debt: How They (and You) Caused the Great Recession, and How We Can Prevent It Happening Again* (Chicago: University of Chicago Press, 2014).

6 M. Lazzarato, *The Making of the Indebted Man: An Essay on the Neoliberal Condition* (Los Angeles: Semiotext, 2012). For a related perspective, see D. Graeber, *Debt: The First 5,000 Years* (New York: Melville House, 2011).

7 A. Ross, *Creditocracy and the Case for Debt Refusal* (New York: OR Books, 2014).

8 Richard Dobbs, cited in R. Atkins, 'Debt mountains spark fears of another crisis', *Financial Times*, 5 February 2015.

9 A. Turner, *Between Debt and the Devil: Money, Credit and Fixing Global Finance* (Princeton: Princeton University Press, 2015).

10 'As safe as houses', *The Economist*, 31 January 2015.

11 L. Buttiglione, P. R. Lane, L. Reichlin and V. Reinhart, 'Deleveraging: What Deleveraging?', Geneva Report on the World Economy 16 (Geneva: International Centre for Monetary and Banking Studies, 2014).

12 A morally inappropriate response has been proposed by influential behavioural economists linked to the nudge units in the White House and 10 Downing Street. This is to ban people from over-borrowing. As one enthusiast put it, 'What is the big deal? Let's limit people's ability to hurt themselves in borrowing, like we do with seatbelts in driving.' D. Ariely, *Predictably Irrational: The Hidden Forces that Shape our Decisions* (New York: Harper Collins, 2008). This would be arbitrary, subjective, costly and an obvious intrusion into freedom.

13 Cited in W. K. Tabb, *The Restructuring of Capitalism in Our Time* (New York: Columbia University Press, 2012), pp. 39–40.

14 D. Gibbons and L. Vaid, *Britain in the Red: Provisional Report*, Centre for Responsible Credit, September 2015.

15 A. Traub, *Discredited: How Employment Credit Checks Keep Qualified Workers Out of a Job* (New York: Demos, 2012).

16 J. Kollewe, 'First-time buyers need to earn £77,000 a year to live in London', *The Guardian*, 4 May 2015.

17 M. Taylor, 'Housing is the nation's most urgent and complex challenge. Yet we're para-lysed', *The Observer*, 16 August 2015.

18 'Build it and they will rent', *The Economist*, 19 September 2015, p. 30.

19 D. Gibbons and L. Vaid, op. cit.

20 P. N. da Costa, 'Big banks and the White House are teaming up to fleece poor people', *Foreign Policy*, 23 February 2016.

21 M. Arnold, 'Beyond banking: Lenders face mortgages challenge from P2Ps', *Financial Times*, 13 November 2015. In May 2016 Laplanche abruptly left the company, whose share price has tumbled since its 2014 listing.

22 A. Palin, 'Q&A: Student loan repayments', *Financial Times*, 19 June 2015.

23 W. Hutton, 'Growing student debt is entrenching unfairness for a whole generation', *The Observer*, 9 August 2015.

24 C. Crawford and W. Jin, *Payback Time? Student Debt and Loan Repayments: What Will the 2012 Reforms Mean for Graduates?* (London: Institute for Fiscal Studies, 2014).

25 'Graduates paying off student loans into their 50s – IFS/Sutton Trust', Press Release, Sutton Trust, 10 April 2014.

26 A. Williams, 'Hard-up students spend less on partying', *Financial Times*, 11 March 2016.

27 A. Andriotis, 'Debt relief for students snarls market for their loans', *Wall Street Journal*, 23 September 2015.

28 J. Rothstein and C. E. Rouse, 'Constrained After College: Student Loans and Early Career Occupational Choices', NBER Working Paper No. 13117, National Bureau of Economic Research, May 2007.

29 B. W. Ambrose, L. Cordell and S. Ma, *The Impact of Student Loan Debt on Small Business Formation*, Federal Reserve Bank of Philadelphia, July 2015.

30 H. Warrell, 'Students take on more paid employment as living costs rise', *Financial Times*, 10 August 2015.

31 L. Bachelor, 'Flatscreen TVs, chic interiors … and rents of up to £300 a week', *The Observer*, 16 August 2015, pp. 8–9.

32 J. Farrell and D. Hellier, 'Northern Rock mortgages worth £13 billion sold to US investment firm', *The Guardian*, 14 November 2015, p. 42.

33 This was widely reported, amid allegations in the Northern Ireland Parliament. See, for instance, 'Cantillon: Cerberus and the Northern Rock deal', *Irish Times*, 14 November 2015.

34 Human Rights Watch, 'US: Courts rubber stamp corporate suits against poor', Press Release, 21 January 2016.

35 C. Reinhart and K. Rogoff, *This Time is Different: Eight Centuries of Financial Folly* (Princeton: Princeton University Press, 2011).

36 See, for instance, S. Mullainathan and E. Shafir, *Scarcity: Why having too little means so much* (London: Allen Lane, 2013). For a general treatment of resilience, see N. N. Taleb, *Anti-Fragile: How to live in a world we don't understand* (London: Allen Lane, 2012).

CHAPTER 5

1   See, for example, P. Kilby, *Forest Camera: A Portrait of Ashdown* (Poundgate: Sweethaws Press, 1998), edited by R. Bowlby.

2   P. Linebaugh, *The Magna Carta Manifesto* (Berkley: University of California Press, 2008), p. 79.

3   I. Illich, 'Silence is a Commons', Asahi Symposium on 'Science and Man – The computer-managed society', Tokyo, 21 March 1982.

4   'The new age of crony capitalism', *The Economist*, 15 March 2014.

5   World Bank, *The Changing Wealth of Nations: Measuring Sustainable Development in the New Millennium* (Washington DC: World Bank, 2011), p. 9.

6   Magna Carta came into being in 1217, not 1215 as schoolchildren are taught, alongside the Charter of the Forest. Certain clauses in the Charter of the Forest were taken from the original 1215 Charter of Liberties, which was renamed Magna Carta.

7   Linebaugh, 2008, op. cit., p. 230.

8   E. Gosden, 'Fracking rigs could surround national parks under Government plans', *Daily Telegraph*, 11 July 2015.

9   E. Marrington, 'National protections for national parks? What a load of potash...', Campaign to Protect Rural England, 24 July 2015.

10 R. Graham, 'Water in the UK – public versus private', Open Democracy, 19 December 2014.

11 N. Flynn, *Public Sector Management* (London: Sage, 6th edition, 2012).

12 G. Monbiot, 'Putting a price on the rivers and rain diminishes us all', *The Guardian*, 7 August 2012.

13 A. D. Guerry et al., 'Natural capital and ecosystem services informing decisions: From promise to practice', *PNAS – Proceedings of the National Academy of Sciences*, 112 (24), 2015: 7748–55.

14 C. Mayer, *Unnatural Capital Accounting*, mimeo, 15 December 2013, p. 3.

15 P. Barkham, 'Introducing "treeconomics": How street trees can save our cities', *The Guardian*, 15 August 2015.

16 J. Vasagar, 'Public spaces in Britain's cities fall into private hands', *The Guardian*, 11 June 2012.

17 See, for example, A. Minton, 'What I want from our cities in 2015: Public spaces that are truly public', *The Guardian*, 30 December 2014.

18 K. Allen, 'Speculative investors head for the exit in Nine Elms development', *Financial Times*, 10 July 2015.

19 P. Stevens, 'BIG reveals design for Malaysia Square at Battersea Power Station', designboom, 1 December 2014.

20 S. Sassen, 'Who owns our cities – and why this urban takeover should concern us all', *The Guardian*, 24 November 2015.

21 Vasagar, 2012, op. cit.

22 Vasagar, 2012, ibid.

23 Standing, 2014, op. cit.

24 D. Boffey, 'Tory right-to-buy plan threatens mass selloff of council homes', *The Observer*, 28 June 2015.

25 R. Booth, 'Londoners miss out as homes built as "safe deposit boxes" for foreign buyers', *The Guardian*, 30 December 2014.

26 O. Wright, 'The government has no idea how many houses have been built on publicly owned land that has been sold to developers', *The Independent*, 24 September 2015, p. 14.

27 R. Mendick, L. Donnelly and A. Kirk, 'The PFI hospitals costing NHS £2bn every year', *Daily Telegraph*, 18 July 2015.

28 J. Owen, 'Crippling PFI deals leave Britain £222bn in debt', *Independent on Sunday*, 12 April 2015.

29 The Private Finance Initiative Watchdog, 'Meet the investment firms that own your PFI-funded public schools and hospitals', pfeyeblog, 18 February 2015.

30 Youssef El-Gingihy, *How to Dismantle the NHS in 10 Easy Steps* (Hampshire: Zero Books, 2015).

31 N. Kochan and J. Armitage, 'Companies supplying NHS could cost £1bn a year in fraud', *The Independent*, 24 September 2015, p. 49.

32 J. Harris, 'We're ignoring the crisis of our most democratic public transport: buses', *The Guardian*, 24 August 2015.

33 Harris, ibid.

34 O. Bowcott, 'Court fees jeopardise Magna Carta principles, says lord chief justice', *The Guardian*, 8 October 2015.

35 Cited in P. Toynbee, 'Support the National Gallery strikes while they're still legal', *The Guardian*, 11 August 2015.

36 P. Mason, 'Welcome to a new way of living', *Guardian Review*, 18 July 2015, p. 3.

37 D. Boffey and W. Mansell, 'Academy chain's fees for "consultants" put schools programme under scrutiny', *The Guardian*, 24 October 2015.

38 W. Mansell, 'Taxpayers to pay investment firm annual £468,000 rent for free school', *The Guardian*, 11 August 2015, p. 35.

39 Standing, 2009, op. cit.

CHAPTER 6

1 G. Standing, 'Tertiary time: The precariat's dilemma', *Public Culture*, 25 (1), 2013: 5–27.

2 J. Manyika, S. Lund, K. Robinson, J. Valentino and R. Dobbs, *Connecting Talent with Opportunity in the Digital Age* (New York: McKinsey Global Institute, June 2015).

3 C. Christensen, *The Innovator's Dilemma: The Revolutionary Book That Will Change the Way You Do Business* (Boston: Harvard Business Review Press, 1997).

4 C. Christensen, M. Raynor and R. McDonald, 'What is disruptive innovation?', *Harvard Business Review*, 2015.

5 M. Harris, 'Uber: Why the world's biggest ride-sharing company has no drivers', *The Guardian*, 16 November 2015.

6 S. Jackman, 'Crowdsourcing may hold key to unlocking Japan's working potential', *Japan News*, 2 January 2015.

7 Cited in S. O'Connor, 'The human cloud: A new world of work', *Financial Times*, 8 October 2015.

8 Associated Press, 'US companies increasingly turning to temporary workers to fill positions', Fox News, 8 July 2013.

9 Cited in *The Economist*, 13 June 2015, p. 57.

10 B. Solomon, 'Leaked: Uber's financials show huge growth, even bigger losses', *Forbes*, 12 January 2016.

11 Unsurprisingly, some drivers found ways to game the system. Uber discovered that some drivers were signing up with as many as ten smartphones, booking phantom trips during peak times on all of them simultaneously.

12 Cited in 'Will crowdsourcing put an end to wage-based employment?', L'Atelier, 29 September 2015.

13 Reported in *Financial Times*, 20 June 2015.

14 Freelancers Union and Elance-oDesk, *Freelancing in America: A National Survey of the New Workforce*, 2015.

15 L. Katz and A. Krueger, 'The Rise of Alternative Work Arrangements and the 'Gig'

Economy', draft paper cited in R. Wile, 'Harvard economist: All net U.S. job growth since 2005 has been in contracting gigs', Fusion, 29 March 2016.

16 *Financial Times*, 22 September 2015.

17 In June 2015, the California Labor Commissioner ruled that Uber was an employer because it controlled pricing, tipping, driver ratings and type of car. Uber appealed and the case was due to go to jury trial in June 2016. However, in April 2016, Uber reached an out-of-court settlement with the drivers that maintains their status of independent contractors in return for certain concessions. A ruling by the UK's Employment Tribunal was also expected in 2016.

18 S. Harris and A. Krueger, 'A Proposal for Modernizing Labor Laws for Twenty-First-Century Work: The "Independent Worker"', The Hamilton Project Discussion Paper 2015–10, Brookings, December 2015.

19 S. Madden, 'Why Homejoy failed … and the future of the on-demand economy', techcrunch.com, 31 July 2015.

20 J. Hullinger, '16 things you might not know about Uber and its drivers', mentalfloss. com, 19 January 2016. Uber agreed in the April 2016 settlement that not accepting enough rides would no longer be a cause of 'de-activation'.

21 Cited in C. Garling, 'Hunting task wabbits', Medium.com, 2 December 2014.

22 As part of the April 2016 proposed settlement, Uber has agreed to stop de-activating drivers 'at will' and institute an appeals process, but it remains to be seen how this will be implemented.

23 J. Dzieza, 'The rating game: How Uber and its peers turned us into horrible bosses', *The Verge*, 28 October 2015.

24 D. Streitfeld, 'Airbnb listings mostly illegal, New York State contends', *New York Times*, 15 October 2014.

25 T. Wadhwa, 'On-demand economy goes white collar: The rise of the lawyer-entrepreneur', Forbes, 26 October 2015.

26 A. Kittur et al., 'The Future of Crowd Work', paper presented at the 10th ACM Conference on Computer Supported Cooperative Work, OSCW, 2013.

27 R. LaPlante and S. Silberman, 'Design notes for a future crowd work market', medium. com, 2015.

28 Cited in M. Z. Marvit, 'How crowdworkers became the ghosts in the digital machine', *The Nation*, 5 February 2014.

29 A. Wood and B. Burchell, 'Zero hours employment: A new temporality of capitalism?', CritCom, 16 September 2015.

30 Standing, 2009, op. cit.

31 R. Susskind and D. Susskind, *The Future of the Professions: How Technology Will Transform the Work of Human Experts* (Oxford: Oxford University Press, 2015).

32 E. Cadman, 'Employers tap "gig" economy in search of freelancers', *Financial Times*, 15 September 2015.

33 H. Ekbia and B. Nardi, 'Inverse instrumentality: How technologies objectify patients and players', in P. Leonardi et al., *Materiality and Organising* (Oxford: Oxford University Press, 2012), p. 157.

34 Cited in H. Ekbia and B. Nardi, 'Heteromation and its (dis)contents: The invisible division of labour between humans and machines', *First Monday*, 19 (6), June 2014.

35 S. Butler, 'Employers claw back living wage in cuts to perks, hours and pay', *The Guardian*, 16 April 2016.

36 Standing, 2014, op. cit.

37 For example, J. Matthews, 'The sharing economy boom is about to bust', *Time*, 27 June 2014.

38 L. Weber and R. E. Silverman, 'On-demand workers: "We are not robots"', Wall Street Journal, 27 January 2015.

39 L. Mishel, 'Uber is not the future of work', *The Atlantic*, 15 November 2015.

40 J. V. Hall and A. B. Krueger, 'An Analysis of the Labor Market for Uber's Driver-Partners in the United States', Working Paper 587, Princeton University, Industrial Relations Section, 2015.

41 In the April 2016 proposed settlement, Uber agreed to 'facilitate and recognize' drivers' 'associations'. The city of Seattle has passed a law granting independent contractors the right to unionise.

CHAPTER 7

1   E. Goldberg, E. Wibbels and E. Mvukiyehe, 'Lessons from Strange Cases: Democracy, Development, and the Resource Curse in the US States', *Comparative Political Studies*, 41, 2008: 477–514.

2   J. Nichols and R. W. McChesney, *Dollarocracy* (New York: Nation Books, 2014).

3   M. Ross, 'Does oil hinder democracy?', *World Politics*, 53 (3), 2001: 325–61.

4   There is a nice story, which this writer has heard from Karl Polanyi's daughter, that Hayek and Polanyi, who were to influence post-1945 thinking in profoundly opposite ways, were employed at the same institute in Vienna in 1930, and used to walk past each other in the morning with just a polite 'good morning' exchange.

5   M. Fourcade, 'The construction of a global profession: The transnationalization of economics', *American Journal of Sociology*, 112(1), 2006: 181.

6   J. Weeks, *Economics of the 1%: How Mainstream Economics Serves the Rich, Obscures Reality and Distorts Policy* (London: Anthem Press, 2014).

7   G. Readfearn, 'Research reveals almost all climate science denial books linked to conservative think tanks', Desmog, 20 March 2013.

8   The bin Laden family is also on intimate terms with the Saudi royal family. Shafiq bin Laden, Osama bin Laden's half-brother, was 'guest of honour' at Carlyle's annual investor conference at the time of the 9/11 attacks, and left afterwards on the same plane as the Saudi royals.

9   'Rise of the distorporation', *The Economist*, 26 October 2013.

10 A. Giddens, *The Third Way: The Renewal of Social Democracy* (Cambridge: Polity Press, 1998).

11 S. Johnson and J. Kwak, *13 Bankers: The Wall Street Takeover and the Next Financial Meltdown* (New York: Pantheon, 2010).

12 A. B. Atkinson and A. Brandolini, 'On the Identification of the Middle Class', Working Paper 2011-217, Society for the Study of Economic Inequality, 2011; R. Bigot, P. Croutte, J. Muller and G. Osier, 'The Middle Classes in Europe: Evidence from the LIS data', LIS Working Paper Series No. 580, Luxembourg Income Study, 2012.

13 M. M. Funke, M. Schularick and C. Trebesch, 'Going to Extremes: Politics after Financial Crises, 1870–2014', CEPR Discussion Paper No. 10884, Centre for Economic Policy Research, 2015.

14 A. Mian, A. Sufi and F. Trebbi, 'Political constraints in the aftermath of financial crises', VoxEU.org, 21 February 2012.

15 John Curtice, cited in O. Jones, 'Time for decent Tories to speak up', *The Guardian*, 3 December 2015, p. 41.

16 J. Thomas, *10 Million Missing Voters* (London: Smith Institute, November 2015).

17 'Britain's missing voters', Hope Not Hate, 9 September 2015. One reason for non-registration is that registration determines eligibility to do jury service. Another is that registration must be done well in advance of elections; by the time someone becomes interested by the debate on topical issues, it is too late to register.

18 Indicative of the special treatment of the Murdochs, Rupert Murdoch's son James was forced to resign as chairman of the Sky satellite television business over the phone-hacking scandal when he had been in charge of the family's UK newspapers. A 2012 report by the regulator, Ofcom, concluded that his conduct 'repeatedly fell short of the conduct to be expected of him as a chief executive officer and chairman'. In early 2016, he was re-appointed to the Sky post.

19 J. Mayer, *Dark Money: The hidden history of the billionaires behind the rise of the radical right* (New York: Doubleday, 2015).

20 D. Boffey, 'The super-rich helping to plan a glamorous Tory fundraiser', *The Observer*, 7 February 2015.

21 'Not more Lords!', Electoral Reform Society press release, 8 August 2014.

22 M. Taibbi, 'The great American bubble machine', *Rolling Stone*, Issue 1082, 9 July 2009.

23 *The Five Presidents' Report: Completing Europe's Economic and Monetary Union* (Brussels: European Commission, June 2015).

24 M. Taibbi, op. cit.

25 T. Braithwaite, G. Chon and H. Sender, 'Banking: Firefighting at the NY Fed', *Financial Times*, 4 December 2014.

26 M. Skapinker, 'How to run a school-business partnership', *Financial Times*, 4 December 2007.

27 D. Lippman, D. Samuelsohn and I. Arnsdorf, 'Trump's week of errors, exaggerations and flat-out falsehoods', *Politico*, 13 March 2016.

28 'The Washington wishing-well', *The Economist*, 13 June 2015.

29 M. R. Mizruchi, *The Fracturing of the American Corporate Elite* (Boston: Harvard University Press, 2013).

30 E. Eichelberger, 'See how Citigroup wrote a bill so it could get a bailout', Mother Jones, 24 May 2013.

31 L. Drutman, *The Business of America is Lobbying: How Corporations Became Politicized and Politics Became Corporate* (Oxford: Oxford University Press, 2015).

32 I. Traynor et al., '30,000 lobbyists and counting: Is Brussels under corporate sway?', *The Guardian*, 8 May 2014.

33 C. Dowler, 'Trusts exodus from Capita HR contract', *Health Service Journal*, 18 June 2014; B. Clover, 'Three trusts end Capita HR contracts', *Health Service Journal*, 30 September 2014.

34 P. Gallagher, 'Is Simon Stevens really the right person to run the NHS?', *The Independent*, 24 October 2013.

35 C. Molloy, 'Milburn, the NHS and Britain's "revolving door"', Open Democracy, May 2013.

36 R. Mason, 'Andrew Lansley takes post advising drugs firm involved in dispute with NHS', *The Guardian*, 16 November 2015.

37 H. Watt and R. Prince, 'Andrew Lansley bankrolled by private healthcare provider', *Daily Telegraph*, 14 January 2010.

38 A. Lutz, 'These six corporations control 90% of the media in America', Business Insider, 14 June 2012.

39 J. Jackson and J. Martinson, 'Osborne met Murdoch twice in run-up to BBC licence fee deal', *The Guardian*, 19 December 2015, p. 8.

40 M. Margan, 'Afghan couple who have nine children and receive £5,000 a month in benefits have asked for free IVF treatment after arriving in Austria (and the wife is 44)', MailOnline, 22 April 2016.

41 A. Perkins, *The Welfare Trait: How State Benefits Affect Personality* (London: Palgrave Macmillan, 2015).

CHAPTER 8

1 S. Sierakowski, 'Open letter to the Parties: Time for the Neo-Dissidents', *Dissent Magazine*, Spring 2013.

2 The latest to try is Matteo Renzi, social democratic Prime Minister of Italy in 2016, who has made it easier to fire employees, provided more subsidies to firms, reduced their taxes and cut social spending. The social strikes are eroding his support base with predictable speed.

3 Standing, 2014, op. cit.

4 They include the UK government-commissioned *Gowers Review of Intellectual Property* (HMSO, 2006), as well as activist and IP practitioner associations and NGOs.

5 Standing, 2009, op. cit.

6 S. O'Connor, 'UK companies look for loopholes around living wage', *Financial Times*, 30 March 2016.

7 J. Kotkin, 'A $15 minimum wage is a booby prize for American workers', Forbes, 5 April 2016.

8 Standing, 2009, op. cit.

9 In Japan, compensation to employees for inventions patented by their firm used to be left to the courts. In a pivotal case in 2001, one employee was awarded $200 million (later reduced to $8 million). He went on to receive a Nobel Prize for helping to invent an energy-saving light source. The law was reformed to enable firms to draw up contracts promising employees 'reasonable compensation' for any invention stemming from their research. The Nobel Prize-winner attacked that rule, saying it would lead to an exodus of talent to the USA. Ironically, that was where he had gone, under the old system.

10 'Norwegian blues', *The Economist*, 10 October 2015, p. 68.

11 C. Wedmore, *Funding the Future: How Sovereign Wealth Funds Benefit Future Generations* (London: Intergenerational Foundation, November 2013).

12 G. Alperovitz and T. M. Hanna, 'Socialism, American Style', *New York Times*, 23 July 2015.

13 J. R. Blasi, D. I. Kruse and R. B. Freeman, *The Citizen's Share: Reducing Inequality in the 21st Century* (New Haven, CT: Yale University Press, 2015).

14 BIEN holds an international congress every two years. In 2014, it was held in Montreal; in 2016, in Seoul. Membership is open to all. See www.basicincome.org.

15 For a fuller review of those claims, see Standing, 2014, op. cit., Article 25, pp. 306–37.

16 T. Paine, *The Political Writings of Thomas Paine, Vol. II* (New York: Solomon King, 1830), p. 422.

17 G. Standing, 'Why basic income's emancipatory value exceeds its monetary value', *Basic Income Studies*, 10 (2), 2015: 193–223.

18 A major hedge-fund guru, Ray Dalio, has argued in much the same way: R. Wigglesworth, 'Helicopter money on the horizon, says Ray Dalio', *Financial Times*, 18 February 2016. A senior staff member of Goldman Sachs has, rather predictably, argued against the idea. F. Garzarelli, 'Central banks have safer options than a helicopter drop', *Financial Times*, 27 April 2016.

19 M. Blyth and E. Lonergan, 'Print less but transfer more: Why central banks should give money directly to the people', *Foreign Affairs*, September/October 2014.

20 This is a point made by other economists, such as Anatole Kaletsky. It is also consistent with Jeremy Corbyn's notion of QE for People, although he favours using the money for public infrastructure, which would not have as good distributional effects.

21 J. Sutter, 'The argument for a basic income', CNN Opinion, 10 March 2015.

22 S. Davala, R. Jhabvala, S. K. Mehta and G. Standing, *Basic Income: A Transformative Policy for India* (London and New Delhi: Bloomsbury, 2015).

23 Atkinson, 2015, op. cit., p. 219.

INDEX